An Untouchable
Community
in South India

An Untouchable Community in South India

STRUCTURE AND CONSENSUS

Michael Moffatt

PRINCETON UNIVERSITY PRESS

PRINCETON, NEW JERSEY

Contents

CONTENTS

List of Tables

List of Maps

List of Figures

List of Myths

Glossary

AaDi Draavida, Adi Dravida: original Dravidian. Part of a claim by some Untouchables that they were either first in the original birth order of caste ancestors, or that they are historically the descendents of the pre-Aryan peoples of south India.

abiiSegam: a ceremonial bathing and cooling, done for a god, generally before puja.

adimai: slave or tied laborer. A traditional role, including "rights" (*urumai*) with respect to the patron of the *adimai*.

adjusted acre: a rough weighting of land, used here to convert varying types of Harijan land into their approximate equivalent in dry land. Adjusted acres = (dry land times 1) + (wet land times 2) + (pumpset-fed land times 3).

Ambattan: the barber caste.

aNNan-tambi: elder brother-younger brother. The relation between two lineages who cannot intermarry because each has intermarried with a third lineage. "Parallel" relatives.

asura: a primordial antigod, against whom the gods had to wage heroic battles in order to gain control of the universe.

bambai: a large, double-ended drum, shorter and fatter than a *tavul*, associated in Endavur with possession by the goddess. One of the goddess's powers.

bhajan: a religious gathering during which devotional, bhakti songs are sung.

bhakti: devotion. An individual's direct relation to a personal deity; one of the three classical paths to enlightenment.

bhut: a ghost.

bolikaran: a sacrifice doer. A low role played by Harijans in the festival to the village goddess Selliyamman.

Candala: the proto-Untouchable mentioned in the ancient Sanskritic texts, a cremation-ground attendant.

ceeri: the older term for the hamlets inhabited uniquely by Untouchable castes in Tamilnadu.

ceeri-nattam: the *ceeri* land as rightfully reserved as the sole prerogative of an Untouchable caste.

Colony, *Kooloni*: the preferential term of reference for the *ceeri*, for the Untouchable hamlet, in northeastern Tamilnadu.

darkhast, dargos: petition. A system instituted by the British, whereby a person who cultivated a piece of waste land for five years could lay claim to it.

devam: a god.

devata: a goddess, generally low in character.

dharma: duty. The code for conduct of a given caste, lineage or person. A north Indian term.

dharmasastra: a lawbook, one of the Sanskritic texts containing codifications of dharma.

dominant caste: the caste which in a given village or region dominates economically and politically. Said by M. N. Srinivas generally to control most of the local land, to be relatively high in rank, and to form a good portion of the total local population.

doree, durai: lord, an honorific term applied to respected Indians, and to Westerners in general, in village Tamilnadu.

Endavur: the fictitious name of the village in Chingleput, Tamilnadu, where principle fieldwork for the present ethnography was conducted.

grade: an internal division in the Harijan caste (and in other castes) in Endavur, ranked with respect to other grades within the caste.

gurukkal: honorific form of *guru*. Applied generally to Brahmin temple priests; applied by the Harijans of Endavur to their now defunct caste overseers.

Harijan: child of god. Gandhi's neologism for Untouchables. In Endavur, the preferred caste title of the Paraiyan caste.

holi: a village festival practiced in north and central India, in which ordinary relations of respect toward humans (based on caste, age, and sex) are relaxed or inverted.

ista devam: chosen god. The god whom a given person decides is all-powerful for him or her.

jaaDi, jati: genera or caste, here restricted to its reference to a caste as a local endogamous unit ranked relative to other such units.

jajmani: a long-term vertical relation between a single family in a service caste and a single family in a dominant caste. A north Indian term.

kapu: a ceremonial black thread, associated with the chastity of the being on whom it is tied.

kapukaran: a *kapu*-wearing person.

karanam: a village accountant.

karma: action, generally connoting the accumulated good and bad actions of a person in past lives. Said in north India and in the ancient dharmasastras to contribute to a person's caste rank in his or her present life.

kiraaman: a village, a bounded social space including the living sites of all the castes in local caste hierarchies in northeastern Tamilnadu.

kiraama devata: village goddess.

kottu: bunch; a lineage or sublineage among the Harijans of Endavur.

kuDumbam: family.

kula devam: lineage god.

kulam: lineage or community.

kuLi: wage; a daily wage laborer, the root of the English term "coolie."

kuṛi meedai: the foretelling platform; the act of foretelling when possessed by a goddess.

maaDu: cow; cow, bullock, and water buffalo.

Maariyamman, Mariyamman: the goddess who changes, the goddess of rain and of epidemic disease, a fallen form of Parvati. The goddess of the *uur* and of the Colony (in two different forms) in Endavur.

mamaan: mother's brother; wife's father.

mamaan-machan: mother's brother/sister's husband. The relation between two lineages who exchange women in marriage. "Cross" relatives.

maniyam: the agricultural land that it is the right of a village service caste to cultivate in partial recompense for its service to the village.

mantram, *mantiram*: a sacred word said by Brahmin priests and by other priests, thought to be powerful in itself.

mantravaadi: a mantram-person, generally one who uses mantrams for black magic.

Mariyattai: an inauspicious family goddess; a term for Mariyamman in her lower form.

meestri: a mason.

mirassi: joint-village responsibility for land revenue.

munsif: a village policeman.

nagarigam: civilization; the personal quality of being civilized.

outcast: a person who has been ostracized from his or her caste for violating its code for conduct, most commonly for a sexual or marital offense.

outcaste: The deceptive term applied to Indian Untouchables, implying perhaps incorrectly that all Untouchables derived historically from outcasts, and implying entirely incorrectly that Untouchables are "outside" the caste system.

paDiyaaL: vegetarian offerings for a village god.

pandal: a temporary pavilion with auspicious connotations, built in front of a household at marriage, and in front of a temple during a festival to the god.

pangali: sharer; persons related by common patrilineal descent from a known ancestor.

pangu: share.

paNNaikkaar, Pannaikkar: field-person (honorific). Among the Harijans, a caste headman; alternatively, one of the three Harijan grades.

paNNaiyaaL: field-person (non-honorific). An agricultural

laborer, usually an Untouchable, with a long-standing relation to a single member of a dominant caste.

parai: a single-headed, tambourine-like drum, made from the
skin of a calf, the drum from whose playing the Paraiyan
caste derives its name.

Paraiyan, Paraiyan: *parai*-drum player, the largest Untouchable caste of Tamilnadu, the main subject of the present
ethnography.

Parangudi: the fictitious name of the village in Trichinopoly,
Tamilnadu, in which preliminary fieldwork for the present
ethnography was conducted.

peey, peey-pisasu: a demon or evil being, usually the spirit
of a human who died unhappily or inappropriately.

piratanai: a vow, usually to a god.

prasadam: the leftovers of a food offering to a god (of a
puja offering), eaten by the god's devotees to demonstrate
their inferiority and devotion to the god.

pucari: puja-person or temple servant. In Endavur, the functionary who deals with the goddess in her lower, possessed
form, and who conducts bloody sacrifice.

puja: a food offering to a god.

pural: a sacred thread, worn by Brahmins and others with
Brahminic pretensions.

purohit: classically, the Brahmin domestic priest. In Endavur,
applied by the Harijans to the person who acts both as
temple priest and domestic priest for them.

puuvaaDai: an auspicious family goddess.

ryotwari: a direct settlement for land revenue, between the
state and the peasant cultivator.

saami: a god; a common term of address of a superior by an
inferior.

saamiyaaDi: a god-dancer, one who is possessed by a god.

saivam: pure food-eating practices.

sannyasin: a religious renouncer or mendicant.

Sanskritization: the process by which a low caste makes a
status claim by adopting features of the code for conduct
of higher castes, of the local Brahmins in particular.

Scheduled Caste: a census category, conterminous with Untouchable as used here; from the schedules or lists drawn up district by district to identify the local Untouchable castes.

Selliyamman: a form of Mariyamman; the village goddess in Endavur.

shakti: divine power.

silambu: ankle bracelets of the goddess, musical rattles that are played to induce her possession, and that are part of her power.

standard acre: an official conversion ratio of land, for land ceiling legislation, in which any type of land is converted into its equivalent in the best quality of wet land.

tai: mother.

tai viiDu: mother's house; in Endavur, the groom's side in a marriage of the goddess Selliyamman, a part played by the Harijans.

Talaiyaari, Talaiyari: assistant to the village *munsif*, a Harijan prerogative in Endavur. One of the three Harijan grades.

taluk: a territorial division, a subdivision of a district.

tavul-nadeswaram band: a band consisting of a *tavul*, a double-ended, barrel-shaped drum, and several *nadeswarams*, double-reed instruments.

tiiNDaamai: not touching, not polluting. The term in Endavur that labels the idea of untouchability in the personal sense.

tiruviRaa: a festival.

tittu: impurity, especially the severe impurity of birth, of menstruation, and of death.

tiv artanai: showing the light, a gesture of respect toward a god or a respected human.

tooTTi: digger, the Harijan role as cremation ground attendant.

toRil: action or service, the "traditional occupation" to which a given caste's identity and rank is referred in Endavur.

untouchability: the state of being untouchable in the personal sense.

Untouchability: any property of Untouchable castes or of persons of Untouchable castes.

untouchable: a person who is personally polluting by touch to another person, due to his or her temporary or permanent impurity.

Untouchable: a member of a Tamil caste excluded from residence in the *uur*, and from other interactions with higher-caste persons, due to his or her caste-defined extreme lowness and impurity.

urumai: right, especially of an inferior with respect to a superior.

uur: the hamlet of the "higher" castes in Tamil villages, of all those castes who are not Untouchable.

vagaiyara: division; in Endavur, grade.

Vannan: the washerman caste.

varam: a boon, usually asked of a god by a devotee.

varasai: a donation, a marriage gift.

varayan: an announcer, often of bad news. In Endavur, a Harijan prerogative.

varna: one of the four major caste categories of the Sanskritic texts; Brahmins, Kshatriyas, Vaishyas, and Sudras, in rank order.

veelai: work or individual occupation, as opposed to *toRil* or caste-defined occupation.

VeTTiyan, Vettiyan: the roles of cattle scavenger, cremation ground attendant, and village watchman, the archetypal Harijan roles in Endavur. One of the three Harijan grades.

viiTTu devam: household god, a god worshipped in common by all the members of an undivided household.

zamin: the territory of a zamindar.

zamindar: a person with dominant rights over land, usually a large tract including several villages.

zamindari: an indirect settlement for land revenue, with a large zamindar or a series of zamindars standing between the state and the peasant-cultivators.

Acknowledgments

THIS book is dedicated to the memory of Dr. Elbert Marston Moffatt, of the Methodist Episcopal Church of North India.

In India, I would like to thank first and foremost the subjects of this study, the Harijans of "Endavur" and "Parangudi," for their patience, courtesy and hospitality under conditions often as strange and inexplicable to them as to myself. My work in Endavur would have been impossible without the approval of "KTR," and I thank the staff of the Endavur leprosy hospital for providing me with comfortable quarters. Dr. Paul Sandegren and Bishop Carl Diehl gave me invaluable aid in my initial settlement in the Pudukottai area. The research assistance of Mr. P. T. Chandran in Endavur was always of the highest quality. In Madras, my thanks to Miss Meena Krishnasami of the American Institute of Indian Studies, to Mohan, Stephanie, and Grischa Chandy for their friendship and hospitality, and to Leila and Ernest Dane for extraordinary help and kindness during a period of personal difficulty. Finally, my appreciation to Robert Falk for friendship and for keeping the mind alive while in the field.

My thanks to my dissertation advisor, Dr. McKim Marriott, for his thorough and intellectually challenging supervision of an earlier version of this work. My appreciation also to the other members of my advisory committee, Drs. Ralph Nicholas, S. J. Tambiah, and Terence Turner. Dr. Brenda Beck provided me with a great deal of help and encouragement in prefield training for India, as did Dr. Steve Barnett. My profound appreciation to Professor Rodney Needham for his teaching and example of scholarship, and to Professor Louis Dumont for the challenge and inspiration of his structural studies of south Indian society. My gratitude to my parents for their interest, encouragement and vicarious participation in nearly all of this project. Melanie Z. Strub accomplished heroic feats of typing with several of the worst manuscripts she'd ever received. Finally, I would like to commend Yanet Baldares and Alan Dalsass for having the good sense to enter my life after the worst phases in the write-up of this material were largely accomplished.

Research was made possible by prefield grants from the National Defense Foreign Languages Program, and by a Junior Fellowship from the Foreign Area Fellowship Foundation. The final draft was considerably assisted by a summer grant from the Rutgers University Research Council.

Note on Orthography

In Tamil words, the following transcriptions are used:

a	அ	s,c	ச	p,b	ப	R	ழ
i	இ	t,d	த	m	ம	v	வ
u	உ	T,D	ட	y	ய	L	ள
e	எ	N	ண	r	ர	l	ல
k,g	க	n	ன	ṟ	ற		

Long vowels are represented by the double vowel in English. As indicated above, I have transcribed certain consonants (க , ச , த , ட , and ப) with two different consonants, which approximate allophonically related sounds in Tamil, according to which English consonant is closer to colloquial Tamil in Endavur.

In general, I am transcribing Tamil orthography given to me on the spot in Endavur. Otherwise I am following the spelling found in V. Visvanatha Pillai, *A Tamil-English Dictionary*, Madras, 1963.

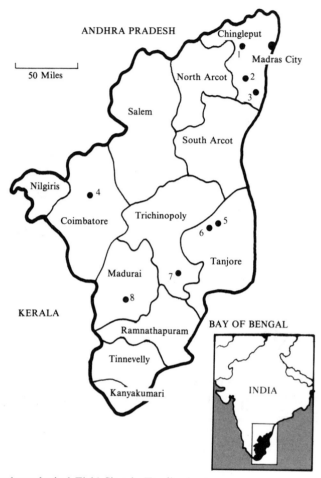

Anthropological Field Sites in Tamilnadu

Field sites mentioned in the present thesis, by name, location and name of associated ethnographer:

1. "Nallapakkam," central Chingleput, Steven Barnett.
2. An area in southern Chingleput, Jean Mencher.
3. "Endavur," southern Chingleput, Michael Moffatt.
4. Olappalaiyam, central Coimbatore, Brenda Beck.
5. "Sripuram," western Tanjore, Andre Beteille.
6. "Kumbapettai," western Tanjore, Kathleen Gough.
7. "Parangudi," southeast Trinchinopoly, Michael Moffatt.
8. An area in central Madurai, Louis Dumont.

Preface

ON DOING FIELDWORK WITH UNTOUCHABLES

THE ethnography that follows is based on two very different encounters with Indian Untouchables, with members of the Paraiyan or "Harijan" caste in rural Tamilnadu, south India.[1] The first was with Harijans in the old princely state of Pudukottai. Pudukottai is a dry, upland area of about one thousand square miles just southwest of the Tanjore delta, the cultural heartland of Tamilnadu (see map, facing page), and it retains in the 1970s a traditional and conservative tone. I conducted research in the Pudukottai region for about eight months, from November 1970 through July 1971, first living on a Brahmin street in the town of Pudukottai (population 50,000) and later settling for a few days a week in the Harijan hamlet of the small village of Parangudi (this name is fictitious), eight miles north of Pudukottai town. In Parangudi, I lived on my own with the Harijans, with no links to the higher castes, with no Indian research assistant, with no non-Indian companion. I believed at the time, and I still do, that this Malinowskian method is, for all its flaws and its

[1] "Untouchables" can be defined as persons belonging to a discrete set of lowest castes in Indian village caste hierarchies. In Tamilnadu, these persons are considered very low and impure because of their caste-defined occupational association with polluting substances or death. Tamil Untouchables invariably live in separate hamlets at some distance from the main village hamlets of the higher castes. The Paraiyans, whose name means "*parai*-drum players," are one large Untouchable caste or caste-category with an all-Tamilnadu distribution (there are two other large Tamil Untouchable castes, and scores of smaller ones). In the two villages where I worked, the Paraiyans preferred to refer to themselves as "Harijans," an honorific term coined by Mahatma Gandhi, meaning "children of God."

xxiii

romanticism, the best way to do anthropological fieldwork. I was not at the time, however, prepared for the psychological stresses of the method, and after about three months of intermittent residence in the Parangudi Harijan hamlet, I left the village and the region with the intention of abandoning my fieldwork in India.

My flight from India stopped in Madras City, where I was fortunate enough to meet some people who could help me with what I then thought of as my total failure as an anthropologist. About a year later, I returned to fieldwork in a different rural region, to the village of Endavur (also a fictitious name) in southern Chingleput, fifty miles south of Madras City and two hundred miles north of Pudukottai. The Endavur region is known for its large *zamindari* landholdings, a pattern of land tenure relatively rare in south India; but it is more like the rest of Tamilnadu historically than is Pudukottai, for it was under direct British rule from the late 1700s until 1947. Because of this, and because of its proximity to Madras City, Endavur has a less "traditional" tone than Pudukottai, though it is still very much a part of village India. My research method in Endavur was far less participatory than in Parangudi. Here, I lived separately from the Harijans, and from the higher castes as well, in the staff quarters of a small leprosy hospital one mile from the village. In Parangudi, I had moved around quietly on bicycle; here, I owned a motorcycle. In Parangudi, I had worked alone in my rudimentary Tamil; in Endavur I had the help of an Indian bilingual research assistant, who was generally with me whenever I entered the Harijan hamlet. I spent eight months in Endavur, from April to November 1972.

Most of my data on Tamil Harijans, and virtually all the analysis that follows, come from my second field site, from Endavur. My most vivid impressions of the nature of Harijan social life, however, of tones and nuances of "being an Untouchable," derive from my Parangudi experience, and I will occasionally mention such unanalytic factors below. As a prefatory note, however, I would like to describe in more detail the conditions of my fieldwork with Tamil Harijans. I see any kind of participant observation with low-status groups in India as presenting very particular tactical problems—problems quite different from those presented by fieldwork with high-status, dominant groups. My own adaptations to these problems are part of the data here, part of what the reader should know in evaluating the ethnography that follows. These adaptations say something about the Harijans, and something about me. The stress that I experienced was due only in part to the particular situation, to the difficulties of working with Tamil Harijans, and the following account is intended to cover only these situational factors, not my own problems as they emerged under the stressful conditions that are a part of cross-cultural fieldwork anywhere in the world.

When I first went to India in September 1972, after four years of prefield preparation at Oxford University and at the University of Chicago, I had two immediate research goals. I wished to study rural Tamil Untouchables in as traditional a region as was available in south India in the early 1970s, and I wished to conduct my research not only without Indian assistance or non-Indian companionship, but without visible relations to the higher castes of the region I chose. My first goal was set by a flaw that I perceived in the anthropological literature on Untouchables at the time: virtually all studies of Untouchables concerned themselves with "change" (cf. Mahar 1972), but few established a thoroughly analyzed "traditional" baseline against which such putative change could be evaluated. I hoped to construct such a baseline. My second goal had two motivations. First, I considered that the reasons for lone, unmediated research were well established in the anthropological literature. The ideal is simple enough. By working alone, the researcher exerts the minimum control effect on the data, disturbing as little as possible the object of his study by his presence in it. And by working alone, he is forced to learn the local language quickly, and—it is hoped —to make some sort of empathetic jump to his subjects equally quickly. This latter ideal strikes me in retrospect as the most tenuous of the lot. Second, I was aware from such personal accounts of Indian fieldwork as Berreman's *Behind Many Masks* (Berreman 1965) how much any higher-caste mediation can affect one's perception of low-caste Indians. Since I was interested in getting as frankly as possible the Untouchable point of view, I wanted no suspicion in the minds of the local Harijans that I might be reporting what they told me to the higher castes. Hence I should work alone; and hence I should not be introduced to local Untouchables in my "traditional" region by any local high-caste agents.

Brenda Beck suggested before I went to India that Pudu-kottai might be the sort of region I was looking for, and once I was in India, Rev. Paul Sandegren, a Swedish Lutheran missionary based in Pattukottai (on the Tanjore coast forty miles from Pudukottai) quickly provided me with a means of making initial contact with rural Untouchables in Pudu-kottai without higher-caste intervention. He told me that he would be delighted if I studied the "Senyar Paraiyan" sub-caste of the Pudukottai area, since his church had not suc-ceeded in making a single convert from them in that area in 146 years, and he would like to know why. He then provided me with the temporary services of Murugan, a Christian whose parents had come from the Senyar Paraiyan caste but migrated out of Pudukottai a generation ago, and later con-verted. Murugan and I began touring by bicycle the villages in the area of Murugan's old home village, north of Pudu-kottai town, for about a month. We found it possible to approach local Harijans directly, at least to make initial in-quiries and to explain my purpose. Murugan was able to con-vince the Harijans quickly of his common caste background with them, though what he was telling them about me at this point I am not entirely certain. He was instructed to tell them that I was interested in the "customs" (Tamil: *PaRakko-vaRakkom*, literally "old customs" or "old traditions") of their community, and that I was looking for a hut to live in in a Harijan hamlet. Most of the Harijans we met at this point were polite to us. Occasionally they seemed confused or frightened, and asked us to see the local dominant caste leaders before talking to them further. They all seemed disbelieving about my intention to live with them, however, and it was clear that no one in a crowded Harijan hamlet left a hut vacant for possible rental to a wandering anthropologist.

We finally found an exceptional Harijan family in the Parangudi hamlet, a family who had educated one of their sons to the precollege level; he was therefore the best educated person in the village, Harijan or higher caste. The boy, Raman, had slightly better control of English than I had of Tamil, and between Murugan, Raman, and myself, a negotiation began whereby his family would build me a hut, on contract, next to their own, on the outer edge of the Harijan hamlet, which in turn lay one hundred yards southeast of Parangudi's main caste hamlet. During these negotiations, Dennis McGilvray, then in his second year of fieldwork in lowland Tamil Ceylon, paid me a visit, and explained to the Parangudi Harijans in most definite terms—in his impressive high Tamil—that I *was* going to live with them, and that they *were* to build me a hut just like their own, mud-walled and palmyra-palm roofed, for payment on an honestly itemized bill. Murugan at this point returned to Pattukottai.

I now had to deal with the dominant caste of Parangudi, who were Kallars, the same caste described in a subcaste variant sixty miles south by Louis Dumont in *Une Sous-caste de L'Inde du sud* (1957a). Raman's family had asked me on my first day to show my police permit to the Kallar village policeman, but after this, the Harijans had demonstrated in my presence no concern about the Kallars' reaction to my living with them in the Harijan hamlet. In light of the fierce reputation of the Kallars (who were classed as a "criminal caste" several generations ago), I was puzzled, and still am to a degree, by this lack of concern. I did discover later that Raman's family had a measure of economic independence from the Kallars; they had five acres of their own dry land, and Raman's father had had until recently a regular paying job as night watchman at a nearby cotton mill.

I decided to make my own courtesy call on the Kallars, and with the help of a bilingual schoolteacher from a neighboring village, I told them what I had told all non-Untouchables in the villages about my research. I was, I said, interested in Tamil culture, a valid interest from the point of view of any Tamil. Much was known about various Tamil "communities," I continued, and there were already many excellent books about Brahmins and Mudaliyars and Kallars. No one, however, had studied the Harijans in detail (a considerable exaggeration), and this was my "duty." When I was feeling defensive, I would suggest that I had no particular personal preference for studying the Harijans, that it was my "duty" to study them because my professors in America had assigned me this topic.

That I was interested in the Harijans as a group was not incomprehensible to village Tamils. So much official social inquiry has been directed at the Scheduled Castes (an administrative equivalent of "Untouchables") in the last twenty years that most villagers are aware of these groups as an object of outside interest. That I was interested in the "culture" of the Harijans was more outlandish; in the words of one old high-caste, English-speaking schoolmaster in Tanjore, "the *culture* of Harijans? What culture!?" That I actually wanted to live with the Harijans was, in the eyes of non-Untouchables, just plain silly. The Kallars of Parangudi listened to my plans politely, and, without objecting to my interest in the Harijans, pointed out that since the Harijan hamlet was one hundred yards from the main village hamlet, I could easily stay with the Kallars and walk over to the Harijan hamlet anytime I wanted to pursue my studies.

I protested that I had to be "with" the Harijans all the time to do my research correctly. I think I tried to tell the Kallars something about informal observation of behavior. I certainly did not tell them my other prime motive: that I wanted to remain solidly identified, in the Harijans' eyes, with the Harijans, that I wanted no suspicion on their part that I was returning to the Kallars daily with information the Harijans had just imparted to me. The Kallars replied that I did not have to live with them if I did not wish to, but requested that I might have the decency to build my hut in the fields outside the Harijan hamlet, rather than inside its boundaries. I once again protested, and the Kallars seemed unhappy about my plans but made no demands that I cease and desist. When I left them, I felt that I would be tolerated in Parangudi, but that my warmest ethnographic relationships were not going to be with Kallars. My stay in Parangudi was too short to predict whether or not I could eventually have gained some rapport with individual Kallars, but long enough to suggest that no overt pressure would have been put on me, or on Raman's Harijan family, to make me leave the hamlet. It was necessary to remain careful in what I admitted to the higher castes, however. Raman's family coached me carefully to deny that I ate with them, and to suggest to outsiders that I somehow survived for three or four days at a time on the tea and biscuits that I had in my hut in the Harijan hamlet.

For about three months, during the hottest part of the Tamil summer (April to June), I lived in the Parangudi Harijan hamlet part of each week and commuted by bicycle back to a small house I had rented in Pudukottai town for the remainder of the week. The house in Pudukottai town was originally a base for my survey work and a place to store my minimal equipment: some books, a camera, and a tape-recorder. It increasingly became a refuge, a place where I could lock the door and be alone, a context in which I could talk non-ethnographically to non-Untouchables, mostly to educated Brahmin men who worked in the schools and businesses of Pudukottai town. These people had some awareness of what I was doing and with whom I was living in Parangudi, though they rarely quizzed me about my work directly. I was asked once or twice not to tell a Brahmin elder anything about my work, for it might upset the elder. Since my contact with Harijans was eight miles out of sight, however, I was treated by the Pudukottai Brahmins like any other Westerner, and exactly like the American Peace Corps volunteer in the town. I was invited to some Brahmin homes as an honored dinner guest, where on most occasions I was fed first and separately, but where I was twice fed—on feast occasions—sitting at the head of a line beside other Brahmin males. I was invited to more *bhajans* than I could attend, where I again sat with the men, and was occasionally given hand cymbals to click along with the music. Had I been living and working in the "slum" of Pudukottai town, mostly Paraiyan and Pallan (another major Tamil Untouchable caste) residentially, I doubt the Pudukottai Brahmins would have taken me in as thoroughly as they did.

My hut (*kurichi*) in the Parangudi Harijan hamlet was constructed by Raman's family. Raman presented me with an itemized bill for its costs, which proved to be about twice the local rate item by item (Rs 550 on what should have been about Rs 275, 1970 prices). I felt that it was important initially to establish that I wasn't a complete idiot, even if I did apparently willingly choose to live with Harijans. We bargained the payment down to the local level, and I finished the argument by pointing out that I was not going to take the hut back with me to America when I left Parangudi. In the first weeks in the hamlet, I felt l was being continually tested for how much I was worth by Raman and his relatives. Would I make them a "loan" of Rs 500 for a pair of bullocks? Would I loan a relative Rs 50? All such requests I declined on two, somewhat inconsistent, grounds: I was "only a student," and my funds only covered expenditures directly relating to research; and, if I loaned money to one Harijan how would I refuse another? Where would I draw the line?

My first reason was hard to believe. Though I thought that I had cut my standard of living to the bone, to the Parangudi Harijans my house in town, my wardrobe (six shirts and a few pairs of trousers), my new bicycle, and my ability to take the train to Madras or Tanjore every month or so, all suggested a very unstudentlike degree of affluence. My second reason for refusing money was easy enough for the Harijans to answer: I should help those who helped me. I remained stubborn, since I did not want my relationship to the Harijans to turn into one of moneylender. I attempted to keep all money transactions contractual: a "wage" for Sundaram on the days he helped me in my work, Rs 2 a day to his family's food budget on the days I was in the hamlet, occasional emergency donations for medical expenses, and donations on ritual occasions. This last was the easiest time to give, and later in Endavur I always made donations at marriages and temple festivals I attended, which were duly noted down and announced together with others' donations. I had thought before coming to India of making more economically rational self-help donations to the Harijans with whom I worked—a well, for example. Such pragmatic donations would always have left someone out, however, someone dissatisfied. They would also have placed me in an unusual position among the Harijans, that of a benefactor to whom countless additional petitions were in order. Donations for ritual display, on the other hand, were very much part of the system, were appreciated and commented upon favorably, and did not disrupt my other daily interactions.

Life in the Harijan hamlet was an intensely face-to-face experience. Things were—quite literally—more out in the open than in the main village hamlet, or than in the town of Pudukottai. My hut had no front door on it—it was too hot to have used one anyway—so I was on display at all times, while eating and sleeping and dressing and undressing. I was extremely ambivalent about my lack of personal privacy. The unrelieved staring, which was worst when my Tamil language abilities were minimal and there was very little I could say to people, was a constant irritant—an intrusion of my personal space with which I never grew comfortable. However, I felt that the situation was an unavoidable part of participant observation. I had put myself in this position so I could observe anything that occurred among the Harijans. In effect, I was invading their privacy totally; why shouldn't they do the same to mine? I also felt some guilt about my hard line with the Harijans on money matters, and I decided that one of my payoffs for them was my prestige and entertainment value. Raman's family took obvious pride in my residence next to them, and I was very reluctant to tell them or others, even occasionally, to go away. I was an obvious source of interest and amusement among people whose leisure-time activities are not elaborate; how could I object to this kind of reciprocity in return for the trouble I was putting them to? Finally, there was a touchingly warm quality about the care with which Raman's family saw to it that I had as little privacy as possible. I would wake up frightened, they decided, if I slept in my hut without company; therefore some of the younger children in the family were told to go and sleep on my floor next to me. One morning I woke up unaccountably depressed, and my gloom increased under the stares of a half dozen people watching me struggle to tie my waist-cloth. To clear them out, I shouted an unexpected cry of rage. My apparent temporary insanity had, of course, the opposite effect on them, and the family gathered around me, looking very worried, and asking me what was wrong. "I only want to be alone," I shouted back at them, and they finally left me, slowly and reluctantly, coming back every ten minutes or so to see if I was all right, and if the unusual mood had passed.

In retrospect, I could have made more personal space for myself in the hamlet. Raman's family was very sensitive to my moods, and they made adjustments for me, and dealt with others on my behalf, when I made my feelings clear to them. I was obviously a very odd person—we would joke in the evenings that my very presence among them proved that I was a little crazy—and there is definite tolerance of oddities and strange habits in India, especially for those of prestigious foreigners. Eventually people were told to leave me alone when I was sleeping or napping. I had two other times when privacy was allowed to me: when I used the fields as a latrine in the mornings, and any time I wandered out of the hamlet at night. I was warned half-jokingly that if I went out alone at night, without a light, one of the *peeys* (evil spirits or demons) who lived in various trees in the fields might "catch" me. As soon as I noticed that my usual crowd of hangers-on, mostly children, did not accompany me on these occasions, however, I made use of the chance for privacy—disappearing for perhaps a half an hour after sundown every day. Either the belief was only a half serious one, or I was less susceptible to the *peeys* than the Harijans: when the Harijans had to account for what they considered my failing health toward the end of my stay with them, they never to my knowledge considered the *peeys* as a possible explanation (though perhaps *peey* possession had different symptoms from those I was showing).

Physical comfort was the least of my problems in the Parangudi Harijan hamlet. This had been one of my biggest concerns in my earlier fantasies of what lay ahead: a mental image of sullen, depressed, underfed people, living in over-populated, squalid slum-like conditions. My visual image was based on pictures of the slums of Indian cities. Most Tamil Harijan hamlets present quite a different aspect. Though the small hamlet site in Parangudi was packed densely with twenty-one residential structures, my housesite on the far side of the hamlet faced the open fields, and gave me a sense of space that I would not have had elsewhere in the village. The season was very hot, but it was acceptable among the Harijans to walk around shirtless (as it would not have been among the higher castes), and my hut was well adapted to the climate. Its palmyra palm roof was a better insulator against the sun's heat than the tiles of my house in the town of Pudukottai, and there was a continuous air space between the top of the mud walls and the bottom of the roof, which allowed breezes from any direction to circulate through the hut. The hamlet was as clean as any Tamil village, and far cleaner than parts of the town of Pudukottai, or of Madras City. Raman's mother swept out my hut and "compound" every morning and evening, and there was no source of running sewage anywhere in the area. I ate with Raman's family; with my contribution to family finances and with Harijan meat-eating practices, the diet was ample and balanced. The food was cooked carefully and cleanly, and conventional Tamil rules of personal purity were observed, such as cleaning the mouth, teeth, and throat thoroughly in the morning before eating, and strict use of the right hand in eating. Initially I was fed separately, before everyone else. Soon I was more integrated, however: I was addressed by kinship terms within the family, and I ate in a semicircle with the men of the household.

During the three months I was in the Parangudi Harijan hamlet, I never overcame the feeling that I was playing an elaborate self-presentational game, one that the Harijans saw through to a degree, but were too polite to call me on. My initial attempts to appear nonaffluent in their eyes had not been a success, and I was continually reminded of how impossible it was for me to blend in in the hamlet—to exist there nonobtrusively, just like any Harijan. People would constantly examine my skin, wonder what the freckles were (mosquito bites?), and tell me admiringly, "you are very white, we are very black." There were no rules for dealing with my presence among them, and the Harijans alternated between attitudes of extreme respect appropriate toward a high-status guest, and a joking relationship that I encouraged, one that was easiest with teenagers and with members of Raman's family, and which made for my most relaxed times in the hamlet. Joan Mencher and Kathleen Gough have commented on their greater sense of personal ease in field-work interactions with Tamil Untouchables than with people from the higher castes (Gough 1973; Mencher n.d.: 39), and though I feel they both considerably overstate the contrasts between Untouchable and non-Untouchable ethos, the Harijans of Parangudi were easier to coax into attitudes of often vulgar and irreverent humor than were, say, the Pudu-kottai Brahmins.

As for my participation in the daily life of the Harijans, Untouchable jobs included a range of activities so inappropriate to my status—even when I lived in the hamlet—that after a few months I began to feel that the activities were as inappropriate for me as the Untouchables did. Field labor was out of the question: I didn't have the skills, I couldn't bear up under the heat, and the attention any charade on my part would have caused would have disrupted the normal work schedule. I could always observe, of course, sitting with the Kallar landowners, or watching Raman's father work his own field from under the shade of a tree or an umbrella. People were always upset when I went out in the sun without my umbrella: the sun wasn't healthy for me, and I would grow too dark from it. I was allowed to go swimming with the children in large wells in the fields in the afternoons. To assimilate me occasionally with children was a useful ploy both for the Harijans and for me; I pointed out to them that in many ways, functionally and verbally, I was "like a child," and they agreed. Within the hamlet, there was very little I could do for myself. I was not permitted to tidy up my own hut; any time I tried to wash out a piece of clothing myself it was snatched from me disapprovingly by Raman's mother or by Raman; and of course I could not cook for myself. I did make a stand on the arcane matter of boiling my own drinking water, and here the Harijans gave way before my peculiar belief that water had to be boiled for twenty minutes before it was safe to drink.

In my three months in the Parangudi Harijan hamlet, I was in no way becoming an Untouchable. The Kallars were unquestionably unhappy with my presence in the hamlet, but their concern about my eating with the Harijans (which they suspected I did, in spite of my prevarications) centered on my becoming sick from the food, or on its affecting me in some other unspecified negative way. This also seemed to be the focus of the Pudukottai Brahmins' explanation of my subsequent problems of health. In my second month in the Harijan hamlet, I began a survey of the temples of Parangudi village, and Raman led me one day to the stone of the Karuppan, the "black god" who guarded the southern boundary of the village. Though we thought our visit to this temple had gone unobserved, Raman was summoned by the Kallars the next day and reprimanded for approaching Karuppan too closely, a definitionally incorrect act for an Untouchable. Significantly, however, he was not reprimanded for taking me to the temple, nor for my closeness to the god.

Thus, in my experience, participant-observation with the Harijans, and identification with them, had its strict limitations. There were positive sides to all this, however. Although the Harijans and the villagers clearly never saw me as becoming "like a Harijan," the Harijans did know that whatever I was and whatever my purposes, I was closer to them than to anyone else. They at least had some reason to believe that I was not a Kallar spy, and this was a basis for trust. It was utterly strange for me to be living in the Harijan hamlet, but my presence there was a source of prestige and pride to Raman's family. I was never invisible, but I could enter the hamlet unobtrusively, by bicycle, through the fields: my lack of a motor vehicle or of an entourage did lower my visibilty. Occasionally, in the hamlet, I felt that my presence was temporarily forgotten, that things were going on around me but not at me. The Harijans' habituation to me, and my declining control effect on what I was observing, would have increased over the months, had I stayed longer. After three months in the hamlet, my control of Harijan conversational Tamil had reached a point where—with Raman's family, at any rate—I could begin to ask questions of an ethnographic nature. I had somewhat deliberately avoided being too inquisitive in the first month or two, and had concentrated on settling in. In the third month, I was beginning to collect genealogies and stories, to draw rough sketch maps of the area, and to survey the gods who were present in the village.

But my hard anthropological data from Parangudi are sketchy, at best.

In early July, a personal crisis which had been building for some months came to a head, and I decided, much too precipitiously for the Harijans to understand, to break off fieldwork in Parangudi. The Harijans had noticed in the previous weeks that I was failing—I complained to them mostly of headaches—and they attributed my distress in part to *kaNNu druSTi*, "evil eye." People in the main hamlet of the village, the Harijans said, had been saying "bad words" against me, though they never told me who these illwishers were or what they had said. But I was suffering from the bad thoughts directed against me, and twice Raman's mother performed a ritual action, also called *kaNNu druSTi*, to draw off these bad influences. On my last night in the hamlet, she fastened three kerosene-soaked wicks to a piece of cactus, which she then rotated three times around my head clockwise, three times counterclockwise, and threw outside the hamlet boundary. In a final effort of ethnographic curiosity, I walked out later to inspect and to sketch the cactus, a move that upset everyone. The whole point of the ritual action was to separate the evil from me, and here I was walking back towards it. When I returned to visit Parangudi briefly six weeks later, Raman had moved into my hut and made it into his study. In the northwest corner of the hut, my photograph had been framed, together with a picture of the goddess of Kannimangalam, who is in fact a Virgin Mary worshiped by many Hindus. The two of us had been receiving the daily benefits of the ritual *tiv artanai* ("showing the light"), Raman's parents explained to me.

I began my second round of fieldwork with Tamil Harijans nearly a year later, in the village of Endavur in southern Chingleput. My fieldwork in Endavur was everything my fieldwork in Parangudi wasn't: strongly mediated, formal, minimally observational, nonparticipatory, and straight to the ethnographic point. I began visiting the area in April 1972, and by June I had decided to study the Harijans of

Endavur. I made arrangements to stay in the staff quarters of a malaria hospital, run by western doctors with a large Indian staff, one mile southeast of the village. I had a number of reasons for not attempting to repeat my efforts in Parangudi. First, I was simply not yet ready to subject myself again to the personal pressures of living full time among Harijans. Second, only eight months remained on my Indian visa, and I needed data quickly. In the Parangudi hamlet, arrangements to have my hut constructed had taken three months in themselves. My Tamil had not improved much since I had left Parandudi, so I could not afford the luxury of what I felt was necessary for any kind of fluency: another six months in a totally non-English-speaking environment, among the Harijans. I therefore had the assistance of Mr. P. T. Chandran, a man who had worked with anthropologists before and who knew the southern Chingleput area well; most of my work in Endavur was done in translation, through him.

Our first move in Endavur, and the reason we originally visited the village, was to pay our respects to KTR, the young head of one of the largest ex-zamindar families in the region, and a high-caste Reddiyar. I told KTR my research interests very frankly, and he immediately suggested we work in the Endavur hamlet, of whose "prosperity" he seemed proud. He also offered us his guest house, immediately adjacent to his own house in the main caste hamlet of the village, as our living quarters. We declined both suggestions as politely as possible, but after surveying the area around Endavur for another two weeks, we decided to concentrate on the Endavur hamlet, for the Harijans there had proved most open with us, and least suspicious and fearful of our purposes. One reason for their attitude, obviously, was that KTR had approved of us and had passed the word down. I was concerned that we might be too closely linked in the Harijans' minds with the Reddiyars, and I hoped that our residence in the more or less neutral hospital, with our almost exclusive attention to the local Untouchable hamlet, would overcome any suspicions about us. We discovered later that there were some other factors working in our favor in Endavur. The hospital had a good reputation among the Harijans, for a number of them had been treated success-fully there. Its presence had also accustomed local Harijans to the sight of European visitors: several visitors a year for over twenty years had been given tours of Endavur village and hamlet. Finally, as I will explain, the economic position of the Endavur Harijans was relatively strong; they conse-quently proved to be less concerned about the opinion of the dominant caste, and about our relation to the dominant caste, than were the Harijans in most villages. During our research in Endavur, we paid regular courtesy calls on KTR, and though we once asked his help with a suspicious high-caste village accountant, we generally talked to him about subjects unrelated to my research. After our initial explana-tion of my research, he never questioned us further on what we were doing in the Harijan hamlet, though he was un-doubtedly getting reports from some of the many Harijans who worked for his family.

In Endavur, from the point of view of the Harijans, I was playing much more by the rules; I was behaving much more comprehensibly like a *doree*[2] than I had in Parangudi. Chan-dran and I drove into the Harijan hamlet mornings and evenings on my Indian motorcycle, and Chandran opened negotiations for me. Chairs would be brought out for us, or we would be invited to sit on the veranda of our host's hut, and we were sometimes offered coffee or betel, but never food until we had strongly indicated our willingness to eat with Harijans. Our interviews were very loosely structured, but they were interviews, in which one or two men respond-ed to my questions, and a group of onlookers—men, wom-en, and children—listened and occasionally interrupted. I would take notes while Chandran translated, and the two of

[2] "*Doree*" is an honorific term, literally "lord," which is applied to Westerners all over village Tamilnadu. It is roughly equivalent to the north Indian *sahib*.

us would often discuss between us, in English, the meaning of some ambiguous response, or another way of probing for the information I wanted. After an hour or two devoted to my business, things would become more informal, topics might be raised casually and spontaneously that called for more investigation on another day, and questions would be directed back at me. Some of our best information came to us after the formal interview was over, in the twilight, when most people had lost interest in us and gone away, and someone would collar us more privately and tell us the "real" answer to what we had been asking, some fact that it was indiscreet to divulge in the eternal public glare of a Harijan hamlet. On one occasion we set up a confidential interview with some care. I wanted to discuss with the Harijan Adimelem the sensitive matter of the relations between the three ranked "grades" within the caste. We asked Adimelem if we could talk to him inside his house, rather than on the veranda, and when the subject became clear to him, he further posted a guard at the door, to chase away eavesdroppers, and afterwards complimented us profusely on our delicacy. His chief rival in the Colony, however, Periyasami, seemed fully informed on what had gone on, and the next evening met us alone in the fields and countered Adimelem's claims point by point. Occasionally we asked individual Harijans to come and talk to us in our rooms at the hospital in the evenings, and discussions there were very frank. Not all my work required this degree of secrecy, but intracommunity conflict and the workings of the ranked structures within the caste were matters whose public discussion was not easy, and where the lack of privacy within the caste affected the Harijans as much as it did me.

There was probably considerable speculation in Endavur about my purposes, though I gave people the same explanation that I had offered in Parangudi for my interest in the Harijans. I was initially confused with the doctors at the hospital, and one genuinely imaginative rumor did get back to me. Chandran and I observed the Harijan Mariyamman

festival in the second week we were in Endavur, and this was
the first time many of the Harijans had seen us. It was also
our longest stay in the Colony as of that date, from dawn
until midnight on the day of the festival. The papers had in
recent weeks been full of accounts of an international cartel
of art thieves, who ran Indian antiquities out of the country
and sold them in the West. It was decided by a few of the
Harijans that this explained our presence in the hamlet and
our unusual interest in the festival: we were casing the moveable image of the goddess.

There was no ambiguity in how I was treated in the Endavur Harijan hamlet, however, for I was clearly defined by
my behavior: I was a *doree*, whose visits to the hamlet were
a source of pride to those I talked to. I felt none of the personal pressure that my more undefined status in Parangudi
had led to. I had by this time the advantage of much more
experience with Indian etiquette patterns, and I had at least
temporarily come to terms with a fact that had caused me
anxiety in my earlier fieldwork: it was better, or at least far
easier, to accept and use the status ascribed to me by the
Harijans, than to aim for a nonexistent equality that left my
position always undefined, always ambiguous, always open to
further testing. The other side of this social comprehensi-
bility, however, was a loss in flexibility. It was assumed that,
as an important outsider, I would only be interested in talking to important Harijans. Adimelem, who as a road inspector at the local block headquarters had the most prestigious job in the hamlet, was the first of my "big men"
among the Harijans, and he jealously guarded his evening
conversations with me in the first few months of fieldwork
in Endavur; others were not allowed to interrupt or contradict
him when he was talking to us. Though he seemed genuinely
interested in talking to us, and what he told us was helpful
and basically correct, the prestige factor of our presence on
his veranda every evening was clearly as important to him as
anything that was said. As his rival Periyasami told us, with
his usual cynical directness: "Yes, Adimelem is now paying

a great deal of attention to you, because you come every evening on that motorcycle. But suppose tomorrow another American comes in a motorcar. Adimelem will forget completely who you are." In Endavur, I had to make a conscious effort to be allowed to talk to the less prestigious Harijans in the hamlet. The process of detaching ourselves from our initial identification with Adimelem, however, did teach us a good deal about status, power, and differing points of view within the caste.

Chandran's assistance also constituted a change from my loneness in Parangudi, and of course added to my visibility when I came into the hamlet and to the formality with which I was received. His assistance made me lazy in acquiring further Tamil language competence, and I am well aware of the ethnographic inadequacies of working in translation on a subject in which meaning is so important to the analysis. My Tamil was sufficient, however, for me to sense when I was getting an inadequate translation, or when something was being left unsaid, or when a key lexical unit seemed to be recurring and called for further elucidation (examples below include the terms "*toRil*," "*shakti*," "*suttam*," and "*kottu*"). My Tamil would never have been sufficient to understand rapidly spoken overheard conversation and comments, and here Chandran's help, and his own particular insights, were invaluable. His education is in economics, and his insights and suggestions on matters having to do with people's material self-interests were often clarifying and helpful, as was the opportunity to talk over hypotheses on the spot with another outside observer. Chandran could also discover certain things from the Harijans on his own that they were less willing to mention in my presence, either because of the sensitivity of the subject or because the Harijans were afraid the matter was too trivial for my ears. When I use the "we" form in my description of Endavur below, I am not just being editorial; "we" rather than "I" did most of the actual fieldwork on which this analysis is based.

My lone fieldwork in Parangudi resulted in little hard data

but in a strong feeling for the tenor of Harijan social life. The Endavur experience was far more instrumental. I often felt I was literally charging in and wrenching the data loose from the people. We were always very intrusive in Endavur: the roar of the motorcycle coming in to the hamlet, the formality of our reception, the distraction of my clipboard and later of my tape-recorder and camera—all these could not fail to draw attention to us. Only a few times did our presence in Endavur seem forgotten or irrelevant: during the most intense moments of the goddess festival, or at points in the Harijan marriages we observed. I am reasonably confident of the accuracy of the data I collected in Endavur, but I always missed from Parangudi the directness of my relation to the Harijans, the serendipity and the explorative nature of my ambiguously defined status there, the intensity and of course the newness of those original impressions. It was as though what should be two intertwined aspects of anthropological fieldwork were for me spatially and temporarily separated. Parangudi was all tenor, tone, informal observation, and limited participation; Endavur was all carefully mediated ethnographic inquiry. I hope what follows reunites the two levels of understanding.

An Untouchable
Community
in South India

CHAPTER I

Models and Theories of Indian Untouchability

THE present work is about Untouchables in the village of "Endavur," south India. It is intended as an ethnography, as a reasonably comprehensive description of the social and cultural context of "being an Untouchable" in a rural south Indian setting. But it is also intended as an argument, set in a structuralist mold. Briefly, the argument and the structuralism are as follows.

To be an Untouchable in a rural Indian caste system is to be very low in, and partially excluded from, an elaborately hierarchical social order. The consequences of this lowness and partial exclusion, however, are not those argued in much of the anthropological literature on Untouchability and caste. Untouchables do not necessarily possess distinctively different social and cultural forms as a result of their position in the system. They do not possess a separate subculture. They are not detached or alienated from the "rationalizations" of the system. Untouchables possess and act upon a thickly textured culture whose fundamental definitions and values are identical to those of more global Indian village culture. The "view from the bottom" is based on the same principles and evaluations as the "view from the middle" or the "view from the top." The cultural system of Indian Untouchables does not distinctively question or revalue the dominant social order. Rather, it continuously recreates among Untouchables a microcosm of the larger system.

More formally, the present argument is for fundamental cultural consensus from the top to the bottom of a local caste hierarchy—a consensus very much participated in by the Untouchables. "Consensus" here does not refer to simple and uniform agreement between actors of every rank in their

3

spontaneous statements about caste and its cultural matrix, for no such consensus exists in south Indian villages. It refers, instead, to deeper and often unarticulated identities of cultural construction. The subject of these identities are such matters as the human and nonhuman units in the world, and the appropriate relations of these units one to another. The present argument for cultural consensus is not meant to rule out the possibility that power plays a role in the maintenance of this consensus. Nor is it meant to rule out the existence of certain types of cultural variation from caste to caste. But the argument is meant to suggest that these variations exist within, and must be interpreted within, a framework of shared definitions and values.

In what follows, cultural consensus will be demonstrated in a number of ways. First, cultural consensus or even identity will be illustrated descriptively, by setting side by side important collective representations of the Endavur Untouchables and of higher-caste actors. Second and more interestingly, cultural consensus will be demonstrated by a structural analysis involving the concepts of inclusion and exclusion, and complementarity and replication. Untouchables are defined in the present study as persons of a discrete set of low castes, excluded for reason of their extreme collective impurity from particular relations with higher beings (both human and divine). The same Untouchables are included, however, in other relations with these same higher beings. It is then shown that, in contexts in which Untouchables are included, they complement. They play the appropriate low roles necessary to the maintenance of the human and divine order. Complementarity is interpreted as an indicator of cultural consensus, but it is a weak indicator. For the Untouchables might be acting in accord with the definitions and norms of the total system because of the power of the higher castes, not because of strongly internalized agreement with the postulates of the system. The Untouchables might be "role playing."

There is a stronger indicator of cultural consensus in the

present analysis, however. Structurally, it is here shown that where the Untouchables are excluded, they replicate. They recreate among themselves the entire set of institutions and of ranked relations from which they have been excluded by the higher castes by reason of their extreme lowness. Replication is a stronger indicator of cultural consensus than complementarity, since it operates within the Untouchable subset of castes, where the power of the higher castes does not directly operate.

In the following ethnographic analysis, this argument and its structural framework will become both more concrete and more complex. Ethnographically, the subject will be investigated in two broad domains: social relations (caste) and relations with the divine (religion). The description will proceed in opposite directions in the two domains. First, social relations will be unpacked, Chinese-box fashion, from large units (village and caste) to smaller units (grade, lineage, and family), to show the progressive unfolding of complementary and replicatory structures among the low castes of Endavur. Second, the same units will be reassembled, from small to large, in a description of the ritual relations between Untouchables and the deities of person, family, and territory. The structural vocabulary will become somewhat more involved as the analysis proceeds, and it will eventually include such terms as isomorphic transformation, code-switching, conflation, differentiation, many-to-one mappings and one-to-many mappings. But the general argument will remain the same throughout: for a pervasive cultural consensus between the Untouchables and the higher castes of Endavur.

The argument for a pervasive culture of caste among those whom the caste system appears to benefit least—the Untouchables—is in clear opposition to a set of disjunctive approaches to Indian Untouchability, approaches that argue that the essence of being an Untouchable is seeing the system in a different way. These disjunctive approaches in turn reflect quite different approaches to culture, to caste, and to comparative social inequality. "Consensus," in particular, is a fighting word in contemporary sociology, with a whole range of functionalist connotations often set in simplistic opposition to those of a more Marxian "conflict" perspective. Before we begin specific analysis of the present material, therefore, let us review in more detail these disjunctive approaches to Indian Untouchability and the theories of caste and social stratification to which they contribute—as well as the general and comparative framework to which the present approach to Untouchability is intended to contribute.

Early Images of Indian Untouchability

Perhaps the earliest and simplest Western image of Untouchability is embodied in the term "outcaste." In this view, to be an Untouchable is to be beyond the reach of Hindu culture and society, to be almost cultureless. Thus the Abbé Dubois, a remarkable French missionary with first-hand knowledge of village India between 1792 and 1823, contrasts the Untouchable "Pariahs" with those higher-caste Hindus on whom the system has had its beneficent moral effect: "We can picture what would become of the Hindus if they were not kept within the bounds of duty by the rules and penalties of caste, by looking at the position of the Pariahs, or outcastes of India, who, checked by no moral restraints, abandon themselves to their natural propensities." Dubois accomplished his protoethnographic goals in south India in the immediately pre-British period by acting as Brahminlike as possible, and his Brahminocentric view of the Pariahs includes a catalog of their "natural propensities" that includes drunkenness, shamelessness, brutality, truthlessness, uncleanliness, disgusting food practices, and an absolute lack of personal honor (Dubois 1959 [1815]: 29, 54–55). The word "pariah," which derives from the Tamil name for the caste to be described in the following pages (*Paraiyan*), has accordingly moved into the English language as a synonym for the socially ostracized and the morally depraved.

The early outcaste image, as it is articulated by Dubois,

implies a major disjunction between the higher "caste Hindus" and the lowermost Untouchables, or outcastes. The very terms express the disjunction. The main body of the Hindu population "has caste," and is regulated by its social and cultural conventions, while the Paraiyans are outside the system and its restraints, and are thus in the grip of their distinctly reprehensible natures.[1] The Paraiyans, Dubois continues, both deserve and accept their low and asocial state. "The idea that he was born to be in subjection to the other castes is so ingrained in his mind that it never occurs to the Pariah to think that his fate is anything but irrevocable. Nothing will ever persuade him that men are all made of the same clay" (50).

Implicit in this last statement of Dubois', however, is a contrary early image of Indian Untouchability, a simple consensus model. If Untouchables accept their status, they believe in the legitimacy of the system. If they further possess their own caste organization, they also act in accordance with the system. Dubois knew very well that Paraiyans and other low groups had caste organization, but he failed to draw out

---

[1] The term "outcaste" or "outcast" has two different referents relevant to the present discussion. If a person violates his caste's code for conduct, he can be temporarily or permanently "outcast" for the offense. He is then without any caste at all, and must either seek readmission into the caste of his birth, or be admitted to a much lower caste, or lead an asocial existence. Since the ancient *dharmasastras* account for the origins of many low castes in a single mythic act of outcasting (usually for an improper mixed marriage), and since persons expelled from higher castes are occasionally incorporated by Untouchable castes (usually when their offense is a sexual alliance with a person of that Untouchable caste), some early Western explanations of caste assumed that all Indian Untouchables were historically derived from individual higher-caste outcasts and their descendants. When these low castes were then labelled "outcastes," the assumption stole in that there was no caste organization among them. This second assumption is emphatically incorrect. To keep the two referents of the terms straight, it is convenient to define "outcast" as an individual expelled from his caste, and "outcaste" as a largely deceptive synonym for the partially excluded lowest castes.

7

the implications of the fact. However, another Western observer of the same period did. Dr. Frances Buchanan, who surveyed newly acquired territories in Mysore for the British in 1799, describes the Untouchable Madiga as follows: "[The Madiga] are divided into small tribes of ten or twelve houses, and intermarry with the daughters of these houses only, in order to be certain of the purity of their race; of which they seem to be as fond, as those castes that are esteemed infinitely superior in rank" (Buchanan 1807: 640). Buchanan thus sees the Madiga as acting in the same way as higher castes, and in terms of the same values—concern with the "purity" of their group.

These two views of Untouchables and caste, the outcaste image and the simple consensus image, dominated Western thinking through the British period. Often they were held simultaneously and inconsistently by the same observer, but they could be brought together. Rev. Stephen Fuchs accomplishes this in a descriptive monograph on the Untouchable Balahis of Madhya Pradesh, by interpreting Balahi culture as consistent with the culture of the higher castes, but as entirely imitative: "[The Balahis'] social customs and conventions are not their own invention, but are copied after the pattern of other castes. Their moral laws and the regulations of public life are not based on high moral ideas, but mainly on fear of public opinion. . . . The rites and ceremonies . . . are each and all imitations of the rich ceremonial of their Hindu environment. Their religious ideas are no less confused . . . than those of the other castes in the [region]." (Fuchs 1950: 434). Balahi culture may thus be in agreement with higher-caste culture, but this represents a weak, copied consensus. To be an Untouchable is not to be excluded from the culture of caste, but it is to possess this culture in a thinner and less convincing form.

Contemporary anthropological perspectives on the situation of Untouchables in caste represent both continuations of and reactions to these earlier Western views. Three sets of approaches can be distinguished in the literature since 1950.

8

The first is a continuation of the "outcaste image": the cultural and social forms of Untouchables are determined by their being at some remove from a single high Brahminic culture. The second set, which are usually stated more explicitly, can be termed "models of diversity": Untouchables are the carriers of differentially valued alternate traditions, which have historically archaic or ethnically distinct roots, or which somehow express the distinct needs and experiences of those at the bottom. The third set of analytic frames is, like the first, a continuation of an older view, and can be termed "models of unity." Several of these models have been argued for the caste system in its higher reaches, but the model of unity has never been extensively argued in the contemporary anthropological literature on Untouchables. It is a form of this model that will be applied in the present work, one that states, most simply, that there is nothing distinctive about Untouchables culturally or socially, other than their placement at the bottom of a consensually defined hierarchical system. Let us look at the disjunctive models and the models of unity in more detail.

OUTCAST IMAGES

A modern example of an outcaste image can be found in Kathleen Gough's analysis of the Untouchable Pallans of south India. Unlike Dubois, and like most modern ethnographers of Indian Untouchables, Gough is empathetically biased in favor of the low castes and against what she sees as the hierarchical, etiquette-bound high castes. If Dubois viewed the "nature" of the Paraiyans as uncivilized and degraded, Gough reverses the evaluation, and sets up tacit oppositions between the inhibiting "culture" of the Brahmins and the freer "nature" of the Untouchables. She discerns in the Pallans a looser, more psychologically healthy, approach to life. In their relation to sexuality and aggression, for example, the Pallans are said to be less restricted than the Brahmins: "The expression of aggression toward elders and

9

peers [among the Pallans] is not strictly inhibited [as it is among the Brahmins]. . . . Similarly, the lower castes do not favor ascetic control of sexuality in marital relationships. . . . The ascetic control of sexuality for its own sake does not increase a man's spiritual strength" (Gough 1956: 847).

The cultural dimension of Gough's approach is "certain moral values deriving from the Sanskrit religious tradition, of which [the Brahmins] are the main carriers" (1956: 826). Since the Pallans are among the lowest castes, farthest spatially and socially from the Brahmins, they are of all the castes in the village most free of the restraints of this Sanskritic culture. As with her psychology, most of Gough's cultural typifications of the low castes are framed in opposition to negatively loaded Brahminic traits: "The low castes place much less emphasis than do Brahmins on other-worldliness and on the fate of the soul after death. Engaged in the practical business of earning a living through manual labor, the low castes care more for health and prosperity in this life" (Gough 1956: 846).

Gough's positive restatement of the outcaste image is stated psychologically, but it is set within a broader materialist analysis. A closely related example of the modern outcaste image is found in the work of Joan Mencher and Gerald Berreman. This image is similarly materialistic, but it frames the cultural component differently. Here, Untouchables are seen to have demystified caste and its accompanying ideology. They view the caste system in an objective and culture-free way for what it really is—a system of oppression. Thus Joan Mencher feels that Paraiyans in south India have a more "explicitly materialistic" view of the system and their place in it than do those at the top, and that "those at the bottom of the hierarchy have less need to rationalize its inequities" (Mencher 1974: 476). The term "rationalize" expresses a particular view of culture held widely in the anthropological literature on Untouchability: that the culture of caste is a mask for what is in fact occurring in the sociomaterial world. It is a form of false consciousness. Since this consciousness

10

serves only the interests of the high castes, the oppressors in the system, it is accordingly weak or absent among the low castes. What form of consciousness is present among the low castes is not, however discussed systematically in Mencher's work.

Gerald Berreman applies the same image in a comment on the consciouness of rural Untouchables in a Himalayan village in north India. In a short critique of Louis Dumont's structural theory of caste, Berreman claims that when he presented his version of the Dumontian model to rural Untouchables, "they laughed, and one of them said, 'you have been talking with Brahmins' " (1971: 16-23). Like Mencher, Berreman maintains that Untouchables in some way reject a high-caste model of the system, but he does not tell us what alternate model of the system is held and enacted among them. None, perhaps. In their realistic view of the system, Berreman seems to tell us, the lowest castes are uninterested in rationalizations and ideology. Untouchables act in accordance with the system because they are forced to so act, but they cannot be forced to believe.

Berreman's interpretation of Indian Untouchables is part of an explicit defense of the "caste school of race" in American sociology (found in the work of W. Lloyd Warner, John Dollard, Gunnar Myrdal, and others). In its original form, this school constructed a comparative analogy between the racial system of the American south in the 1930s and 1940s and the Indian caste system. In both systems, there are said to be two or more rigidly ranked groups between which individual mobility is impossible. Membership in each group is permanent and defined at birth (or "birth ascribed"); each group is endogamous; and each system is maintained by prohibitions on intergroup contacts, especially on sexual ones between males of the low groups and females of the high groups. Ultimately, each system is maintained by the power of the high groups—by coercion rather than by consensus.

The black sociologist Oliver Cox criticized this equation of caste and race at length in 1948, before the postwar ethno-

11

graphic data on the Indian caste system became available in the United States. His critique contrasted the simple consensus model of caste given above with American race as it was known first-hand from the monographic studies of the sociologists. Cox's theoretical point is that race is a highly specific and historically recent phenomenon, tied as ideology and practice to Western capitalism and imperialism. Caste, on the other hand, Cox views as a social system adapted to a noncapitalist economy. Cox's comparative point is that race in the American South violates the dominant egalitarian ideology of the society in which it occurs, while caste operates within a homogeneous set of nonegalitarian values, which are equally accepted by its superordinate and subordinate groups. "[Caste] carries in itself no basic antagonisms" (Cox 1948: 502).

Berreman's position on Untouchables is a return to the functionalist comparisons of the caste school of race, adding to them insights from the more detailed anthropological fieldwork on caste carried out in the 1950s in India. Berreman points out that the power of high Indian castes does have a role in maintaining the caste system, and that caste is rife with manipulation and conflict. Thus it does not differ from race in terms of these sociological abstractions. To show further that Untouchables are no more in agreement with the dominant ideology of caste than are Southern blacks with the dominant ideology of race (and that Southern whites are as undefensively hierarchical as Indian Brahmins) is once again to bring race and caste together as sociological equivalents (see Berreman 1960, 1972b).

The modern outcaste image of Indian Untouchables has another comparative affinity, though this one is less explicit. It is with Oscar Lewis's "culture of poverty" hypothesis for the urban poor in Western societies. In Lewis's restatement of the concept, the culture of poverty is a thin one—"the poverty of culture is one of the crucial aspects of the culture of poverty" (1970: 78). This thinness is a consequence of the purely rational adaptation of the urban poor to the situation in which they find themselves. The poor in capitalistic societies have less reason than the middle class to act in terms of middle-class values, since these values do not pay off for them. Nor do the urban poor have an alternate tradition or system of meaning available to them, other than the weakly structured and negatively defined "culture of poverty." Likewise, Untouchables in India do not accept high-caste culture because this culture has no rationalizing value for them. The Untouchables' alternatives vary according to the image. For Dubois, Untouchables are in a state of unbridled license, while for Gough, they are in a state of psychologically healthy removal from an obsessive high-caste culture. For Mencher and Berreman, they are the sceptics and demystifiers of caste—perhaps even its existentialists and protorevolutionaries.

MODELS OF DIVERSITY

The second set of contemporary anthropological approaches to Untouchables and caste argues for essential cultural diversity, and is itself an exceedingly diverse set. Like the outcaste images, the models of diversity are disjunctive; they stress contrasts between Untouchables and the higher castes. Unlike the outcaste images, however, they do not state these contrasts in terms of culture versus lack of culture. Rather, they view Untouchables as the bearers of alternate social and cultural systems, or of variants of the dominant system particularly adapted to the needs and experiences of those at the very bottom of the system. These needs and experiences vary according to the particular model. Their analytic cruxes include historical, communicative, psychological, economic, and political determinants. Each particular model of diversity tends to be tighter analytically than the outcaste images. Each generally makes a clear statement about the nature of the Untouchable subsystem, and about the mechanisms that have produced this subsystem. Taken as a whole, however, the predictions for "difference at the bottom" of all of these models of diversity form a rather heterogeneous set.

Consider, for example, Bernard Cohn's analysis of the Untouchable Camars of north India. Cohn sees the Camars as differing from the high castes for the same reason that Gough's Pallans differ from the Brahmins: for reason of the social and spatial separation between Untouchables and higher castes. Because Untouchables cannot hear the Vedas, or be served by Brahmins, or enter high-caste temples, they suffer from a kind of communications block. The result of this block, however, is not a form of culturelessness, but the retention of a historically prior pre-Aryan little tradition. Unlike the great tradition of the higher castes and of the Brahmins in particular, the little tradition of the Camars contains a "pre-Aryan and non-Brahmanic" religion, which emphasizes the propitiation of goddesses of disease, and the use of mediums and exorcists (Cohn 1955: 58). Cohn has to qualify these disjunctive contrasts considerably, however: "It is almost impossible to sort out those traits which are Sanskritic and those which are non-Sanskritic . . . and . . . what is idiosyncratic to the Camars as a group and what is a common body of ritual and belief held by other low castes and high castes as well" (Cohn 1954: 175). Given this qualification, then, Cohn's analysis amounts to a set of tentatively specified contrasts within an unanalyzed framework of cultural continuities.

Cohn's subcultural dichotomies, however, form only the baseline for his treatment of social change. For the Camars have in the last fifty years attempted to Sanskritize, to raise their status by adopting symbols of higher status in their local hierarchy. In doing so, they have abandoned many of the features of their distinctive little tradition, and have adopted the dominant Thakur's traditional caste code, which includes a nonbeef diet, a tighter joint family, and more "Brahmanic" ritual practices. Therefore, although the Camars may have possessed a somewhat distinctive culture of their own in the base-line period, it is not a culture that they distinctively

14

valued in any way, for they were quite willing to abandon it in an effort to raise their status.

The Camars' attempt to raise their status has been largely futile, however, according to Cohn. At the same time that the Camars were Sanskritizing in the direction of the high-ranking Thakurs, the Thakurs were moving toward a more "Westernized" life style. This included "Western" education, "secularization," extensive urban contacts, a loosened caste and family structure, and more equality between husband and wife (Cohn 1955: 67). Thus, in the end, the original little tradition/great tradition dichotomy between Untouchables and high castes was simply replaced by a newer cultural dichotomy, an obsolete great tradition versus a more prestigious "Westernized" tradition. And the Thakurs have retained their political dominance over the Camars during the same period, permitting them to frustrate two attempts by the Camars and other low castes in the late 1940s to force electorally based rank concessions from them. In Cohn's analysis, then, the Camars are on a perpetual treadmill, culturally always a step behind the Thakurs. The difference between the Camars and the Thakurs expresses only this dynamic of change and of blocked communication: the Camars differ only because they can never catch up.

A second model of diversity is found in Pauline Kolenda's treatment of karma doctrine among a caste of Untouchable Sweepers in north India, and turns on a psychological argument. Of the models of diversity that we are considering here, Kolenda's is the most minimal and the most carefully stated. Kolenda begins her analysis by demonstrating that the basic themes in the Sweepers' religion are common not only to higher-caste religion but to themes found in the ancient Sanskritic texts. She then deals with a single disjunction— with the question of how the Sweepers deal with one unpleasant implication of the linked doctrines of karma, dharma, and transmigration. According to these doctrines, which the Sweepers understand in abstract form, one's caste status in a given birth is the result of the total score of one's good or bad

15

karma ("action" in accord with one's dharma, "duty," as defined in a given caste) in past lives. If the Untouchable Sweepers were to apply the karmaic explanation to their present low status, they would be admitting that they deserved such a status—that they had been unusually wicked in past rebirths. This admission, according to Kolenda, would cause them "religious anxiety." Why it would do so is not entirely clear. The hidden psychological assumption seems to be that no one wants to accept bottommost status in a ranked system, or that no one wants to accept the idea that they deserve so low a status.

In any case, Kolenda reports that the Sweepers refuse to apply karma doctrine to their own low status. Instead, they refer their present status to collective myths which state that they were once of much higher caste, and fell due to a terrible accident motivated by the best of intentions. According to one myth, for example, the original Untouchable was a Brahmin who came upon a cow mired in the mud. Intending to help the cow (a meritorious intent), he pulled on its tail. But the cow died, and since he was in contact with a dead cow—a polluting contact—his older brothers outcast him and he became the first Untouchable (version reported by Cohn 1954: 113). Not only do myths like this protect Untouchables from the "anxiety" of karmaic explanation, according to Kolenda, but they provide them with a positive sense of having once been much higher (see Kolenda 1964: 74-76). Kolenda considerably qualifies the idea that such avoidance of karmaic thinking is distinctive of Untouchables alone, however: "Since [these] legends are so commonly found among middle and low castes . . . we may ask whether, in fact, the transmigration doctrine does justify the differences in caste rank for these castes, or whether it is usually outweighed by myths explaining the injustice of the low status of the group. Perhaps the theory is a justification of rank for only the highest castes, as Max Weber has suggested" (Kolenda 1964: 75).

For a third model of diversity for Untouchables in caste,

we must turn once again to Kathleen Gough. Though Gough's explicit analysis of culture and Untouchability amounts to an example of the outcaste image, her clearly formulated analysis of the material determinants of Pallan social organization also makes major predictions for evaluative and normative differences between the high and low castes. Gough's analysis can thus be seen in another light as a model of diversity, in which cultural differences are generated by political and economic variables.

Gough's explanation of Pallan social organization begins with the highly asymmetric political and economic relationship between the dominant Brahmins and the Untouchable Pallan laborers of the village. Traditionally, not only did the Brahmins have direct authority over their Pallan laborers, but they held most of the land in the village. As the result of the Pallans' lack of land and movable property, says Gough, there are no material bases for ranked differences within the Pallan caste. The internal social organization of the Pallans is therefore characterized by "lack of privacy . . . fanatical emphasis on equality, and the extreme control of the street over individual affairs." "The street" here refers to Pallan political organization. The Pallan caste is divided into four streets, each with its own assembly and its own headman, and these assemblies affect the individual Pallan "at the slightest sign of individual nonconformity or in the smallest crisis of family life." And the tightness of this political organization is a consequence of two factors: the need to present a solid front to the Brahmins, who hold an entire Pallan street collectively responsible for an offense committed by any member; and the weakness of an alternate internal authority system, the family (Gough 1960a: 43-44).

The weakness of the family Gough again attributes to the Pallans' relationship to the land. She posits a direct relationship between landholding and the depth of the patrilineage: "the *Aadi-Draavidas* [the Pallans] do not own land . . . [and] their patrilineal group is therefore very shallow." As agricultural laborers, Pallan women are independent wage-earners,

17

as are sons from early adolescence. Thus, an economic base of the husband and father's authority is missing—the common working of a common piece of land. This factor then feeds back as "equality" within the kin group: "rank is underplayed in the low caste kinship system and great stress is placed on the equivalence and solidarity of peers" (Gough 1956: 845-46).

Starting with a material factor and a political factor, then —the relation of the Pallans to the land and the relation of the Pallans to the Brahmins—Gough derives a distinctive social and cultural subsystem at the bottom of a local caste hierarchy. The solidarity and egalitarianism of the Pallans are said to be in particularly strong contrast to comparable patterns in the Brahmin caste, for the Brahmins have no internal caste organization, and they predicate every social relationship on rank. Gough sums up these contrasts in a personal statement about the ethos of Pallan life: "Pallans show an almost fanatical passion for equality within their caste group. In fact, I found the equal and comradely style of life in the Palla street a great relief from the obsessive ritualism, hierarchy, and envy in the Brahmin street. . . . [The Pallans] react to their poverty (of which they are well aware) with a combination of anger, resignation, wryness and humor" (Gough 1973: 232, 233-34). Gough does not, it should be noted, include in her analysis a consideration of the relations between subunits of the Pallan caste, the "streets." Nor does she discuss the relations between this caste of Pallans, the Devandra Pallans by subcaste, and another Pallan subcaste (the Tekkatti Pallans) that lives separately in the same village.

Though Gough does not argue the point explicitly, the distinctive features that she discerns in the Pallans—solidarity, egalitarianism, and the weakness of traditional kinship authority—might be expected to preadapt them to radical anticaste political action. Robert Miller, who has presented the last example of a model of diversity to be considered here, claims that the Untouchable Mahars of central India

18

are already engaged in such political action. And unlike Cohn's Camars, who are attempting to diminish the despised cultural disjunction between themselves and the higher castes, Miller's Mahars are said to be actively constructing a radical cultural disjunction between themselves and the higher castes, to be in a sense revaluing their little tradition. The Mahar, Miller writes, "have been building a tradition which can hardly be called 'a distinctive variant of *the* Great Tradition cognate to those of the four major *varnas* of Hindu society' [quoting Singer 1958: 194]." In fact, the Mahars are building on a counter-great tradition which has always existed in India, as an antithesis to the Brahmanic great tradition (which Miller never defines). In this counter tradition, "equality is opposed to inequality; individual ability is opposed to merger of the individual in the group; emotionalism is opposed to ritualism; escape *from* the system is opposed to movement *within* the system." Miller's discussion amounts to an assertion that bhakti devotionalism, Mahar militance, and the eventual emergence of neo-Buddhism from the Mahar caste, attest to the strength of these alternate values. To the possible objection that bhakti and militance are very much part of the great tradition, Miller replies that he is not concerned with individual cultural traits, but with the total pattern, which among the Mahars must be seen "not as a variant of *the* system, but as an entirely different system in itself" (Miller 1966: 26, 28 and *passim*).

Miller's evidence for the contours of this entirely disjunctive cultural system among the Mahars is mostly formal and decontextualized, however. He cites oral tradition and the written statements of politicized Mahar groups, but gives no detailed information on the baseline for Mahar change, on social organization, on behavior, or on how their "escape from the system" is in fact working out.[2]

[2] For a more detailed and sophisticated treatment of a low group that is manipulating the "great civilization" in a politically self-conscious way, see Martin Orans' *The Santal: A Tribe in Search of a Great Tradition* (Detroit: Wayne State University Press, 1965). I am

19

What are we to make of all these models of diversity, other than that they reflect a very real empirical diversity in India, which became apparent after the first round of anthropological fieldwork in the 1950s? One way to sort them out is to note that two, Kolenda's and Gough's, are nonhistorical. These two make synchronic predictions about necessary differences between the high and low castes in a traditional village hierarchy. Since the determinants of the differences are very general—psychology and karma, material asymmetry—it will not therefore be unfair in what follows to test them, to note and analyze the degree to which the data from Endavur agrees with these predictions. The other two models of diversity, Cohn's and Miller's, are stated as models of change. As such, both could be basically accurate at different points in time. See, for example, Owen Lynch's study of Untouchables in a north India city, where a particular caste of Leatherworkers has pursued a strategy of Sanskritization in the early part of the century (more successfully than Cohn's Camars), and then switched over to a mixed strategy including an anticaste ideology (with less cultural reconstruction than Miller's Mahars) (Lynch 1969). Nevertheless, both Cohn's and Miller's .models of change also include statements about the traditional baseline, and as such can be

---

not considering Orans' analysis here because of the additional complexities introduced into the argument by the Santals' recent tribal background. There is yet another model of diversity relevant to just this variable, however: the idea that the present Untouchable groups in India, or some of them at any rate, are the historical precipitate of ethnically and culturally distinct tribal entities that have been Hinduized and introduced to the "bottom rung" of local caste hierarchies. Such is the thrust of Irawati Karve's "agglomerative" interpretation of caste, though Karve does not actually argue that Untouchables are more likely than higher castes to bear the markers of their former tribal backgrounds (see Karve 1961). Nor am I aware of any other anthropologist who has tried to sustain this kind of argument of tribal diversity for any of the major contemporary Untouchable castes of India.

empirically commented upon in light of the Endavur data. We will reserve these empirical critiques for later.

For now, let us consider the theoretical implications of these models of diversity, particularly their approaches to culture, to caste, and to comparative social stratification. To begin with, the models of diversity as a whole assume a different theory of culture than do the outcaste images. Outcaste images imply that culture (or the culture of caste, at any rate) is only a manipulative rationalization, and that culture-free perception and action are to some degree possible. In the outcaste image, some cultures can be more realistic than others, some can be thinner than others. Models of diversity make no such assumption. For this set of approaches, all the varying cultures of caste are equally thick and equally relativistic. The culture of a given caste varies with its position in the system, but none of these cultures is necessarily truer than any other. Models of diversity attempt to explain the determinants of cultural difference from caste to caste, not to determine the objectivity of these differences as judgments of a system of oppression.

Despite a different underlying treatment of culture, however, models of diversity can have the same implications for general theories of social inequality as outcaste images. For both, approaches to Indian Untouchables are disjunctive. To the extent that models of diversity analyze only difference and ignore cultural continuities between castes, they can then be taken to imply that power and oppression alone account for caste stratification. Models of diversity then differ from the outcaste images only in that the latter imply that Untouchables have some awareness of their own oppression, while the former contain no such implication.

To see how these equations between cultural disjunction and power are made, consider a recent typological article by Berreman, in which the analogy between caste and race is extended several steps further, to include ethnic stratification and even class as comparable sociological phenomena.

21

Berreman begins with a point similar to Cohn's assumption of blocked communication between high castes and Untouchables. To make this point, he shifts from his earlier outcaste image to a model of diversity: "In the caste system, 'Because intensive and status equal interaction is limited to the caste, a common and distinctive culture is assured. This is a function of the quality and density of communication within the group, for culture is learned, shared and transmitted' [quoting Berreman 1967: 51]" (Berreman 1972b: 400). Berreman jumps from this characterization of the cultural context of caste, where each social unit (each caste) is imagined as a tightly bound cultural unit (a "distinctive culture"), to the following generalization: "Caste, race and ethnic stratification, like all plural systems therefore, are systems of social separation and cultural heterogeneity, maintained by common or overriding economic and political institutions rather than by agreement or consensus regarding the stratification system and its rationale" (*ibid.*). Berreman does back off slightly from his total denial of consensus, stating that there is a common understanding in caste and in other stratified systems about "the objective facts . . . who has the power . . . and how it is likely to be exercized" (*ibid.*). But his basic comparative point remains: only power, and consensus about power, determine caste and all other systems of structured social inequality.

Berreman's position is admittedly extreme, but some of its comparative assumptions are shared by other anthropologists who have analyzed Indian Untouchables disjunctively. Also shared by these anthropologists is a more diffuse attitude toward caste. Gough, Mencher, Berreman, and Miller, in particular, make manifestly clear at some point their personal distaste for caste, for its social inequities, and for its oppression. Their egalitarian values run clearly against the system, and in favor of those people whom the system seems most obviously to be exploiting: the bottommost Untouchables. Given this empathetic attitude, it is particularly difficult for these analysts to specify possible continuities between the positively viewed Untouchables and the negatively viewed system in its higher reaches.

It should be noted, however, that there is no necessary connection between such empathy and a critical view of caste as a system of oppression. One can, for example, incorporate cultural consensus into a radical Marxist interpretation of caste, as evidence of false consciousness, or of the operation of ideological domination, among the lowest castes.[3]

There is one other reason for the degree to which disjunctive models—outcaste images and models of diversity—have dominated analyses of Indian Untouchability. This reason is both pragmatic and perceptual. Ethnography that discovers something new is rewarding, while the overt payoff may seem minimal in an extended study that concludes that the only surprise is that there is no surprise, that there is nothing new culturally. The degree of commonality and cultural sharing between Untouchables and higher castes may seem self-evident and trivial to any Indianist with field experience; why run through a tedious litany of all the resemblances? The alternative, however, is to reify part cultures as if they were whole cultures, and to lose sight of systematic interconnections between the parts. Charles Valentine has made a similar criticism of the culture of poverty studies which, he notes, generally start with some statement that the culture of the poor in complex Western societies is really a "subculture." These studies then go on, he says, to describe the subcultures of the poor as if they were self-contained wholes, emphasizing distinctiveness and failing to weigh continuities with the larger culture. Valentine calls of a countervailing attempt to "discern what cultural features are shared by different but related subsystems, and how subcultures are articulated with universals in the total system" (Valentine 1968: 115). It should be clear by now that we are here

[3] For an example of such an interpretation, see Djurfelt and Lindberg 1975.

making a similar call with respect to the cultural system of Indian Untouchables.

MODELS OF UNITY

There are two important models of unity among the contemporary approaches to India, the structural model of Louis Dumont and the "ethnosociological" model of McKim Marriott, Ronald Inden, and Ralph Nicholas. Unlike the disjunctive approaches above, both of these models are fundamentally concerned with "ideology" or culture; neither treats culture in caste as an epiphenomenon of something more sociologically universal (such as stratification, power, or oppression). Both models state that there is a consistent set of underlying principles that structure Indian cultural conceptions, that these principles are found universally within India, but that they are also unique to India. Both models contain principles of diversity, but in each model diversity is either "encompassed by," or generated from, a more basic unity. And both models assume agreement on the basic cultural principles as profound among Indian Untouchables as among anyone else in the caste system.[4]

The framework for the following ethnographic analysis is inspired by Dumont's structural model of Indian society. The ethnosociological approach, however, and its particular application to Indian folk religion by Susan Wadley (Wadley 1975), are also conceptually useful in attempts to grasp the indigenous cultural categories of the Endavur Untouchables.

What, then, is Dumont's structural approach to Indian society, and what are its implications for "being an Untouchable?" To begin somewhat simplistically, Dumont does not see caste as an inexplicably "unequal" system that requires an explanation because of the way in which it violates the more fundamentally egalitarian "nature" of man. Rather,

---

[4] There are profound differences between the two approaches as well, though they are not central here. For a pro-Dumontian gloss of the disagreements, see Barnett, Fruzzetti, and Ostor, 1976. See also Marriott 1969, Dumont 1971, and Marriott and Inden 1974.

Dumont reverses the comparative question, and suggests that it is Western egalitarian ideology that is the social-scientific puzzle, and that rank or hierarchy is more transhumanly comprehensible: "man does not only think, he acts. . . . To adopt a value is to introduce hierarchy, and a certain consensus of values, a certain hierarchy of ideas, things and people, is indispensable to social life. . . . In relation to these more or less necessary requirements of social life, the idea of equality, even if it is thought superior, is artificial" (Dumont 1970: 54-55). Caste represents the institutionalization of hierarchical values, the most elaborate known working out of a set of values that we in the West have been systematically denying for the last three hundred years. To understand fully this egalitarian effort in the West, Dumont says, we must confront its polar opposite in India, hierarchy.

In his comparative epistemology, Dumont differs radically from Berreman and from other conflict theorists and functionalists. For Dumont, to compare is not to search for abstract, ahistorical essences common to caste, race, and ethnic stratification, and to dismiss ideological specificities as unimportant detail. To compare is to construct a structural analysis of each ideological and social formation, and then to confront these fully and specifically analyzed formations with one another (see Barnett, Fruzzetti, and Ostor 1976: 627-28). The purpose of the confrontation is dialectically to improve the understanding of each structure. Thus a provisional understanding of caste as a total ideological and social formation might contribute to a better understanding of race, and further insights about race similarly analyzed might be dialectically fed back to a more adequate understanding of caste.

At present, Dumont's comparative analyses contain a suspicious number of simple logical oppositions, but they are nevertheless interesting.[5] For example, on caste and race, Dumont returns to Cox, but not to Cox's materialism. Caste,

[5] Dumont has pushed his comparison of *homo hierarchicus* and *homo aequalis* considerably further in Dumont 1977. We are not considering this elaborated comparison here.

Dumont says, is a homogeneous moral system that values hierarchy and does not isolate and value the individual as the "measure of all things." Racism, on the other hand, is ideologically linked to egalitarianism, individualism, and to the Western denial of hierarchy. According to Dumont, in denying hierarchy in the social realm as a legitimate innate quality of the relations between humans, Western ideology must resituate it in a rigorously differentiated natural realm as racism, referred exclusively to natural difference (see Dumont 1960; Dumont 1970: 35-55).

Thus in Dumont's approach, Indian Untouchables are not the abstract sociological equivalent of racially subordinate groups in Western society. What, then, are Indian Untouchables, and how do they fit into the specific ideological and social formation? To begin indirectly, there is in Dumont's conception of Indian hierarchy an unstated implication about the "view from the bottom." For if, in India, hierarchy can be apprehended as a positive value, it must therefore be satisfying for actors throughout the system, even for those at the bottom. Either that, or power must suddenly intrude somewhere in the system, to hold down a set of people who have made a cognitive break from these hierarchical values. Dumont's position assumes the first possibility, and denies the second. There is a further possible implication of Dumont's argument for a positive view of hierarchy: that it represents an unmodified return to the old "simple consensus model" of caste, in which caste is seen as a system almost idyllically free of strife and conflict. Such is the implication that Berreman in particular draws from Dumont (see Berreman 1971: 18-19). Dumont, however, explicitly denies this particular implication of hierarchy, and points out that hierarchy in fact generates conflict. "India . . . emphasizes [hierarchy] to the point that situations tending to equality are unstable and conflict is called for to solve them by the establishment of a gradation. This might well be the basic reason why dispute is so endemic in India: however developed it might be, the system has not succeeded in establishing a perfect gradation of the whole of social life" (Dumont 1957b: 18). Therefore hierarchy, like "consensus" above, is not a term intended to deny the existence of dispute, but rather to frame the matters that are appropriately the subject of dispute. Dumont sees most disputes about rank in caste as disputes about one's legitimate position in a ranked system, not about the legitimacy of the ranked system itself. And this is as true for Untouchables as it is for higher-caste actors.

Dumont is more specific about the relation of Untouchables to the Indian social order, however. In his holistic conception of caste, hierarchy is expressed in an Indian cultural code of relative purity and impurity, in a continuously graded status order whose extremes are the Brahmin at the top— the most pure of men—and the Untouchable at the bottom —the least pure of men. Brahmin and Untouchable are conceptually opposed in a number of ways that contribute to their archetypal purity and impurity, according to Dumont. The Brahmin lives in the center of the village, and is a "god on earth," while the Untouchable lives outside the village and is apparently excluded from religious life. The murder of a Brahmin is as heinous a crime as the murder of a cow, while the Untouchable is the scavenger and the eater of dead cows. The Brahmin purifies himself in order to approach the gods, and thus mediates between man and god. The Untouchable makes personal purity possible by removing the strongest sources of organic impurity, and the Untouchable mediates between man and the maleficent "demons." For Dumont, however, this opposition of Brahmin and Untouchable is also a complementarity—the completion of a "whole" by two equally necessary but unequally ranked parts. "The impurity of the Untouchable is conceptually inseparable from the purity of the Brahmin." Since "the execution of impure tasks by some is necessary to the maintenance of purity for others . . . society is a totality made up of two unequal but complementary parts" (Dumont 1970: 92, 93).

But what exactly does this discussion of the relation of

Untouchables to the structural whole of Indian society tell us about the possible consciousness of the Untouchables? Dumont never explicitly states his conception of the "view from the bottom," perhaps because he considers the continuities among Untouchables too self-evident ethnographically to require comment. However, his analysis of status, power, and "encompassment" in caste does imply a particular type of commonality between top and bottom. For Dumont's model, unlike the disjunctive models above, situates diversity in the middle of the system rather than in its lower reaches.

The argument is as follows. Dumont sees rank in caste as a case of pure ritual status, not as a reflection or an expression of political and economic power. But caste as a social institution must accommodate itself to power, and it does so by "encompassing" power within status. In the varna scheme, the Brahmin, who is at the apex of the status order, is clearly ranked above the Kshatriya or king, who is at the apex of the power order. This same structural relation is found in contemporary Indian villages, according to Dumont, where the Brahmin caste, however poor and powerless, always ranks above the dominant caste, the local power holders. Power is then given a range in which to operate, in the middle range of local caste hierarchies. In this region of the hierarchy, Dumont believes, a great diversity of caste codes is permitted to represent dominant rank, and the unilinear ranking of castes is less clear and consistent due to struggles based on power and wealth. Ritual status as the unambiguous basis for rank then reemerges at the bottom of caste hierarchies, thus "encompassing" or bracketing power as a modifier of the rank order (see Dumont 1970).

What this means for Untouchables is fairly simple. If we follow Dumont's logic through, rank defined in unambiguous terms of relative purity and impurity should be as clear among Untouchables as it is among the highest castes. Diversity and dissension should be sought instead among the middle-ranking castes in the system.

28

The middle castes are not the subject here, nor is Dumont's "encompassment" theory central to the interpretative problems that we are raising for the Untouchables of Endavur.[6] More important for the present purpose is the general idea of a pervasive and continuous social hierarchy marked by relative purity and impurity. More specifically important is the possibility that Untouchables might define their own internal social organization as consistently in these terms as do the higher castes, and that they might be as pervasively "rank-conscious" as the higher castes. These simple ideas we will be testing with the data which follow.

The structural model that follows is also based on Dumont, though it is considerably more formal in its present statement. In his analysis of the lineage cults of the Pramalai Kallar of south India, Dumont in effect shows that orthodox cultural structures are replicated among a low and territorially isolated dominant caste. The Kallars divide the "divine" into two categories, Dumont says: high, pure gods who receive only vegetarian offerings, and lower, less pure gods who receive bloody sacrifice. This dichotomy of the divine is isomorphic with a basic human dichotomy: that between the pure but powerless Brahmins and the impure but dominant Kallars. By worshipping among themselves a divine world so organized, Dumont suggests, the Kallars admit to their own status inferiority vis-à-vis the Brahmins, and reaffirm the holistic interdependence between high and low god, between Brahmin and Kallar. The Kallar also state and rank the dichotomy according to orthodox cultural principles, relative purity and impurity (here expressed by the type of offerings to the respective gods) (see Dumont 1957a: 415-19; Dumont 1959). This model of structural isomorphism and of structural replication will be formalized and elaborated in what follows, to make a similar argument

---

[6] An empirical problem is that transactional and opinion analyses of caste-rank orders do not show any greater indeterminancy in the middle ranges than at the extremes of caste (see Marriott 1968). For some interpretative and theoretical problems, see Marriott 1969.

for a deep sharing of cultural codes among a group of Untouchables.

As for "ethnosociology" and its use here, this approach, whose purpose is to describe the "pervasive indigenous assumptions" (Marriott 1974: 1) behind social action in India, is a model of unity even more radical than Dumont's. A linguistic analogy might give a sense of its relevance to the issue of Untouchables and Indian culture. Ethnosociology is presently endeavoring to construct a model of Indian cultural assumptions so basic that it can be compared to the categories of a language grammar. To suggest that low-ranking actors who act in terms of a culture so analyzed might also "reject" its categorical assumptions is then logically equivalent to suggesting that some speakers of a given language might similarly reject its grammar. Neither, of course, is possible. The principles are too deep; they are the very stuff of thought and of action.[7]

Ethnosociology accordingly makes no specific predictions about Untouchables; it simply assumes them to be sharers in a deep cultural grammar common to everyone in Hindu village India. Nor does ethnosociology in its present formulations (Marriott and Inden 1973; Marriott and Inden 1974; Marriott 1974; Inden and Nicholas 1972; Inden 1975) have much to say about social or cultural comparison, other than an essentially negative comparative point—that exogenous models of society, drawn from Western social experience, are unilluminating when applied to Indian social reality. As a relativistic view from within, ethnosociology can be taken as antithetical to Dumont's structuralism. But as a model of unity, with a distinct, more carefully cultural focus, it can

[7] In one article, Marriott does generate a diverse set of transactional strategies from the fundamentally unitary ethnosociological model. Without going into the technicalities of his argument, let us only note that this approach to diversity—like Dumont's, but for very different reasons—also predicts most of its diversity in the middle ranges of local caste hierarchies. Here also, Brahmins and Untouchables are more like one another than they are like the middle castes, for both are restricted to "asymmetric" strategies (see Marriott 1974: 23-24).

also be taken as complementary to Dumont's approach, and we shall so take it here. Ethnosociology is currently generating some useful propositions about indigenously defined units of action, and about the semantics of the relations between these units. It is becoming increasingly clear, for example, that "purity/impurity" is too simplistic and too misleading a gloss of the relation between high and low-caste actors, that the indigenous definition of rank also contains ideas about auspiciousness, power (as it is culturally understood), and control. Similarly, the concept of a "transaction," which in its initial statement was a type of raw behavior (Marriott 1968), has recently been rethought in cognitive terms (Marriott 1974), and as such constitutes a more precise and specific tool for decoding the meaning of a given caste's status and identity than does anything found in Dumont. Finally, ethnosociology is considerably revising our perhaps ethnocentric ideas about the relations between humans and gods in Indian culture (Wadley 1975), as we shall see below.

Ethnosociology thus provides us with more precise approximations of certain Indian cultural conceptions than does Dumont's approach. Where it does, we will adopt its insights. Ethnosociology is, however, at present less explicit about the total structure of the Indian social order than is Dumont's model. It has virtually nothing to say about the relation between culture and behavior. And its suggestions for transsocietal comparison are neither as explicit nor as interesting as Dumont's. For this reason, the Dumontian structural model of caste and Untouchables will very much "encompass" ethnosociology in the following ethnographic analysis.

CHAPTER II

Untouchability in South India: A Historical Review

THERE was in the prewar Indian Independence movement a fundamental dispute between Mahatma Gandhi and B. R. Ambedkar concerning the relation of caste to Untouchability.[1] Gandhi felt that Untouchability was an "excrescence" of Hinduism, an institution to be rooted out by reformist change "in the hearts" of high-caste Indians, so that the Untouchables might be integrated into the Sudras in a reformed, unranked, varna system. Ambedkar, himself of Untouchable Mahar origins, maintained that caste implied Untouchability and could not be thus "purified" of it. Varna, the great fourfold textual organization of classical Indian society into the categories Brahmin (Priest), Kshatriya (Warrior), Vaishya (Merchant), and Sudra (Servant), likewise implied rank and caste, and could not be realistically recreated as a set of cooperative, egalitarian social groups. India's Untouchables, Ambedkar felt, would not win an improved position in Indian society by voluntary reform from above, but by a forced change in their economic and political subordination, and by internal India-wide political organization around initially separatist principles. They might then eventually become reintegrated as "citizens" into a modern secular Indian state.

Neither of the futures envisioned by Gandhi or Ambedkar has come to pass for Indian Untouchables in the 1970s. Am-

---

[1] I am indebted to David Ludden, a historian of south India at the University of Pennsylvania, for a critique of this chapter. I have incorporated some of Mr. Ludden's points where noted. Otherwise, the interpretation—in particular, its occasional speculations—remains my own responsibility.

32

bedkar's legacy is the official government policy of protective discrimination—positions reserved for Untouchables in the civil service, in legislatures, and in higher education—and the constitutional illegality of Untouchability. Gandhi's legacy is a mostly verbal unease among educated Indians about the continued existence of Untouchability in Indian villages, and a relaxation of "Untouchability behavior" in the larger temples of India.

As for the past, Ambedkar's conception of the relation between varna, caste, Untouchability, and political action is far more realistic historically than is Gandhi's revitalistic vision. Both caste and Untouchability are deeply rooted in Indian history, in the agrarian social order that dominated the Indian economy until the advent of the British, and which remains today India's largest economic sector. Though the relation of India's rural Untouchables to this social order has shifted in subtle ways in the past two centuries, there remain pervasive continuities, especially of meaning and of cultural construction, with this deeply rooted past. Let us review this historical context, then, not only for cultural continuities, but for an understanding of the political and economic forces that have been acting on south Indian Untouchables both in pre-British and in modern times.

The earliest evidence for caste and Untouchability is textual, and dates back more than two thousand years. Varna is first mentioned in a late Vedic text (c. 1000 B.C.), and by the time of the lawbook of Manu (c. 200 B.C. to A.D. 200), varna and *jati* (or "caste") coexist as isomorphically ranked social orders. A vast number of extant castes of this period are explained and ranked by Manu according to a theory of mixture between the varna categories. According to Manu, marriage within a varna is best, and produces children of the same varna as their parents. Intervarna marriage is also recognized, and its offspring are generally lower than either parent. However, the offspring of parents who marry hypergamously or "with the hair"—a higher varna male marrying a lower varna female—are not so low as are the offspring of parents who marry hypogamously or "against the hair"—a lower varna male marrying a higher varna female (see Tambiah 1973 for a more systematic analysis of the logic of varnaic mixture in Manu).

According to Manu, the most extreme of these extravarnaic marriages produces the Candala, a being with many of the social attributes of Indian Untouchables two thousand years later. The Candala is the result of a hypogamous marriage of the most unequal type, between a Sudra male and a Brahmin female, and he is described as the "lowest of men": "The dwellings of the Candalas . . . shall be outside the village . . . and their wealth shall be dogs and donkeys. Their dress shall be the garments of the dead, they shall eat their food from broken dishes, black iron shall be their ornaments, and they must always wander from place to place. A man who fulfills a religious duty shall not seek intercourse with them; their transactions shall be among themselves, and their marriages with their equals" (Manu 10: 51-53). Thus, like contemporary Untouchables, the Candalas are excluded from the village and from the religious life of the high born. They are similarly recipients of low and inauspicious things (broken dishes and garments of the dead). They are not pictured as solitary outcasts, but as an endogamous community with "transactions . . . among themselves."

The Candalas may be excluded from close interaction with the high born, but they are not excluded from the continued operation of the principles of admixture that generated them. In another passage, Manu carries the description of improper mixture two steps further, to describe the generation of a social type even lower than the Candala, the Antya-vayasin. While hypogamous marriage between a Sudra male and a Brahmin female produces the Candala, hypergamous marriage of the same distance, between a Brahmin male and a Sudra female, produces the Nishada (Manu 10:8), also a low mixture but not so low as the Candala, since this marriage is not "against the hair" but with it. Finally, a hypogamous union of a Nishada female and a Candala male, a mixture doubly "against the hair," generates the Antyavayasin, who is "employed in the burial grounds, and despised even by those excluded from the Aryan community" (Manu 10:39) (see Figure 2-1). Just as the Candala can be seen

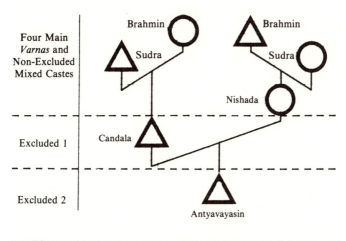

Four Main *Varnas* and Non-Excluded Mixed Castes

Brahmin

Sudra

Brahmin

Sudra

Nishada

Excluded 1

Candala

Excluded 2

Antyavayasin

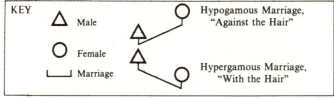

KEY

△ Male

◯ Female

⌐⌐ Marriage

Hypogamous Marriage, "Against the Hair"

Hypergamous Marriage, "With the Hair"

FIGURE 2-1. Levels of Exclusion in the Genealogy of the Antya-vayasin

as a proto-Untouchable, the Antyavayasin corresponds conceptually to relationships among contemporary Untouchable castes, in which particularly low groups are excluded by the excluded; they are Untouchable to the Untouchables.

Thus in the lawbook of Manu, Untouchables are very much part of the logic of the system, and to be an Untouchable is not to be cut off from the operation of this logic. Untouchability is thus very old as an Indian social fact. For whatever the actual historical relation between varna and caste two thousand years ago, it is likely that low and excluded groups were part of Indian society at the time, in order for Manu's codification to have had a social referent.

The codifications of Manu applied to the great Hindu kingdoms of north India two millennia ago, and in north India today varna categories are still used indigenously to group castes into larger categories. Varna has apparently always been a less common way of conceiving of rank in South India, but textual sources from the south almost as old as Manu suggest the existence there of similarly ranked relations between humans, and of behavioral expressions of these relations reaching the extremes of Untouchability and of Unapproachability. The Sangam grammarian Tolkappiar (c. A.D. 300-600), for example, divides the south Indian society of his time into four varnalike categories: Brahmin, Arasar or King, Vaniyar or Merchant, and Vellalar or Peasant. Unlike varnas, however, in this system the Brahmin has no clear precedence over the Arasar. Furthermore, the Vellalar category is divided into "superior Vellalars" and "inferior Vellalars." Superior Vellalars have the right to intermarry with Arasars or kings, unlike inferior Vellalars, who are the "only class . . . considered *fit* to be employed as farm laborers" (Subrahmanian 1966: 280).

In addition to these broad categories, the Sangam literature of south India mentions much lower groups, though these groups are not generated by improper marriages from the varnalike categories. Goldsmiths and Cobblers are described as "low-born" beings who must live in settlements away from those of the highborn. The term *ceeri*, a pejorative term for Untouchable hamlets in contemporary Tamilnadu, is in the earliest Sangam literature a neutral designation meaning the "quarter" of a town inhabited by any community, but it soon comes to label only the settlements of the "low-born ones." Other low groups besides Goldsmiths and Cobblers are mentioned, including a "community" (*kudi* rather than *jati*) called the *PaaNar*—"people at the lower rungs of society and wandering minstrels." Within the *Paa-Nar* are two subtypes: the *TuDiar* (who play the *tuDi* drum) and the *Paṟaiyar* (who play the *paṟai* drum) (Subrahmanian 1966: 116, 225, 251, 258, 280, 282).

Many of the attributes of contemporary south Indian Untouchables were thus apparently present fifteen hundred years ago, in the Sangam period. We do not know how these features were structurally combined at the time, however. Society may have been pervasively ranked, its lowest members polluting by proximity those who were "higher born"; or it may have been simply segmented, without pervasive rank except with regard to certain groups, whose particular powers made their avoidance advisable by others. Whether the state of these avoided groups amounted to "pollution" in the modern Indian sense, or to more generalized "magical danger," we also do not know.[2] It should be noted, however, that the proto-Untouchable groups were explicitly said to be "low." In particular, lowness was associated with leather, with drumming, and (in the case of the two types of Vellalars) with agricultural labor. *Paṟaiyans* existed, though we might assume that they were only one small group among others.

From the Sangam period to the Chola period of south Indian history (c. A.D. 600 to 1200), political consolidation proceeded in the south Indian "nuclear areas," zones ecologically adapted to irrigation or to tank-fed agriculture. In these regions, state-level political authority was in the hands of relatively low, Vellalar chieftains, who endowed local and nonlocal Brahmins with land and honor, and were in turn legitimized by them (see Stein 1967). It is probable that during this period the ideological lineaments of caste were more formally established, along more all-India lines. There is

[2] My thanks to David Ludden for this particular point. The latter interpretation, that groups such as the Paraiyans were magically dangerous rather than polluting during the Sangam period, is made by the historian George L. Hart III (Hart 1975).

little mention in the written sources of this period (most of which are temple inscriptions) of nondominant groups, but one clear reference to Paraiyans and to the spatial distancing of the very low is found in the period of Rajarajacola (c. A.D. 1000). This is a temple inscription that specifies the tax-exempt status of certain sections of a village (*uur*) under the Chola rulers, and mentions the *uur-nattam* (the main village), the *kammaancceeri* (the hamlet of the Kammalars or Artisans), and the *paraiceeri*—the hamlet of the Paraiyans (Sastri 1955: 535). There is also mention of "Paraiya chieftainships" in the eighth and tenth centuries, however, though what these were, and how they were integrated into the diffuse overarching Chola political integration, is not known (Ludden, personal communication).

Another type of evidence for the nature of caste and of Untouchability in medieval south India is found in the literature of the bhakti movement, which swept the region between the seventh and ninth centuries A.D. Bhakti devotionalism postulates that one's personal devotion to god is more important than one's birth or one's use of Brahmanic ritualism, and apparently constitutes a challenge to a caste order founded on worship mediated by a hierarchy of human specialists. The "saints" of both the Saivite and the Vaishnavite bhakti movements (the sixty-three *Naayanaars* and the twelve *Aalvaars*, respectively) include one (and only one) Untouchable figure—Nandan in the case of the *Naayanaars* and Tiruppan in the case of the *Aalvaars*. The stories of Nandan and of Tiruppan are similar. Each is a character who, for reason of his low birth, cannot enter the temple of the god to whom he is devoted. And each is, after years of intense devotion to the god, miraculously absorbed by his deity, by Siva or Vishnu (see Sastri 1963).

In a text from the twelfth century, there is a description of the Untouchable *ceeri* into which the saint Nandan was born. In its high-caste stereotyping, the text is consonant with modern high-caste views of the Untouchable milieu:

In the threshold of the huts covered with the strips of leather, little chickens were seen moving about in groups; dark children who wore bracelets of black iron were prancing about . . . there were mango trees from whose branches drums were hanging. . . . The music of many instruments accompanies the drinking *fetes* of Pulaiya women . . . who staggered in their dance as the result of increasing intoxication. In this abode of the people of the lowest caste (*kadainar*), there arose a man with a feeling of true devotion to the feet of Siva (*Seekkilaar Periya Puraanam*, in Sastri 1955: 568-569).

Nandan is further described as a temple servant, a leather-worker who supplies straps for drums and gut-string for stringed instruments to the Saivite temple at Srirangam—which he himself is not allowed to enter.

There is evidence that bhakti religious ideology did facilitate certain types of individual mobility for middle-ranking peasants in the period after A.D. 1000 (see Stein 1968: 91). However, bhakti devotionalism in no way undermined Brahmin ritual dominance in the south, and it may have constituted a religious reform that allowed a more popular Brahmanic Hinduism to fend off the challenge of Jainism and Buddhism (see Stein 1967). Nor is the role of the bhakti Untouchable saints evidence that the low were less low, or that Untouchability was somehow more flexibly defined, at the time. The converse is equally possible, in fact. Assuming the existence of a highly developed hierarchical system at the time of early bhakti, Nandan and Tiruppan are powerful symbols, for the very reason of their strong Untouchability, of the specifically religious message of early bhakti—of the personal rather than the social quality of the relation to god entailed in the movement. The message would not be so strong if Nandan and Tiruppan were not so low.[3]

[3] Twentieth-century Brahmins in Pudukottai frequently stressed the personal ethic of their *bhajans*, which were attended uniformly by

Thus around A.D. 1000, some groups or possibly castes in the Chola integration were very low, particularly those whose occupation associated them with leather and with other polluting substances. Though south Indian society underwent major transformations between this time and the advent of the British, those at the bottom did not change their position in any fundamental way. A social category and a set of functional groups that did begin a slow upward climb at this time, however, was the Kammalars or Artisans, who like other proto-Untouchables were relegated to their own *ceeris* in earlier times. Sometime after the thirteenth century, the Artisans began to pursue a strategy of collective upward mobility, supported by an urbanizing trend and by new warrior-kings to whose wealth their "contribution . . . was important and whose protection they enjoyed" (Stein 1969: 195). At present in south India, Artisans usually hold middle-range ranks in local caste hierarchies, following "minimizing strategies" transactionally (see Marriott 1968, 1974) and claiming Brahminlike identities.

For the bulk of south India's Untouchables, however, the only significant change in the next five hundred years was one of numbers. We can speculate that in the Sangam period, Untouchable "communities" were small, specialized groups, most of whose members actually made their living from performing their low function—for instance, from drumming. In contemporary Tamilnadu, on the other hand, Untouchables compose eighteen percent of the state-wide population, and a much greater proportion of the population in the old lowland nuclear areas. Though these contemporary Untouchables have a "right" to perform their caste-definitional occupation, most of them survive by working as agricultural laborers. How do we account for this tremendous demographic change?

Brahmins, by saying that it was purity of heart, rather than of birth, that counted, and by saying that "many low caste" people had been associated with bhakti in the past.

40

The simplest hypothesis for the earlier period of demographic change is "accretion at the bottom." Burton Stein describes a more or less continuous process from pre-Chola times, in which the nuclear areas associated with a fully integrated caste system and with peasant modes of production expanded into the forest and upland areas of tribal and warrior peoples. Some of the nonpeasant peoples of these areas were integrated into the caste system as warrior-retainers, and others may have acquired or retained tribal lands and established themselves as local dominant castes. But most of the new tribal peoples were brought in at the lowest level, as Untouchables, due to "the stigma which must have attached to their previous non-peasant way of life" (Stein 1967: 243). Thus, for example, a new tribal group might begin in a given area to play the *parai* drum, and thus be labeled locally as *Paraiyan*. Or, alternatively, *Paraiyan* might have come in that area to denote a low laboring status group (whether it actually played the *parai* or not), to which the new group might be assimilated by agreeing to serve as an agricultural work force. The group might be motivated to so serve by a "tradeoff" between status on the one hand (which it would lose) and food and security on the other (which it would gain in the more settled peasant zones) (Ludden, personal communication). Eventually the group would either legitimize its new identity by extending its marriage ties to other Paraiyan groups, or it would turn inward as a new and distinct Paraiyan subcaste. It may be that the tremendous number of Paraiyan subcastes noted in the early twentieth century (Thurston 1909, 6: 80) are remnants of this process of caste accretion (see Karve 1961 for an accretive or "agglomerative" approach to the history of caste).

Two other demographic factors may have played a role in the growth of the major south Indian Untouchable castes in the last thousand years: the slow addition to them of outcasts from the higher castes, and higher birth rates than the higher castes. Neither factor seems particularly important in the last hundred years, however. The rate of permanent out-

41

casting is impossible to estimate, though it appears to be very low. The current fertility ratio for Paraiyan women (measured by the ratio of women to children ages 0 to 4) is slightly higher than that of the general population—.64 versus .60—but the unmeasured mortality figures are undoubtedly also higher. And the overall growth rate for the two major Tamil Untouchable castes between 1921 and 1961 is in fact lower than the growth rate of the general population (45 percent for the Paraiyans and 47 percent for the Pallans, compared to 51 percent for the general population) (see Census of India 1961: 22-29).

Whatever the reasons for the disproportionate expansion of the Untouchable castes in the late medieval period, at the time of early Western contact, south Indian Untouchables existed in proportions comparable to those of the present, and at levels at least as low. Duarte Barbosa, who visited the Malabar coast in 1514, mentions "eleven sects" of low and excluded castes, who polluted the higher-caste persons by touch, by proximity, and even by visual contact. The system was, in Barbosa's unadorned account, very much maintained by force. In the case of contact between a dominant Nayar and an Untouchable Pulayar, for example, "whatever [Nayar] woman or man should touch these [Pulayars], their relations immediately kill them like a contaminated thing: and they kill so many of these pulers [Pulayars] until they are weary of it, without any penalty" (Barbosa 1866 [1516]: 143).

An account from Tamilnadu in the late eighteenth century is similarly graphic about Paraiyans and their ability to pollute higher caste persons by sight, sound, and proximity, as well as by touch:

> [Paraiyans] are prohibited from drawing water from the wells of other castes; but have particular wells of their own near their inhabitations, round which they place the bones of animals, that they may be known and avoided. When an Indian of any other caste permits a Paraiya to speak to him, this unfortunate being is obliged to hold his hand

before his mouth, lest the Indian may be contaminated with his breath . . . the Brahmins cannot behold them, and they are obliged to fly when they appear . . . if they are employed in any work [inside a high-caste household] a door is purposely made for them, but they must work with their eyes on the ground; for, if it is perceived they have glanced at the kitchen, all the utensils must be broken (Thurston 1909, 6: 78-79, quoting Sonnerat's *Voyage to the East Indies*, 1774 and 1781).

The situation of Untouchables in Tamilnadu in the immediately pre-British period was not entirely oppressive, however, as extreme as it might have appeared to Westerners at the time. For the village system in south India was a pre-capitalist formation in which, in all its variants, the institution of private ownership of land did not exist. To oversimplify a complex reality, no individual or corporate group had exclusive and alienable rights to land, but rather differential rights existed, with a dominant caste directing and controlling agricultural production (and paying taxes or tribute to an extravillage political authority), and the other castes of a village having traditionally defined "shares"[4] of the produce and of access to the land. And Untouchables were, like all other castes, share holders in this village system.

The rights of the lower service castes in the pre-British village system were diverse. They included rights to well-defined shares of the annual harvest, to individual payments in grain from high-caste patrons, and to *maniyam* land—a small share of the village land over which service castes had dominant cultivation rights in return for their service to the village. Low castes could not be unilaterally evicted from living sites (the *ceeris* for the Untouchables), and in the case of the transfer of dominance, Untouchable field laborers could stay with the land and transfer their service relations

[4] An incisive but still unpublished analysis of the *pangu* or "share" system in southern Tamilnadu is presently being carried out by David Ludden.

to families of the new dominant group (see Kumar 1965: 34 and Gough 1960b: 87).

There were also in the immediately pre-British period formal and informal sanctions limiting the power of the higher castes over the lower castes. Culturally, the high castes were to some degree restrained by fear of the powers of sorcery of the very low. Economically, the noncultivating high castes were exceedingly dependent on low-caste agricultural laborers, giving the low castes a degree of bargaining power. Politically, the high castes needed the support of low-caste retainers in factional disputes; and low castes could appeal to extravillage royal authority if the local dominant castes were unduly oppressing them. The low castes also had the right to boycott a high-caste patron who mistreated one of their members. Cohn describes the operation of this sanction in contemporary north India, where if a dominant Thakur patron wishes to change the Untouchable Camar leatherworker who serves his particular family, he must have the consent of the local Camar caste council. Any new Camar who accepts service from the Thakur without this council's approval can be outcast from the Camar caste for his strike breaking (Cohn 1954: 29).

The British worked largely unplanned changes in the older village system after the beginning of the nineteenth century. In the south, they were concerned with consolidating the enormous areas that they had won in the lengthy Carnatic wars of the eighteenth century, and they needed to generate maximum revenues through land tax to pay the costs of this consolidation. In their search for the originally nonexistent ultimate proprietor of the land, the British eventually created a new economic being, the private landowner (cf. Stein 1969: 196-212). By the end of the nineteenth century, the British had begun to convert ranked economic rights into absolute economic rights, had monetized the rural economy, and had usurped the position of royal overlord to the village dominant castes. The effects on south Indian Untouchables of this British transformation of the village system can be determined only by a far more thorough historical analysis than we are undertaking here, but we can note a few of the trends.

To begin with the most predictable trend, the new private landowners were in most cases the old dominant castes. In some areas, the older relationship between dominant-caste landowners and low-caste laborers then became monetized and more contractual in ways detrimental to the lower castes. For the Untouchables lost their rights under the old system, and they were not always able to benefit from the opportunities of the new rural capitalism.

Kathleen Gough describes the effects of this process on the Untouchable Pallans of Tanjore district, Tamilnadu. In 1843, the British abolished "serfdom" in south India, the *adimai* or "slave" relationship of a field laborer to his high-caste patron. Although *adimai* does in fact mean something like "slave," a field laborer in the old system also had "rights" (*urumai*) with respect to his patron—and these the British were also unwittingly abolishing (a point not noted by Gough). High-caste employers of the period then proceeded to tie the same Untouchable laborers to them monetarily, by making them the cash loans they needed to function in the changing economy. What resulted was a new form of tie between landowner and low-caste laborer that worked more to the advantage of the landowner. The Untouchable could not break the tie because of exorbitant interest rates on the loan. The high-caste landowner could dismiss the Untouchable more easily, however, and could legally evict him from any land but the *ceeri*, by foregoing the (to him) small loan.

It should be noted, however, that this change from "status" to "contract" was intially more legalistic than actual, that existing relations in Tamil villages remained exceedingly mixed. Thus debt was also part of the older *adimai* relationship, which in addition had some contractual features both from the patron's and the client's points of view (Ludden, personal communication). Similarly, noncontractual definitions and attitudes remain very much a part of the relation between high-caste landowners and Untouchable landless laborers in Endavur and in other Tamil villages in the 1970s.

Gough describes the growing economic insecurity under this shifting system over the next one hundred years. In Tanjore, land switched hands more frequently, tied-labor contracts were made increasingly short term, and—with the three hundred percent growth of the general rural population —an increasing number of landless Untouchables became chronically underemployed day laborers (Gough 1960a: 30-31). Gough's analysis predicts the rapid growth of an Untouchable-derived south Indian rural proletariat, and of social movements based on the class interests of this proletariat. And Gough describes such movements in eastern Tanjore beginning in 1948, which involved communist labor organization of Untouchable landless laborers across caste lines, and the abandonment between the Untouchable Pallans and Paraiyans of "all caste restrictions except endogamy" (Gough 1960a, Gough 1973). However, although eastern Tanjore remains in the 1970s a politicized arena, proletarianization has not evidenced itself elsewhere among rural Tamil Untouchables since the 1950s. This may be a reflection of the atypicality of Tanjore and of analyses based on it.

A second countervailing political and economic trend for Untouchables in the last hundred years has had two facets: protection and remedial action on behalf of Untouchables by the British government and later by the Indian government, and land acquisition by Untouchables under the umbrella of this protection. The result of these economic actions has been to lock many rural Untouchables into a modern peasant adaptation, tending to foster political conservatism among the very low.

For a description of early events in this trend, consider the report of the administrator Charles Crole, writing from the vantage point of 1879, of nineteenth-century British experiments at land settlement in Chingleput district, Tamilnadu. Crole's account describes a flirtation with each of the major landownership hypotheses employed by the British in India in the nineteenth century, followed in each case by remedial action designed both to protect the suspended rights of the lower castes and to serve the economic interests of the British—to extract maximum land revenue from the villages.

After the surrender of the district to the British in 1760, Crole writes, the government was "impregnated with the germs of the zemindari heresy" until 1796. This attempt at informal tax farming then required the "reforms" of the Collector Mr. Place in 1796, in which the village level offices of *karanam* (accountant), *munsif* (policeman), and *talaiyari* (policeman's assistant) were restored, as was the *maniyam* land attached to each service—which "had often excited the cupidity of the villagers." *Talaiyari* duty and its *maniyam* land belong to Untouchables in contemporary Chingleput; both presumably had become negotiable in the late eighteenth century, and had to be returned to those to whom they belonged. Between 1800 and 1807, Crole continues, the British experimented with a better organized zamindari settlement, which was as disastrous as the previous one, although the few tax farmers who succeeded were made permanent. In the next experiment, the British instituted ryotwari settlement, a settlement with the individual cultivator, between 1807 and 1822. Here, however, it was often difficult to identify the actual cultivator, and a mixed system of joint-village responsibility (*mirassi*) coexisted with ryotwari. By 1859, however, the private landowners in most Tamil villages had been better defined. In effect, those with dominant rights over the land had converted these rights to "private property." The joint-village system was then abolished.

A second-round of reforms on behalf of the lower village servants was again necessary, however. Between 1859 and 1863, the village-level offices of *karanam, talaiyari*, and *vettiyan* (scavenger) were again reestablished, and regular salaries were attached to each. Vettiyan work, like Talaiyari work, is presently an Untouchable prerogative. Though it is doubtful that anyone but an Untouchable would try to be a cattle scavenger, the attachment of a salary to this position and to the other positions reflected the needs of the service castes for payments in a medium other than grain. At the same time, the British introduced new land rules in Chingleput district and elsewhere that provided the lower castes with an opportunity for land acquisition. Under the *darkhast* ("petition") rules, a person who cultivated a piece of waste land for five years could make a legal claim to ownership of it (Crole 1879: 238-303).

Tamil Untouchables proceeded to acquire land during the next eighty years under British protection. Some was earned directly under the *darkhast* system and under other systems devised by the British in order to define the individual cultivator. Other land the Untouchables purchased with capital from a variety of sources. A local source was wage labor and salary payments for village services; more concentrated sources were found in the cities, in the army, and in plantation labor overseas. Since 1930 or so, and increasingly since 1947, the government-level policy of protective discrimination has meant a higher incidence of government jobs for Untouchables, the salaries from which are often fed back into rural land purchase.

At present, Tamil Untouchables own land in proportions not adequately suggested by case studies from Tanjore. Figure 2-2, constructed from data in the 1961 Census of India, compares landownership in the general population for the ten districts of Tamilnadu. It further shows within each district the percentage of higher-caste families who own land, versus the percentage of Untouchable families who own land. We can note initially that Tanjore ranks last in its proportion of general landowning families, and second to last in its proportion of Untouchable landholding families. One reason for this, in all probability, is that in Tanjore there was very little waste land available for new cultivation in the late nineteenth century; there was nothing available for the Untouchables to buy under the newly relaxed British policies. Ramnathapuram, on the other hand, was much less densely populated, and its caste hierarchy was far less

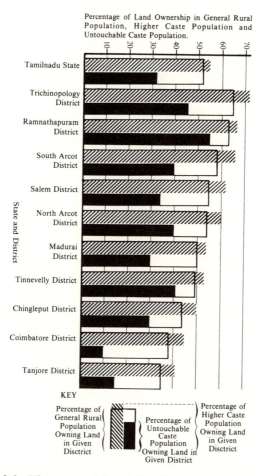

Percentage of Land Ownership in General Rural Population, Higher Caste Population and Untouchable Caste Population.

State and District

Tamilnadu State

Trichinopology District

Ramnathapuram District

South Arcot District

Salem District

North Arcot District

Madurai District

Tinnevelly District

Chingleput District

Coimbatore District

Tanjore District

KEY

Percentage of General Rural Population Owning Land in Given Disctrict

Percentage of Untouchable Caste Population Owning Land in Given District

Percentage of Higher Caste Population Owning Land in Given Disctrict

FIGURE 2-2. Histogram of Rural Landownership in Tamilnadu (General Population, Higher Castes, and Untouchable Castes Compared by District)

Note: This figure and the following two figures are constructed from data found in the individual District Census Handbooks, Madras, Census of India, 1961, and in the report *Scheduled Castes and Tribes*, Madras, Census of India, 1961. The Untouchable castes of Tamilnadu are coterminous with the census category "Scheduled Castes." The higher caste category in the present figures represents the general population minus the Untouchable caste figures; it is intended to represent the non-Untouchable castes in rural areas.

49

complex and involuted than that in Tanjore. For these and other reasons, Ramnathapuran is the district with the highest percentage of Untouchable landownership.

In other districts, the percentage of Untouchable families owning land roughly follows the trend in the general population. Although the land the Untouchables own is usually poorer and drier than that of the higher castes, and though the average size of an Untouchable family's holding is smaller than a higher-caste family's holding (see Figure 2-3), the

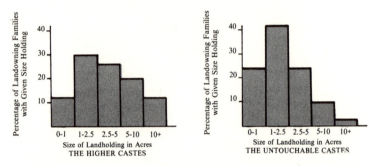

FIGURE 2-3. Size of Landholdings of Landowning Higher-Caste Families and Landowning Untouchable Families Compared on a State-Wide Basis

Tamil Untouchables have done reasonably well in the last hundred years, considering the zero baseline from which they have started, and the continuous economic discrimination to which they have been subjected.

With their developing land base, Untouchables in south India began in the early twentieth century to make new status claims, mostly by Sanskritizing. An extraordinary document from Ramnathapuram in the early 1930s reflects a dominant caste's reaction to an Untouchable caste's attempt to upgrade its caste code for conduct, on the basis of an improved landownership base. In this document (reported by Hutton 1963: 205-206), the dominant Kallars began by forbidding behavior on the part of the local Untouchables (probably Pallans) that was associated with their own dominant caste's code for conduct. Prestigious behaviors forbidden by the Kallar included, for example, males and females wearing anything above the waist, or wearing flowers or saffron paste. No Untouchable was to use umbrellas or sandals, music and mounted bridegrooms were prohibited in the Untouchable marriage ceremony, and nothing but earthenware vessels were to be used in the home. When the local Untouchables did not obey these demands, the Kallars attacked them, beat them, destroyed their crops—and presumably attracted the attention of the British.

In a later set of proclamations, the Kallars went for the new economic bases of the Untouchables' status claims, declaring that the Untouchables were not to own land, and were to sell back any land they owned to the Kallars at reduced prices. The Untouchables were also to remove themselves from any land tenancy arrangements they had, and were to devote themselves to *kuli* wage labor at one-quarter rupee per day. The Kallars threatened further physical attack, and the cutting off of irrigation water, if the Untouchables did not obey them this time. The Untouchables did not, presumably because of British intervention.

The British had thus, in the nineteenth and twentieth centuries, replaced the older royal authority as the court of ultimate appeal, as the authority to which Untouchables could carry their grievances against the local dominant caste. The British were a possibly more liberal court; though they tried not to interfere with the general workings of the caste system, Untouchability struck them as an extreme custom, one that—like widow-burning and *thugee*—could not be treated entirely dispassionately.[5] They were only the court

[5] See Hardgrave (1969) for a fascinating account from nineteenth-century Travancore of the maneuvers of the near-Untouchable Nadars, supported by Christian missionaries, between a conservative Hindu authority and a more liberal British resident, in the "breast cloth controversy" (pp. 55-70).

of last resort, for the local dominant caste retained the most immediate local Untouchables in most cases. The local dominant caste's awareness of the British, however, may have made them less able or willing to control all behavior of the Untouchables. Though this can in no way be proved on present evidence, it appears that in the early twentieth century, rigorous local control of Untouchables (along the lines suggested by Barbosa and Sonneret above) relaxed somewhat, and Untouchables were permitted to add auspicious, "Sanskritic" behavior to their caste codes.

Such Sanskritization did little for the standing of most Tamil Untouchable castes in their local caste hierarchies, however, though it may have effected minor shifts in the relative standing of closely related Untouchable subcastes. M. N. Srinivas notes that all over India Sanskritization tactics were adopted by a wide set of Untouchable castes in the early twentieth century, but that these tactics were uniformly unsuccessful. According to Srinivas, no Sanskritizing Untouchable caste has succeeded in crossing the "touchability" barrier in this century (Srinivas 1962). It is possible, however, that widespread Sanskritization at this time did not invariably signal an Untouchable caste's consciously formulated demand for higher rank. It might more simply have reflected the widespread relaxation of direct upper-caste control over lower castes' codes for conduct in the early twentieth century —and the subsequent adoption by low castes of positively valued, and formerly prohibited, behavior.

The best-known attempt of a low south Indian caste systematically to raise its status in the last hundred years is that of the Nadars. The Nadars, the "toddy-tappers" of Tamilnadu, have a history quite unlike that of the main body of Tamil Untouchable castes. Their movement is therefore instructive for its suggestions of what the main Untouchable castes might require to build a more successful collective challenge to their low status. The Nadar movement also suggests the severe limits of such collective action.

To begin with some differences with the main Untouch-

52

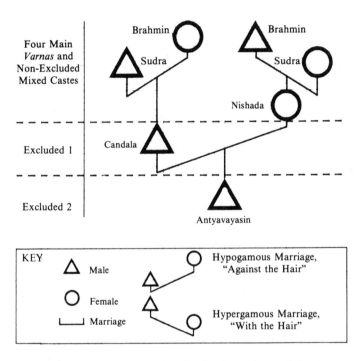

lage as are the Untouchables of neighboring villages. Here as elsewhere, the Harijans and the other Untouchable castes continue to live and worship separately, to show deference to the dominant caste of the village, and to carry out their traditional lowering caste-definitive functions: *parai* drumming, cattle scavenging, leatherworking, and other tasks. Here as elsewhere, those with power and wealth maintain themselves in high and privileged positions in the system, and see to it that others stay in the low positions that the system equally requires. Power and wealth, however, do not explain the specific structure of the system, nor do they explain why all persons in the system share a common cultural construction of it. To set the stage for the description of this cultural consensus among the Untouchable castes of Endavur, we must look at the village of Endavur in a different light: in terms of its formal caste structure.

Caste Structure and the Untouchables of Endavur

The caste system and Untouchability are very much alive and well in Endavur. In Endavur as elsewhere, political and economic dominance must be expressed in terms of caste, and caste relations are not a simple reflection of economic relations. Caste represents, as Dumont would have it, an autonomous order that must accommodate itself to the facts of power and wealth, but that is not explained by political and material inequalities (see Dumont 1970: 196-230). What, then, does it mean to be an Untouchable in Endavur? What are the caste-determined structural relations of the *uur* castes to the Untouchable castes? From what are the Untouchables excluded by the *uur*, despite their relative material prosperity, and in what are they included?

To begin with the term "Untouchable," members of the lowest, partially excluded castes of Endavur are considered personally "untouchable" by members of all the *uur* castes of the village. Literally, "untouchability" refers to a personal interaction or noninteraction: A is "untouchable" to B if A

85

is relatively so impure that direct physical contact with B must be avoided. If contact occurs, B must bathe in order to regain his former state of purity vis-à-vis A. So defined, untouchability is not directed only at Untouchables. Rather, it is found continuously at all levels of the caste system. For example, untouchability in this relational sense exists between a high-caste husband and wife during the wife's menstrual period, between a Brahmin and other members of his caste during the mourning period for the death of a lineal relative, between an outcast and members of the caste from which the outcast was expelled, between members of any lower caste and members of almost any orthodox higher caste, as well as between members of the "Untouchable" castes and all those above them. The personal relationship of "untouchability," which will be marked here by use of a small case "u," is indigenously named in Endavur. Villagers use the term *tiiNDaamai* for "not touching," a negative form of the root *tiiNDu*, which means both "to touch" and "to pollute."

The discrete category of partially excluded lowest castes, the Untouchables, is not marked by an indigenous term in Endavur, however. The local terms that come closest to labeling all of the lowest castes are *ceeri janankal* and *kooloni janankal*, "people of the *ceeri*" and "people of the Colony." But these terms technically do not label those low-caste persons who live both outside the Colony and outside the *uur*. The administrative term "Scheduled Castes" has some limited use among educated villagers, though it is most generally used as a euphemism for the largest Untouchable caste in a region, rather than in its intercaste categorical sense. We will refer to the unnamed category of lowest, partially excluded castes here as "Untouchables," with a capital "U," and will refer by the term "Untouchability" to the qualities of the Untouchable castes.

Now then, what is the relationship between "Untouchables" and "untouchability?" Most simply, it is that of all those in the Endavur caste hierarchy, Untouchables are most strictly and permanently untouchable to everyone else. Their collective impurity is weakly referred to as *aassuttam* ("impurity") and strongly referred to as *tittu*—the extreme impurity resulting from death, birth and menstruation. And this *tittu* is explicitly a collective property of the lowest castes. In the words of a non-Untouchable talking about the Harijans, "it is that caste itself that is *tittu*" (*anda jaadidaan tittu irukku*).

In Endavur and in other Tamil villages, a structured expression of this collective and concentrated impurity among the lowest castes is the qualified territorial and social exclusion that we have sketched above. Members of the Untouchable castes may not live in proximity to higher-caste households and to the gods of the higher castes; they must live outside the *uur* and worship separate images of the gods. They are, however, included in a wider territorial unit, the *kiraamam*, and in the worship of a deity common to the *kiraamam*. In previous times, and in other villages today, Untouchables were kept out of the streets of the *uur*, except on business, and even today higher-caste people who enter the *ceeri* generally must purify themselves when they return to the *uur*. In one interesting inversion of these relations—a prerogative noted for Untouchables in Tanjore in the nineteenth century—a Brahmin who entered a *ceeri* could be driven out by the Untouchables, and was treated as an object of pollution with respect to the *ceeri* (see Beteille 1965: 38, and Thurston 6: 88).

The Untouchables are also prevented from making certain types of transactions with castes above them. If we view "untouchability" as a means of limiting the flow of bodily substance upwards, flow that would reduce the purity of higher humans and other beings, then it is not surprising that, for Untouchables, flow in more loaded media than "touch" is even more strictly limited.[10] Thus members of

[10] This conceptualization, and much of the transactional specification in this chapter, are deliberately stated in terms close to those used by Marriott, Inden, and Nicholas. See Marriott and Inden 1974,

virtually none of the non-Untouchable higher castes will accept cooked food or water from Untouchables, and the upward transactions of substance implied by the relations of sex and marriage are even more strongly abjured. Upward transactions in less loaded media are sometimes made from Untouchable to non-Untouchable, however—transactions in money, in raw rice, and in new clothes.

Prohibitions on the upward flow of substance do not, of course, occur only between Untouchables and non-Untouchables. They are, like the relationship of untouchability itself, found continuously throughout the system. Castes from the top to the bottom of a local hierarchy are progressively excluded from certain interactions with one another by a range of transactional prohibitions. Untouchables are merely the most extreme objects of these progressive differentiations and exclusions, just as they are only the most extreme objects of the relationship of untouchability. The breakpoint between the *uur* castes and the Untouchables is one of many exclusionary break-points in Tamil caste hierarchies. But it differs from others in its particularly clear territorial marking, and in its summative properties. For Untouchables are cut off from more relations than anyone else in rural caste orders.

Inden and Nicholas 1972, and Marriott 1968. It is also possible to see "untouchability" in these terms as one type of transactional prohibition on a continuum between, at one extreme, "not marrying together" and "not eating together," and at the opposite extreme, "not touching," "not approaching," and "not seeing or hearing." These latter extremes, expressions of great differences in the states of purity of the actors in question, have all been described for south India. Examples include the elaborate distance pollution scales between low and high castes in pre-British Kerala (see Barbosa 1866 [1516]), and the "unseeable" castes reported for Tinnevelly (Hutton 1963: 81). Barnett says that the most orthodox high-caste *KondaikkaaTTi VeeLaaLars* of western Chingleput "would take a ritual bath after seeing (*KaaNDa muttu*) or even hearing (*keeTTa muttu*) a Paraiyan before morning puja" (1970: 142). We might predict at the extreme end of this continuum of noninteraction "unthinkability" and "unknowability." No examples of such extremes are known, however.

The structural response of the Untouchable castes of Endavur to their exclusion is replication. That is, the Untouchables recreate among themselves virtually every relation and institution from which they have been excluded for reason of their Untouchability. To understand the specificity of this replication, let us examine in more detail the castes of the village, their relations with one another, and their relations or nonrelations with the Untouchables of Endavur.

In terms of the Untouchables' exclusion, the higher castes of the village, who are listed in rank order in Table 3-4, can be divided into three sets. The first set has one member—the dominant Reddiyars. The second set includes those castes who, in the performance of their traditional, caste-related occupations, deny their services to the Untouchables. This set comprises the Brahmins, the Vettaikarans as temple servants, the Vannans and Ambattans, and, in a special sense, the Harijans. And the third set is made up of those castes who either produce a product available for purchase by all, or who are explicitly willing to provide their caste services to members of any village caste, Brahmin to Untouchable. This set includes, on the one hand, the Sengundar Mudaliyars, the Idaiyars, the Vettaikarans as basketmakers, and the Villis; and on the other hand, the Chettiyars, the Pandarams, and the Acaris.[11] Let us consider these sets in more detail.

The position of the single member of the first set of higher castes in Endavur, the dominant Reddiyars, has already been discussed at some length as a political and economic

[11] The Kannakka Pillais, the Naidus, and the Kavundars are left uncategorized here. The Kannakka Pillais provide the service of "village accountant," a service oriented toward the village as a whole, involving no specific intercaste relations other than liaison with the dominant caste. Little is known about the Naidus or the Kavundars in Endavur. It should be noted that this characterization of the *uur* castes of Endavur is based on limited personal observation, for our time was short in this village, and we were concerned with maintaining our primary ethnographic identification with the local Untouchable castes.

Table 3-4. Caste Composition of the Village of Endavur

Rank order	Caste name	ToRil: Caste-definitive service[a]	Number of households	Percent of village population
Uur castes				
1	Brahmin	Domestic and temple priest	1	0.3
2	Kannakka Pillai	Accountant	3	1
3	Reddiyar	(Dominance)	5	2
4	Sengundar Mudaliyar	Weaver	69	25
5	Chettiyar	Merchant	11	4
6	Naidu	(?)	6	2
7	Idaiyar	Herdsman	32	11
8	Pandaram	Florist	2	0.6
9	Kavundar	(?)	17	6
10	Acari	Artisan	9	3
11	Vettaikaran	Basketmaker, temple servant	24	9
12	Vannan	Washerman	1	0.3
13	Ambattan	Barber, auspicious musician	2	0.6
14	Villi	Forest person	5	2
Untouchable castes				
15	Valluvar Pandaram	Harijan domestic and temple priest	5	2
16	Harijan, Paraiyan	*Parai* drummer	98	30
17	Harijan, Vannan	Harijan washerman	2	0.6
18	Chakkiliyan	Leatherworker	3	1
19	Kurivikaran	Crow-catcher	(2 itinerate)	1
			295 households	

[a] These *toRil* services are an approximation at this point. There is much more to Harijan service than *parai* drumming, for example, as we shall see below. A caste's *toRil* can sometimes be determined from a direct translation of the caste's name. Thus "*kannakka* Pillai" = "counting Pillai," and "Paraiyan" = "*parai* person." More often, however, a caste name has no commonly understood denotation beyond its reference as a name.

fact. As a caste-related phenomenon, however, the Reddiyars' dominance has a slightly different type of significance. For dominance in this sense is the function that maintains the relations that define the caste system. It is to the dominant caste that the service relations of the other castes are oriented; it is the resources of the dominant caste that make these services economically feasible; and it is the power of the dominant caste which keeps the service castes in position in the system. The Untouchable castes of Endavur are very much included in the Reddiyars' dominance. But among themselves, when they seek to construct a replicatory microcaste order in response to their specific exclusion, the Untouchables require an internal function of dominance as well. We shall be looking for this function below.

The second set of *uur* castes is the set that defines the exclusion of the Endavur Untouchables. Each of the castes in this set—the uppermost Brahmins, the nearly lowermost *uur* caste Vettaikarans, Vannans, and Ambattans, and the Untouchable Harijans—deny their caste-related services, their *toRil*, to all or some of the Untouchables of the village. It is these services and relations that are then internally replicated within the Untouchable castes. To understand the logic of this exclusion, and the cultural language of relative rank in Endavur, we must first gloss in more detail the important indigenous term *toRil*, the term that labels the service or occupation by which a given caste's rank is calculated in the village.

The general meaning of the term *toRil* is "action" or "duty." Its specific reference in Endavur, when applied to a caste, is to the action that is the "right" (*urumai*) of members of that caste to perform in the village system. *ToRil* is terminologically distinguished from *veelai*, or "work." Most *veelai* in Endavur is connected with agriculture and is not differentiated strictly according to caste. Every caste in the village, on the other hand, has a distinctive *toRil* to which its rank is referred. Rank is calculated both from what is believed to be the intrinsic highness or lowness of a given *toRil*, and from the relations to others implied by a given

91

toRil. Particularly important in these relational considerations are the types of substance transferred from persons of one caste to persons of another in a *toRil*-based action.[12]

The castes of the village who deny their services to the Untouchables do so for reasons of *toRil*. Let us consider the *toRil*-based reasons of the Brahmins, for a start. It is the *toRil* of the single Brahmin of Endavur to act as temple priest to the high god Siva (who has a temple in the *uur*) and as domestic priest in the auspicious life-cycle rituals of families of the higher castes of the *uur*. The Brahmin's former role is often called *gurukkal* and the latter *purohit*, but "*purohit*" is also used in Endavur to refer to both aspects of the Brahmin's *toRil*. And the *toRil* of *purohit* is appropriate to the Brahmin, the highest and purest of humans in the village. For as temple priest, the Brahmin acts as an intermediary between the high gods who rank above him and other humans who rank below him; and as domestic priest, he acts as a human facilitator for those who wish to achieve higher states of personal purity and auspiciousness.

Yet, though the Brahmin is not by this *toRil* subordinated to beings other than the high gods whom he serves, he cannot mediate too great a difference of human highness and lowness without endangering his own purity. As it is, he pays a status price for his *toRil*, for he takes payments from his clients below him, payments in relatively nonpolluting substances such as money and raw rice. For reason of these payments, he ranks by subcaste (Gurukkal) well below other Brahmins outside the village who do not serve as priests. The Brahmin cannot take even these relatively neutral substances from those who rank far below him, however, and for this

[12] *ToRil* may be a Tamil equivalent of an aspect of *dharma* as it is analyzed ethnosociologically by Inden and Nicholas for Bengal: an aspect of the "code for conduct" considered inherent in the shared substance of the unit (caste, *kulam*, or person) in which it resides (Inden and Nicholas 1972). And like *dharma* in Inden and Nicholas's analysis, *toRil* in Endavur can also be a property of units smaller than castes, that is, of kin groups and persons.

reason he cannot extend his *purohit* services to lowest castes of the village, the Untouchables. The function of *purohit* must therefore be replicated among the Untouchables.

The other members of the second, exclusionary set of castes rank far below the Brahmin, but the logic of their *toRils* similarly prevents them from serving the Untouchable castes. These castes constitute three of the four lowest non-Untouchable castes in the village, and there is a loose analogy between their attitude toward the Untouchables and the stereotypic "poor white" complex toward blacks in the American South: a similar tendency to exaggerate differences with the single bloc of persons over whom one scores in status terms. The least low of these three exclusionary castes are the Vettaikarans, one member of whom acts as temple servant or *pucari* ("puja person") in the temple to the territorial goddess of the *uur*, the *uur* Mariyamman. As *pucari* to this goddess (whose nature will be analyzed in Chapter VI), the Vettaikaran serves a deity of decidedly mixed qualities, both high and low, both pure and impure, and his *toRil* is particularly oriented to her lower form. For the *pucari* assists when this goddess possesses one of her devotees as an angry and bloodthirsty being, and he carries out the bloody sacrifices that this form of the goddess demands. *Pucari toRil* is very much in complementary opposition to the *purohit toRil* of the Brahmin; as the Brahmin mediates upward toward a high form of god, the *pucari* mediates downward toward a lower form of god. *Pucari toRil* is thus appropriately vested in a member of a relatively low *uur* caste, in a Vettaikaran. It is not appropriately vested in a member of a much lower caste, such as an Untouchable, for the Untouchables are by definition excluded from nearness of the goddess of the *uur*.

Since the Vettaikaran *pucari* serves a goddess from whose powers the Untouchables cannot benefit, the Untouchables are thus excluded from the Vettaikaran's services. Nor could the Vettaikaran also separately serve the distinct territorial goddess of the Colony, the Colony Mariyamman, for his

93

toRil makes him an intermediary between human worshippers and low forms of divinity. By serving in the Colony, he would thus be subordinated to the human worshippers of the Colony deity, to the Harijans, and lose at least five steps in the caste hierarchy as it is presently constituted. Such a rank concession the Vettaikarans are not willing to make. Therefore the *pucari* services of the Vettaikarans, like the *purohit* services of the Brahmin, must be replicated among the Harijans.

The remaining two exclusionary castes of the *uur*, the Vannan washermen and the Ambattan barbers, refuse their services to the lower-ranking Untouchables due to the polluting acceptances that their *toRils* entail. Both of these lowest *uur* castes resemble Untouchables in the fact that it is their *toRil* to facilitate the personal purity of those above them by taking impure substances from persons of higher castes. The Vannans and the Ambattans do not accept substances as impure as those accepted by the Untouchables, however, and they are therefore not quite Untouchable themselves. The Vannan washerman takes soiled clothes from his clients, menstrual clothes in particular. The Ambattan barber male takes hair, while the barber female, who serves as midwife to the higher castes, is in contact with the low substances of childbirth. From the acceptance of these impure bodily substances derives the low rank of these two castes. To accept the same substances from the still lower Untouchables would be to concede further rank to the Untouchables, a concession that the Ambattans and the Vannans, like the Vettaikarans, are not willing to make.

The Untouchables of Endavur are not simply cut off from the washing, the barbering, and the midwifery of these two castes, however. For the Vannans and the Ambattans also have, as part of their *toRils*, specific roles of assistance in the life-cycle rituals of their higher-caste patrons. The Vannan performs services connected with the purification of clothing in the marriage and the funeral of the higher castes, and the Ambattan acts as the very important "funeral priest" for his patrons. Finally, a separate subcaste of Ambattans, who are not found in Endavur but who serve Endavur from a neighboring village, act as auspicious musicians—providing the "good music" of the *tavul-nadeswaram* band to the marriages and the goddess festivals of the *uur* castes. All of these additional ritual services of the *uur* Vannans and Ambattans are also denied to the Untouchable castes of Endavur; all these must also be replicated from within.

The last exclusionary caste in the second set of castes, the Harijans, is something of a special case. The *toRil* of the Harijans makes them inferior to all those they serve, because it requires them to accept the most severely polluted substances in the transactional repertoire of the village, substances associated with death. Accordingly, the Harijans deny their services to the three Untouchable castes below them—the Harijan Vannans, the Chakkiliyans, and the Kurivikarans—for the same reason that the lower *uur* castes deny their services to the Harijans: the Harijans are unwilling to make the rank concession that the acceptance of impure substances from these lowest castes would imply. Likewise, though the Harijans perform their own *toRils* for themselves, they are by this reflexive performance of their *toRil* cut off from a relation to lower persons who act as Harijans for them. The Untouchables of Endavur are thus apparently excluded from having their own Untouchables— from having, as do all the *uur* castes, much lower people ranked below them to act as receivers of their most impure substances. We will be examining the very interesting replicatory response of the Untouchables to this last exclusion at length.

The third set of village castes in Endavur is the set of those who either sell a product to anyone, or who provide a service for anyone, regardless of the recipient's caste rank. The Untouchables are thus not excluded with respect to the *toRils* of these castes. Let us run through them quickly.

First, there are the castes who produce a product available for purchase by all. The highest of these are the Sengundar Mudaliyars, who say their *toRil* is a high one because clothes "hide the shame of mankind," because they facilitate human modesty. Though the handloom cotton woven by the Mudaliyars is in theory available for purchase to anyone in the village, all of it in fact goes onto the Madras market. The Untouchables and the other villagers, in turn, buy most of their clothing in the market town of Madurantakam. The product of the second caste in this subset, the Idaiyars, is available for purchase in the village, and when Untouchables have the money and when their own cattle go dry, they can go into the Idaiyar street and purchase milk from the Idaiyars. Likewise, the products of the low-ranking Vettaikaran and Villi castes, baskets and "forest products" (small game animals), can be purchased or bartered for by anyone in the village.

The second subset of the third set of castes, the Chettiyars, the Pandarams, and the Acaris, are more interesting in their relation to the low Untouchable castes. For members of these castes will come into the Colony to perform their *toRils*. One member of the Chettiyar caste has a small shop in a Harijan household in the Colony, where he comes daily from the *uur* to sell foodstuffs and household supplies to the Harijans. Several Acaris have built the Untouchables' temple car, and one of them enters the Colony during annual festival for the goddess of the Colony and supervises her car procession. Likewise, a Pandaram comes into the Colony during the same festival and decorates the moveable image of the Untouchables' goddess with flowers. All of these *uur* persons are paid for their services with money, and the Pandaram and the Acari also receive a new waist-cloth for their ritual actions. The transactions that they make with the Untouchables are thus in auspicious or in neutral media. Also, the Acari and the Pandaram are, during the goddess ritual, serving not the Untouchables but the higher form of goddess. Hence these actions for the Untouchables do not lower their performers in the same way that analogous *toRil-*

96

specific services by the *uur* Vannans and Ambattans would.[13] And since the Untouchables are provided with these important services, especially those of the Pandarams and the Acaris, they need not replicate these *toRils* among themselves.

Given this analysis of rank and *toRil* in the village as a whole, we can now specify very precisely the exclusion and the inclusion of the Untouchable castes of Endavur, as follows. The five Untouchable castes of Endavur are excluded, for reason of their extreme collective impurity, from the *uur* and from worship to the territorial deity of the *uur*. They are included in the village or *kiraamam*, however, and in worship to the territorial goddess of the *kiraamam*. The Untouchables are also excluded from the purity-enhancing and rank-enhancing *toRils* of the Brahmin *purohit*; the Vettaikaran *pucari*; the Vannan washerman and ritual assistant; the Ambattan barber, midwife, ritual assistant, and auspicious musician; and the Harijans themselves. But they are included in the benefit of the *toRils* of the Sengundar Mudaliyar weaver, the Chettiyar merchant, the Idaiyar herdsman, the Pandaram florist, the Acari carpenter, the Vettaikaran basketmaker, and the Villi forest person. And the Untouchables' own *toRils* benefit members of all the castes above

---

[13] These three castes fall into a widely distributed set of castes, generally in the middle of caste hierarchies, and generally merchants and artisans by function. Kenneth David describes them for Ceylon as the "nonbound castes," as castes whose relations with other castes are short-term, symmetric, and nonhierarchical, and whose rank in the total system is created not by their relations with other humans, but by their relations with god (David 1972). Marriott describes them for all of India in somewhat similar terms, as castes who practice a "minimizing" symmetric transactional strategy in substances that convey pollution (and a wider strategy in unloaded substances such as trade goods and money), and whose rank is created by indirect rather than by direct transactional calculations with other humans (Marriott 1974).

them; they make up a complementary "whole" at the level of the village.

If the Untouchables of Endavur were simply an oppressed underclass, cut off from the higher castes and from higher-caste culture by their exclusion from the *uur*, and forced to perform their *toRils* by the power of the dominant caste, we could expect some true disjunctions when we investigated the internal social structure of the Untouchable castes. If the Untouchables were excluded by their position from knowledge of higher-caste cultural patterns, they would be unable to adopt these patterns internally. If they had de-mystified caste and caste ideology, they would be uninter-ested in reproducing the same structure and the same ide-ology among themselves. Or if they were somehow engaged in constructing an alternative social order, we might expect to find the first evidence of this transformation in the in-ternal structure of the Untouchable subset of castes, where such deviance would not be of immediate interest to the higher castes.

As we have adumbrated above, none of these possibili-ties is supported by the Endavur data, for the Untouchables of Endavur replicate among themselves, to the best of their materially limited abilities, almost every relationship from which they have been excluded by the *uur* castes. And this replicatory order is constructed in the same cultural code that marks highness and lowness, purity and impurity, super-ordination and subordination, among the higher castes. It thus implies among the lowest castes of Endavur a deep cultural consensus on the cognitive and evaluative assump-tions of the system as a whole. Let us turn at last from these accounts of the context of Untouchability in south India and in the village of Endavur to a consideration of the internal structure and the cultural matrix of the Untouchable castes of Endavur.

CHAPTER IV

The Replicatory Caste Order
of the Untouchables

THE Endavur Colony lies about two hundred yards northeast of the *uur*, across waste land owned by the big Reddiyar family. The Colony has long since overflowed the old *ceeri-nattam* boundaries, spreading northeast away from the *uur* over Harijan *maniyam* land and over more waste land owned by the big Reddiyars (see Map 4-1). The extension of the Colony, which follows a graded dirt road leading out of the village, is called the "new Colony," while the original site is called the "old Colony." The old Colony is, like the *uur*, a bounded living site, marked on all sides but the northeast by a cactus hedge. The Colony Mariyamman is the deity who protects the boundaries of this social space, as does the *uur* Mariyamman for the *uur*. Among themselves, the Untouchables who live inside the Colony often refer to the Colony as an "*uur*," calling it "this *uur*" in contrast to the Colonies of Untouchables in other villages. The Colony or the *ceeri* is the home ground of the Untouchables, the one spot from which they can never be evicted, the one spot from which they are central and all others are peripheral.

The relative prosperity of the Endavur Untouchables is evident in the Colony. The dwellings are mostly the usual mud-and-thatch huts of Tamil Untouchables and of poorer *uur* castes, but they are in better repair than most Harijan dwellings. There are occasional huts with masonry walls; two roofs are tiled; and three households are electrified. Two of these electrified households have radios, around which the Harijans gather in the evenings. The Colony temple to the goddess Mariyamman is a freshly painted concrete structure bearing the date 1947, and it has a working loudspeaker

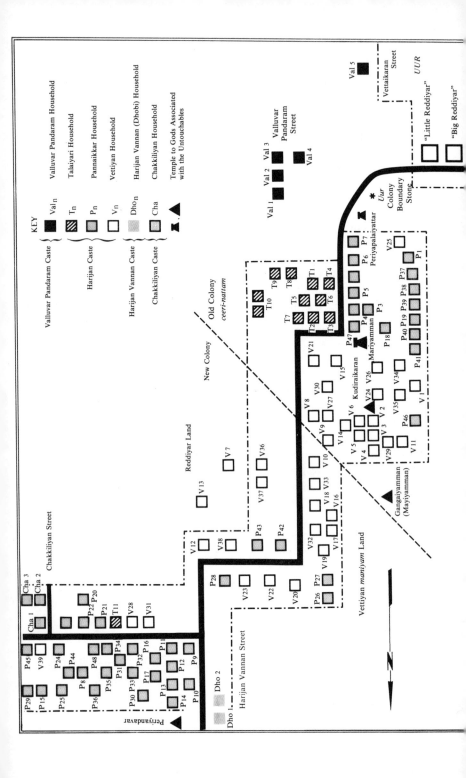

system that is used mostly for cinema music. There is as much livestock in the Colony as in the *uur* (excluding always the Reddiyars' compounds), and there is if anything more living space here—with the new Colony extension—than there is in the unexpanded *uur*.

The four residential Untouchable castes of Endavur live either in the Colony or near its boundaries. Four families of the Valluvar Pandaram caste live in their own "street" midway between the Colony and the *uur*. All ninety-eight households of the Harijan caste live inside either the old Colony or the new Colony. On the northern edge of the new Colony is a separate street for the two families of the tiny Harijan Vannan caste, and on the eastern edge of the new Colony is another "street" for the three families of the Chakkiliyan caste. These two streets were separate territories until two generations ago, when the expanding new Colony engulfed them. Finally, on the other side of the *uur* is the "stopping place" for the lowest caste in the Endavur hierarchy, the wandering Kurivikarans or "crow-catchers."

The Untouchability of three of the five Untouchable castes of Endavur—the Valluvar Pandarams, the Harijans, and the Harijan Vannans—centers definitionally around the low *toRil* of the central caste, the Harijans, for the Valluvar Pandarams and the Harijan Vannans are by their *toRil* bound up transactionally with the Harijans, and thus bound up in their lowness. The Valluvar Pandarams provide the Harijans with *purohit* services and are paid for these services in money, raw rice, and new clothes, while the Harijan Vannans provide the Harijans with washermen (*vaNNan* or *dhobi*) services and take from them impure clothes and cooked food. The lowness of the bottommost two castes in the village hierarchy, the Chakkiliyan leatherworkers and the Kurivikaran crow-catchers, is a function of their low *toRils* with respect to the village as a whole, though these castes are also inferiorized by the fact that they will accept

Opposite: MAP 4-1. Endavur Colony: Castes, Grades, and Temples

101

transactions in cooked food and water from the other Untouchable castes in the Colony.

Each of these five lowest castes calls itself a "caste" (a *jaaDi*), and each is strictly an inmarrying group, finding its marriage partners among its cocaste members in neighboring villages. There has been only one case of an intercaste marriage between Endavur Untouchables in the last ten years, and it will be discussed below.

Let us begin to sketch the replicatory microcaste order of the Untouchables of Endavur by describing these five castes in more detail—their general features, their relations to the village and the *uur*, and their relations to one another. In the next chapter, we will further unpack the structure at the bottom, by analyzing the internal social organization of the largest of these Untouchable castes, the Harijans or Paraiyans. And in a final descriptive chapter, on the religion of the Harijans, we will reassemble these relationships around the formal themes of identity, replication, and complementarity in divine practice. The following caste-wide analysis of the Untouchables treats the lowest, partially excluded castes of the village according to their local rank order in Endavur, top to bottom within the Untouchable subset of castes.

THE VALLUVAR PANDARAM CASTE

The highest-ranking Untouchable caste in Endavur is the *VaLLuvar PaNDaram* caste, defined both in the *uur* and the Colony as the "Brahmins for the Harijans." The Valluvar Pandarams' replication among the Untouchables of the Brahmins' *toRil* among the *uur* castes is thus an indigenously conscious fact. The Valluvar Pandarams of Endavur do not just relate downward to the Untouchables, however; they also serve upward as astrologers to the non-Brahmin *uur* castes. They are thus divided almost evenly between Untouchables and non-Untouchables by their *toRil*, but the balance of these ties is toward the Untouchables. For due to their acceptance of money, raw rice, and betel from the Harijans in exchange for their services, they are excluded from the *uur*. The position of the Valluvar Pandaram street clearly expresses their medial position between the *uur* castes and the rest of the Untouchables. The fifth Valluvar Pandaram household (Val₅ on Map 4-1) appears on casual inspection to be the last house of the Vettaikaran street in the *uur*, but a closer look shows that the cactus-marked boundary of the *uur* runs through the ten-foot space between the outermost Vettaikaran household and this Valluvar household.

The Valluvar Pandarams of Endavur could not tell an origin myth for their caste. But a myth reported by Thurston admirably expresses the Brahminness of the Valluvars, their lowness, and their intermediacy, deriving them from the mixture of a Brahmin and a Paraiyan: "According to one account, the Valluvans are the descendants of an alliance between a Brahman sage and a Paraiyan woman, whose children complained to their father of their lowly position. He blessed them, and told them that they would become very clever astrologers, and, in consequence, much respected" (Thurston 7: 304).

The head of only one of the five Valluvar Pandaram households serves full time as Valluvar *purohit* to the Harijans and to the Harijan Vannans, and as astrologer to the *uur*. This man is landless, while the other four Valluvars in the village are landed agriculturalists. The four landowning families of the Valluvar caste hold an average of three adjusted acres per family; "adjusted acres" is a rough measure we will be using among the Untouchables, an approximate weighting of dry, wet, and pump-fed land.[1] The Valluvar *purohit* has a jurisdiction of Endavur and two neighboring villages, and he estimates his combined income from *purohit*

---

[1] The "adjusted acres" of a given landowning family are its dry acreage times one, plus its wet acres times two, plus its pumpset-fed land times three. Thus a family with .5 acres dry, 1 acre wet and .5 acres pumpset-fed have an "adjusted acres" score of 4.0, which approximates the equivalent holding in purely dry land.

duties and astrology to be a meager two rupees per day, on the average. *Purohit* duties have a variable season, however, for marriages (the main source of income) depend on a cycle of auspicious and inauspicious months among the Untouchables, just as they do among the higher castes.

The services of the Valluvar *purohit* for the Harijans and for the Harijan Vannans are precisely the same as those of the Brahmin for the *uur* castes. The *purohit* is mediator between Harijan worshipers and high forms of divinity, and he is conductor of auspicious life-cycle rituals for the Harijans. The *purohit* once came to the Colony Mariyamman temple on a daily basis to perform evening puja, but he has discontinued this service recently due to a dispute with the Harijans over his payments. But he remains an essential actor in the yearly festival to the Colony Mariyamman, and his role in this festival is strictly contextualized. For the Valluvar *purohit* deals only with the multivalent goddess Mariyamman when she is in her high, pure, and beneficent form. In his own words, he "stays inside with the goddess," inside the temple between the lower-caste worshipers and the high form of the goddess, her immovable image in the inner sanctum of the temple. The *purohit* purifies and "cools" this image of the goddess, and makes to her vegetarian offerings on behalf of her Harijan worshipers. But he strictly avoids the goddess in her lower form, when she possesses a Harijan devotee as an angry and bloodthirsty being. And when bloody sacrifice in made to the goddess outside the temple, both her immovable image and the Valluvar *purohit* are screened from the sight with a white curtain (see Chapter VI).

The Valluvar *purohit* thus stands clearly between the Harijans and a high form of the goddess, just as the Brahmin stands between other humans and deities of a high nature. Like the Brahmin, the Valluvar *purohit* serves only those within a certain range of himself; as the Brahmin excludes all the Untouchables of the village from his *purohit* services, so too the Valluvar refuses his service to the two lowest castes

104

among the Untouchables—the Chakkiliyans and the Kuri-vikarans. As with the Brahmin, it is appropriate that the Valluvar Pandaram plays the *purohit* role to the Harijans and the Harijan Vannans, since the Valluvar ranks above these castes. It is similarly appropriate that the Valluvar *purohit* conducts the auspicious life-cycle rituals of the Harijans and the Harijan Vannans. These rituals include marriage, where the *purohit* conducts the focal ceremonies under the marriage pavilion (the *pandal*); *karumadi*, the ceremony that marks the end of the mourning period sixteen days after a death (where, in exact parallel with the Brahmins' role in *uur* funerals, the *purohit* is fed nonboiled foods); and the name-giving ceremony for a child of three or four.

Not every Harijan has the name-giving ceremony conducted for his children, and it is possible to go through the adult names of Endavur Harijans and determine who has had the ceremony and who has not. Those who have had the ceremony carry the names of gods and sacred places, while those who have not still bear in adulthood the more profane nicknames of early childhood ("white-faced," "lame," "the horse"). Marriage and *karumadi* rituals, on the other hand, must be conducted for all Harijans, and the presence of the Valluvar *purohit* is essential in both.

The Valluvar Pandarams rank above the Harijans, due to their high *toRil* and due to their refusal to accept from the Harijans any transactions except the relatively neutral ones that are payment for *purohit* services. Their caste is said to be purer than the Harijans. The *purohit* himself avoids beef-eating entirely, is a vegetarian four months of the year (*Kaarttihai, PuraTTaasi, MaargaRi*, and *AavaNi*), and the rest of the year eats only chicken, eggs, and fish. He talks of his community still having some *aachiram* ("highness"; the Tamil term is cognate with "ashram"), but complains that it has lost much of this in recent generations, as fewer members have maintained the caste's standards of purity.

The Valluvar *purohit* is very serious about the performance of his *toRil*. He presents himself very Brahmanically to

105

the Harijans, his head shaven into a topknot, his chest bare and covered with sacred ash, his lower body in a clean waist-cloth. He wears a sacred thread (a *pural*) to which, he claims, all of his caste has a right, but few are sufficiently pure these days to wear on a daily basis. The Valluvar *purohit* compares his duties constantly to those of the Brahmins, emphasizing his knowledge of correct actions but not of the written Sanskritic words of the Brahmins:

> We do for these Harijans the things the Brahmin does for the *uur* people in marriage, *arasani kaal, kudai velaikku, kurai sal* [ritual acts in the marriage]. But we don't know what the Brahmins are saying when they are performing those rites.
>
> I learned these rituals from my father, just as the Brahmin learns from his. But, unlike the Brahmin, I did not learn from books.

Brahmin mantrams are among the few genuinely safe secrets of Tamil village life, for they are spoken in a language known to none but a few Brahmins. Though the *purohit* is serious about the performance of his duties, he has virtually no interest in the meaning of the rituals, in their exegetical explanation. Particular Harijan informants were distinctly more sophisticated in interpreting the significance of ritual acts than was the *purohit*. This nonexegetical approach may be a function of the imitative ritualism of the Valluvar *purohits* in general, or it may simply be a personal characteristic of this particular *purohit*—a young man who has only been at his duties about five years.

The Harijans are much less respectful of the Valluvar *purohit* than he is of himself. Their interactions with him, even in the middle of ritual actions, are highly argumenta-tive, and they generally show more deference to some of their own headmen than they do to him. During the Colony Mariyamman festival, for example, the *purohit* and the Hari-jans kept up a running debate over whether a new waist-cloth was to be included in the *purohit*'s fees. The *purohit* finally threatened not to participate in the goddess's car procession, and at the last moment the Harijans capitulated and paid up. One influential Harijan maintained that the Valluvar *purohit* ranked below the Harijans transactionally, that he was "just like a beggar" since he took raw rice in partial payment for his services. Though this Harijan was rebuked by an elder for his slanted analysis of the *purohit*'s rank, he continued to apply an anti-Brahmin analogy to the Valluvar, one reminiscent of Dravidian movement demystifications of the Brahmins: "Brahmins are fighting for rice; the Valluvar *purohit* is fighting for rice" (that is, both perform their *toRils* not out of true religious feeling, but out of greed for the payments involved). But this same Harijan used the services of the *purohit* in the marriage of his son. The Harijans' lack of respect for the *purohit* may also be a reaction to the youth and inexperience of this one in particular; none of the Harijans, in any case, seem to question the general necessity for higher-ranking priests who are willing to serve them.

The Valluvar Pandarams are in general quite emphatic about their distinctness from the Harijans as a caste, and about the fact that they definitely do not live in the "*ceeri*." The single recent intercaste marriage among Endavur Untouchables occurred between a Harijan man and a Valluvar Pandaram woman—and the reaction of both castes to the liaison indicates the degree to which each sees itself as a tightly bound caste or *jaaDi*. The rank difference between the man and the woman was as small as possible in an intercaste context, for the man was a member of the highest of three ranked "grades" within the Harijan caste, and the Harijan caste is next in rank below the Valluvar Pandarams. The marriage was hypogamous, however—in the worse direction in terms of the relative ranks of the man and the woman (the man rather than the woman was "marrying up"). After a secret courtship, the woman became pregnant and the couple decided to marry. Both partners to the marriage were then outcast by their respective castes, and the couple left Endavur for four years and lived in various towns in the region; the man is a competent mason and is capable of self-support. Finally, after a prolonged negotiation involving one of the Reddiyars and the headmen of the Harijan caste, the couple was readmitted into the Harijan caste (the man had to pay the Harijan caste council a large fine). They now live with the man's family, in the Colony. From the point of view of the Valluvar Pandarams, the woman remains outcast and in fact no longer exists; her family, who live fifty yards from the couple's house, in sight of it, declare that they "have no daughter."

The internal organization of the Valluvar Pandaram caste of Endavur is not complex. Four of the five households in Endavur are lineally related and worship in common the lineage god (*kula devam*) Periyandavar. "Streets" of up to ten Valluvar Pandaram households are found in most of the larger villages around Endavur, and it is to these that the Endavur Valluvar Pandarams go for their appropriately related marriage partners. Local caste decisions are made by a consensus of the male heads of household among the five families; no Valluvar Pandaram caste council was reported on an intervillage level.

The Endavur Valluvar Pandarams say they are *Nayinar* Valluvar Pandarams by subcaste, and claim to be superior in rank to three other Valluvar subcastes, none of whom lives in the immediate vicinity of Endavur, and who do not intermarry or interdine. The three, in rank order below the *Nayinars*, are said to be:

1. *Vayiniyan VaLLuvars,* associated with the worship of goddesses, but with possession by them in particular. This caste will adopt the *purohit* duties of the *Nayinars* where the *Nayinars* do not exist.
2. *Taatan VaLLuvars,* who beat the *bambai* drums associated with the onset of the goddess possession.
3. *Sekku MooNDi VaLLuvars,* who work as oil crushers

(shastrically low because of an association with the taking of life) and who have no clear function in relation to the gods.

Whatever the ethnographic validity of these subcastes and of their relative rank (and most informants' subcaste accounts seem to place their own subcaste foremost), the articulated principles of differentiation are interesting. For the division of functions between the higher-ranking *Nayinars* and the lower-ranking *Vayiniyans* and *Taatans* is isomorphic with the division between *purohit* and *pucari* functions in the *uur* and in the Colony, and restates the ritual superiority of the local Valluvar Pandaram's *purohit* duties. Subcaste 3 may be a kind of excluded group among the Valluvars, ranked low by its nonassociation with ritual functions and its association with the taking of life.

As Untouchables, the Valluvar Pandarams are subjected to the same exclusions that define the Untouchability of the four castes below them. In response to these exclusions, the Valluvars have access to the same replicatory subsystem used by the much larger Harijan caste just below them, with one exception. The Harijans use as *purohit* a rather young and inexperienced member of the Valluvar Pandaram caste. Among themselves, however, the Valluvar Pandarams go for their own *purohit* services to a particularly venerable ninety-year-old Valluvar of another village, who performs marriages and other auspicious life-cycle rituals within the caste. A *purohit* should in some way rank above those he serves, but the appropriate candidate of a caste higher than the Valluvars—the *uur* Brahmin *purohit*—will not so serve the Valluvars. The Valluvars have therefore found their priestly service by a device that will become familiar below, and that can be described structurally as "code-switching." Since the Valluvars cannot find a priest who ranks above them in the code of "caste," they make do with a member of their own caste who ranks above them in "age."

109

THE HARIJAN CASTE AND CULTURAL DEFINITIONS OF HARIJAN LOWNESS

The Harijan caste of Endavur is the central and dominant caste among the five Untouchable castes of the village. The caste is central in its spatial position in the Colony. It is dominant in that the services of two other Untouchable castes are directed toward it. In common with dominant castes among the higher castes of village India, the Harijans control most of the resources of the Untouchable subset (89 percent of the land owned by Untouchables is owned by Harijans), compose the bulk of the Untouchable population (92 percent of the local Untouchables are Harijans), and rank relatively high within the subset (the Harijans rank second among the five Untouchable castes of the village). The Harijans are also dominant in that they possess the only active caste council among the five Untouchable castes, a group of five Harijan headmen who make collective decisions for the caste. Their decisions, such as the timing of festivals, have an impact on members of the other Untouchable castes.

Harijan dominance differs from Reddiyar dominance in range and in force, for it operates only within the Untouchable subset, and it operates with far fewer resources than does the Reddiyars'. Nor have the Harijans ever had other Untouchables in *paNNaiyaaL*-like tied labor relations to themselves. The Harijans have, however, recreated newer relations of labor dominance; some of the richer landed Harijans of the Colony employ poorer landless Harijans and other Untouchables (including, in one case, a Valluvar Pandaram) to work as their *kuli* wage laborers.

Thus, just as the Valluvar Pandarams replicate for the Harijans and the Harijan Vannans the high *purohit* function, so too the Harijans replicate dominance among the Untouchables. Furthermore, the major castewise replication of the Untouchables is centered on the Harijans; it is for the

110

Harijans and not for themselves that the Valluvar Panda-rams replicate *purohit toRil*, and that the Harijan Vannans replicate other lowering *toRils*.

The lowness of the Valluvar Pandarams and of the Harijan Vannans is centered on their transactional relations with the Harijans. What then is the source of the Harijans' lowness? How is a Harijan defined from the point of view of the *uur*, and how do the Harijans define themselves? What is their own relation to their low identity, and how far have they reinterpreted this identity among themselves? These intricate and somewhat subtle questions of culturally defined identity can be investigated in two related domains: in the nature and definition of Harijan *toRil*, and in mythic definitions of Harijan origins. Let us begin with Harijan *toRil*.

At the most general level of cultural semantics, the Harijans are low because their *toRil* associates them in a number of ways with the death of higher beings—of humans and of cows, in particular. More specifically, the Harijans take death-substances from the higher castes, including dead cows, dead humans, and food and clothes that carry death pollution (*tittu*). The Harijans also serve as intermediaries between higher beings (both human and divine) and the lowermost divine beings, the *peey-pisasu* or demons, most of whom are the spirits of the maleficent human dead.

There are five distinct roles that make up Harijan *toRil* in Endavur, roles that it is both the obligation and the right of the Harijans to perform, and roles to which the collective rank of the Harijan caste is referred by all persons in the village. These roles are *parai* drummer, cattle scavenger, cremation ground attendant, *varayan* announcer, and village watchman. Each of these roles is associated in a number of ways, some strongly and some weakly, with the death of cows, with the death of humans, and with spirits of the maleficent dead.

The first of the Harijan roles, *parai* drummer, is the action from which the older, now stigmatized caste name was

111

derived: *paṛaiyan* = "*paṛai* person."[2] *Paṛaiyan* is sometimes translated into English as "drummer," but there are many types of drum in a Tamil village, and many types of drummer. Virtually all the other drums of the villages (a set which includes the *uDukkai*, the *bambai*, and the *tavul*) have goat-skin heads, a point that their non-Untouchable players generally emphasize. The *paṛai*, on the other hand—a single-headed tamborine-like instrument—has a head made of the skin of a young cow. A Paraiyan plays his *paṛai* with his hands, not with a stick, and in doing so he is in contact with product of a dead cow. The named *toRil* of the Paraiyans thus represents their physical contact with cowhide, with a substance produced by the death of a cow.

Paṛai drumming also associates the Harijans with the *peey*. The *peey-pisasu* ("demons") and the similar *bhuts* ("ghosts") are believed to be mostly the spirits of the un-happy dead, of humans who have died in inauspicious ways —in childbirth, by accident, by suicide. Due to their unhap-piness, they have not gone on to the next world, but they remain in the vicinity of the village, living outside the *uur*, Colony, and village boundaries, often in particular trees, sometimes at crossroads. The *peey* are low, impure, blood-thirsty and maleficent beings who attack humans without warning, and whose presence is threatening to many ritual occasions. As *paṛai* drummers, it is the role of the Harijans

2 "Harijan" means "children of god" in Hindi. The term was coined by Mahatma Gandhi, to refer to all of India's Untouchables regard-less of caste. The Harijans of Endavur clearly prefer "Harijan" to "Paraiyan," but though they associate the caste title with Gandhi, they do not know its Hindi meaning. Nor do Untouchables anywhere in village Tamilnadu use "Harijan" to label more than one Untouch-able caste. If, in a given village, the Paraiyans call themselves "Hari-jans," members of other Untouchable castes will not use the same term, but will seek out other honorific substitutes for their older caste names. The title "Harijan" is resented by more politicized Tamil Un-touchables as patronizing; these Untouchables generally prefer the caste title *AaDi Draavida*, "original Dravidian."

to protect higher beings, both human and divine, from the attack of these *peey*.

The *peey* are not attracted to all ritual occasions, but only to those in which blood and death are present. The Harijan *parai* band is therefore not used in the auspicious ceremonies of the *uur* castes, such as high god worship or a high-caste marriage. It is only asked to come to more mixed ritual occasions, to festivals of the territorial goddesses Mariyamman and Selliyamman, and to higher-caste funerals. Here, the *parai* band stands at some distance from the ritual focus and plays its noisy beat, while the more auspicious *tavul-nadeswaram* band of the *uur* Ambattan caste stands closer to the center, closer to the goddess or to the body of the deceased high-caste person. The *parai* band serves on these occasions to frighten away the *peey*, who are attracted to the bloody sacrifices that the goddesses require, or to the flesh and blood of human corpses. The "good" music of the Ambattan band, on the other hand, affects the ritual focus more directly and more auspiciously.

The Harijan drummers are lowered by their *toRil*-based proximity to or contact with the absolutely impure *peey*, but they are also in the same position as certain very low guardian gods: they have power over the *peey*. Just as it is fitting that the Brahmin *purohit* mediates with high deities, and that the Vettaikaran *pucari* mediates with intermediate-to-low goddesses, so too it is appropriate that the Harijans, who are among the lowest of humans, mediate between higher humans (and gods) and the lowest of divine beings, the *peey*.

The second definitive role in Harijan *toRil*, cattle scavenger, involves the Harijans directly in the acceptance of dead cows. In Tamil village culture, the cow is an auspicious and beneficent animal, a "puja-worthy animal," "the giver of all things." Cows are not openly or willingly killed; the killing of a cow is equated in the ancient *dharmasastra* lawbooks with the killing of a Brahmin. When a cow (a *maaDu*, which

113

in Endavur includes cows, bullocks, and water buffalos)
does die a natural death anywhere in the village of Endavur,
it is the obligation of the Harijans to remove its body, which
they generally drag into the Colony. The Harijans then have
the right to make use of the cows' carcass. They are universally believed in the *uur* to eat the flesh of the cow; and
they sell the skin and bones to the leatherworking Chakkiliyans. As cattle scavengers, the Harijans are thus accepting
from the *uur* castes transactions in a most inauspicious medium, dead cattle, and as eaters of beef, they are incorporat-
ing these transactions directly into their bodily substance.
One high-caste respondent in the *uur* accounted for what he
had defined as the "low and filthy" language of the Harijans
by saying that since bad things went into the mouths of Harijans, it was not surprising that bad things came out again.

The impurity of cow flesh represents an inversion of the
general cultural logic by which the purity of an animal's
flesh is determined. According to this general logic, which
is quite explicit in Endavur, the purity of a given meat is
directly related to the dietary purity of the animal in life.
Thus goat meat is purer than pork, since the goat is observed to graze on greens in the waste land outside the village, while the pig scavenges around visibly in the village,
eating food leftovers and even human feces. In the case of
the cow, however, the fact of death overrides the animal's
consumate purity in life (and the observed cleanliness of its
diet while living). This inversion may be due in part to the
circumstances of a cow's death. While goats and pigs are deliberately slaughtered for consumption by meat-eating village
castes and consumed quickly, cows die slowly and their
carcasses are not picked up by the Harijans until sometime
after their death. Agents of death and decay—the *peey*, perhaps—have thus penetrated cow flesh by the time the Harijans consume it. This is not the entire reason for the lowness
of cow flesh, however, for even freshly killed beef (available
from Muslim butchers in the town of Madurantakam) is a
very low meat. The only meats lower than beef are crow,

which is eaten by the lowest caste in Endavur, the Kurivi-karans, and dog, an unthinkably low diet. The contradictions in dietary logic that define the lowness of beef have not escaped the attention of some Harijans, as we shall see.

The third role in Harijan *toRil*, cremation ground attendant, implicates the Harijans in the death of humans, and once again places them in contact with the *peey*, mediating downward against the *peey* on behalf of higher beings. At the cremation ground, the Harijans either take over and manage the corpse while it is on the fire, or dig a grave and place the body in it. They thus take dead human bodies from the higher castes. As cremation ground attendants, the Harijans also receive two more death-polluted substances from those above them: they are given the shroud of the corpse (which is a new cloth placed over the body after death, immediately and severely polluted by its contact with the body), and they are fed cooked food by the family of the deceased—at a time when this family is so polluted by the close death that (in addition to the Untouchables) only similarly impure close lineal relatives will take food from them. By having nonrelatives who are willing to be fed by them, the higher-caste family of the deceased wins merit for itself and for the spirit of the deceased, for it is meritorious to feed "the poor" at the end of ritual occasions. In addition to the cremation ground attendant, the Harijan *parai* drummers also make this lowering acceptance of death-polluted food when they play for a higher-caste funeral.

Of all of their specific *toRil*-based roles, that of cremation ground attendant brings the Harijans most markedly and most explicitly into contact with the *peey*. For it is around these grounds that the *peey*, themselves dead beings who are attracted by other dead beings, are thickest. It is to the cremation ground that *mantravaadis*, individuals from a range of castes who practice black magic, are often said to come to draw their powers, to bind *peey* to them as their maleficent servants.

The fourth role in Harijan *toRil*, *varayan* announcer, has

115

most of the same associations as the third, cremation ground attendant, though the associations are slightly weaker here. The *varayan* announces mostly inauspicious news for the higher castes of the village, especially the news of death. It is his responsibility to inform all close relatives in the village and in nearby villages of a death in the family, and of the timing and arrangements for the funeral. The *varayan* also assists the Harijan cremation ground attendant, and takes cooked food from the family of the deceased in partial payment for his services.

The fifth role, village watchman, has weak associations with the *peey* and involves the Harijans in no lowering acceptances of death-polluted substances from the higher castes. It is thus the least low part of Harijan *toRil*, and it is the role to which the Harijans themselves most proudly refer their identity. As village watchmen, Harijans armed with wooden staffs that represent their position guard the village (*kiraamam*) and *uur* boundaries at night. They guard the houses and the fields of the village against human thieves, calling on a high-caste *munsif* (policeman) if he is needed. Since the Harijan watchmen are moving around at night, a time when the *peey* are thought to be most active, they are once again guarding higher beings against these low demons. They are in particular guarding the boundaries of the village and the *uur*, for it is outside these boundaries that the *peey* mostly dwell. In these boundary terms, by the way, the living site of the Colony itself can be said to represent the general position of the Harijans as intermediaries downward: the Colony lies about midway between the center of the village, the *uur*, and its outer boundaries, the *kiraamam* stones beyond which the *peey* live. *Peey* also dwell within the boundaries of the *kiraamam*, however, in internal spaces that are not part of the *uur* or the Colony living sites. The Harijan village watchmen are paid for their services with money and with raw rice, not with substances associated in any way with the death of cows or the death of humans.

116

The semantic associations and the specific transactions entailed in the five roles that comprise Harijan *toRil* in Endavur are summarized in Table 4-1.[3] All these acceptances

TABLE 4-1. The Meaning of Harijan *ToRil*

Meaning		The Five Roles of Harijan ToRil				
General lowering association	Specific lowering acceptance or contact	Cremation ground attendant	Varayan announcer	Cattle scavenger	Paṛai drummer	Village watchman
	Acceptance of:					
The death of humans	death-polluted human bodies	+	+	0	0	0
	death-polluted food	+	+	0	$\binom{+}{0}$	0
	death-polluted clothes	+	0	0	0	0
The death of cows	death-polluted cow bodies	0	0	+	0	0
	death-polluted cow meat	0	0	+	0	0
	Contact with: death-polluted cow hide	0	0	+	+	0
Spirits of the maleficent human dead	the *peey* (spirits of the maleficent dead)	+	+	(+)	+	+

of "death" put Harijans in the same general relation to the total system as that held by the *uur* Vannan washermen and Ambattan barbers: they are the acceptors of very impure substances, facilitating by these acceptances the personal

[3] My thanks to McKim Marriott for his critical comments on earlier drafts of this section in particular, for his suggestions that I specify as concretely as possible just what the higher castes were transacting with the Harijans.

and collective purity of the higher castes from whose proximity they remove these substances. The Harijans further facilitate the purity and auspiciousness of the higher castes by standing between them and such low beings as the death-generated *peey*. And the Harijans reinforce by these low acceptances and by this intermediacy their own fundamental lowness with respect to those whom they serve.

Table 4-1 suggests that the different roles in Harijan *toRil* are weighted differently. The roles of cremation ground attendant and cattle scavenger are most negatively marked by four lowering acceptances or contacts each; *varayan* announcer and *parai* drummer are less negatively marked; and village watchman is least negatively marked, by only one lowering contact with "death." These differences in stress are consistent with differences in the way the *uur* castes and the Harijans refer to the identity of the Harijans. An *uur* person in Endavur, asked to comment on the status of the Harijans, will stress the lowness of their cattle scavenging, their beefeating, and their cremation ground duties. A Harijan, on the other hand, is more likely spontaneously to refer his caste's identity to its more honorific duty of village guardianship. This watchman role, in fact, is elaborately enacted by the Harijans in the festival to the village goddess Selliyamman (see Chapter VI). Neither the *uur* person nor the Harijan is ignorant of the respective roles in Harijan *toRil* that he does not stress; higher-caste persons are well aware of the village watchman role, and the Harijans of course know they are also cremation ground attendants and cattle scavengers. The differences in interpretation here do not reflect any cultural disjunction; they are simply differences of attitude, keyed to relative rank and to whether the speaker is looking up or looking down.

Which brings us to the question of the Harijans' own definition of their *toRil*. The Harijans have not stopped performing any of this *toRil* in recent years, so in this sense they still "accept" it. If they tried to boycott their *toRil*, the Reddiyars would stop providing them with agricultural labor until they returned to performing the *toRil*. But even a boycott would not necessarily indicate any change of consciousness about rank and its symbols among the Harijans; more likely, it would simply indicate the desire of one Untouchable caste to raise its status by disavowing a *toRil* whose status is as low among Untouchables as among higher castes.

Among themselves, and in relation to a non-Indian anthropologist, the Harijans do articulate some minor reinterpretations of their *toRil*. One Harijan, for example, tried to say that the "real" name of the *paraimelem* ("*parai* drum") was the "*periya meelum*" ("big drum"). "*Parai*" and "*periya*" are not that close in spoken Tamil, though folk etymologies common in Tamil villages frequently work with differences this great. The shift from "*parai*" to "big," however, would represent the detachment of one Harijan artifact from a word now solidly stigmatized and its reattachment to a more generally and vaguely prestigious term.

Beefeating also has its reinterpretations, though here things become very ambiguous. Many Harijans denied that they ate beef at all, but one who made this denial (and claimed that he ate only chicken and goat) also pointed to the contradiction in the logic by which the cow's impurity was calculated—for the cow, he said, was a cleaner feeder in life than any other animal. The Harijans delight in stories of beef and trickery of the higher castes; most of the stories have the outcome that higher-caste meateaters do not recognize beef when they taste it, but only want to know where such delicious mutton has come from. Beef is also said by the Untouchables to be a strengthening food. In the last Indo-Pakistan war, according to an old Endavur Harijan, there was a tug-of-war in the Indian army between a team of fifty beefeaters and fifty vegetarians—and the beefeaters, of course, won.

Physical strength, however, is not highly valued in Tamil culture, in an agrarian social order where rank is overtly symbolized by the ability to dominate labor rather than to perform it, and the Harijans are well aware of this. Their fundamental attitude toward their *toRil*, their consensus with a culture that defines the performance of such *toRil* as innately lowering, is revealed by the assignment of the *toRil* within the caste. The Harijan caste of Endavur is divided into three ranked divisions or "grades," collectivities said to vary in their collective purity. Members of the highest of these grades perform none of the five lowering services to the village that compose Harijan *toRil*. Members of the second grade perform only one of these services, that of *varayan* announcer, and most persons of the grade dissociate themselves as much as possible from the actual performer of *varayan toRil*. And the third and lowest grade in the Harijan caste is low because its members perform four of the five basic services in Harijan *toRil*. The lowness of Harijan *toRil* is thus capable of producing rank within the Harijan caste, at a second level of internal replication that we will treat in detail in the next chapter.

The second major cultural domain in which we can investigate Harijan identity is that of myth, the origin myths of the Harijan or Paraiyan caste. Here we can be more precise about Harijan self-images and higher-caste images of the Harijans—about possible similarities and differences in the two perspectives—for we have myths from both points of view, two as told by the Harijans, and two as told by higher *uur* persons. Though the four myths are different, all four are basically consistent and mutually supportive as explanatory devices. They vary in one or two attitudinal ways, however, depending on the rank of their tellers. Let us start with the Harijan versions.

The most elaborate origin myth of the Paraiyans was told by an eighty-year-old Endavur Harijan:

M_1 *The Origin of the Paraiyans*

At the origin there was nothing in the world. There was no life. There was nothing except for one woman, *AaDi* ["origin"]. She was all alone, and she wanted a husband.

So she made a sacrificial fire (*yagam*) and started meditating ferociously, fasting and not opening her eyes. Lord
Vinayagar [Ganesha] came out of the fire, and called to
her, "what, mother?" *AaDi* replied, "no, no, I don't want
you. I want a husband, not a son." Vinayagar disappeared and again she started meditating vigorously. Lord
Vishnu came out of the fire and said to her, "what do you
want, younger sister?" *AaDi* said to him, "no, I don't want
you. I want a husband, not an elder brother." Vishnu
disappeared. She again began to meditate vigorously. Finally a handsome man emerged from the fire. According
to her wish, he married her. He was none other than Iswaran [Siva]. The couple lived happily.

After some time four children were born to *AaDi*. The
gods were satisfied that everything was complete, except
for the creation of the castes. So they planned for it. According to their plan, the four children, who had become
adults, were made to cook beef one day. The eldest son
offered to do the cooking. While he was cooking, the other three brothers sat around him, watching him cooking.
While the meat was boiling, one piece fell from the pot.
The eldest son saw it fall on the ground, and thought that
it would bring a bad name to his cooking. So, meaning
well, he hid it under the heap of ash. Immediately the
others accused him of theft, and scolded him for stealing
a big piece of meat for himself. They shouted at him,
"*Paṛaiyaa, maṛaiyaade!*" ["Paraiyan, do not hide (that)"].
Hence the name "*Paṛaiyan.*" Eventually the elder brother
was forced to live separately, and he was called "Paraiyan."

The old Harijan who told this myth immediately added
the spontaneous interpretation: "Even now the same situation continues. We are generally innocent, without any idea
of theft or of cheating. Yet we are branded as dishonest
people. As you find in this story, we do things with good intentions only. But these are misinterpreted by others as

something with bad intention and without any reason. We get blamed."

The Harijan's interpretation is apparently very close to that predicted by Pauline Kolenda for north Indian Untouchable origin myths: that the Untouchables relate their present status to a mythic fall caused by a terrible misunderstanding (Kolenda 1964). In contradistinction to Kolenda's interpretation, however, the fall was hardly an accident. As the myth states, the gods had "planned for it," they had created caste by setting up the incident. The old Harijan was very clear on this point. When on another occasion he was asked why Harijans continue to eat beef if it makes them so impure in the eyes of the *uur* people, he looked surprised. Didn't we remember the myth? "It is the order of the gods, who set up the test," he said; it is just the way things are, it is "fate" (*viidi*).

Nor in a strict sense was the fall of the original Paraiyan an unjust fall, for the Paraiyan acted badly, and bad actions have lowering consequences (in north Indian terms, bad performance of *dharma* leads to bad *karma*). Since the original Paraiyan carried out his bad action with good intentions, the best construction that can be placed on his behavior is that he acted foolishly. An image of themselves as stupid and gullible is found in a number of Harijan self-representations in Endavur.

The bad action that caused the original Paraiyan's fall was not beefeating, however, for all four brothers were apparently sitting down to a meal of beef. *Uur* people who knew this myth admitted to the point with some surprise; yes, all people must have been beefeaters originally in order for the myth to make sense. The old Harijan who told the first myth had another interpretation: only the eldest brother ate the beef, for his younger brothers left him with the cooked carcass after the incident. But in terms of the explicit narrative of the myth, the bad action that created the fall was impure cooking practices, followed by an attempt to hide these practices and the accusation of theft.

122

As a whole, myth M_1 begins as a general origin account, in which the first human being, *AaDi*, whose origin is not explained, is put into relation to the gods Ganesha (as mother), Vishnu (as younger sister) and Siva (as wife). From the union of Siva and *AaDi* comes four sons, not yet differentiated by caste, but differentiated by age. For the original Paraiyan was the first son, and the Harijans in other contexts still refer to this original birth precedence. The Harijan cremation ground attendant, for example, has the right to chant to the *uur* people at the cremation ground:

I was the first born
I first wore the sacred thread
I am Sangu Paraiyan . . .

In other Harijan versions of the myth, the eldest brother wears a sacred thread, which is taken from him by a younger brother after the mythic creation of caste—and this younger brother becomes the first Brahmin.

The central incident of the myth is important structurally, for it represents an inversion and a code-switch around the feature of relative rank. That is, before the fall, the original Paraiyan ranks first in the code of age, while after the incident he ranks last in the code of caste. The intertranslatability of age-rank and caste-rank is a key feature of the replicatory structures among the Untouchables, as we have noted above for the Valluvar Pandarams. Here the intertranslation is made mythically rather than social-structurally, but the symbolic principle is the same—relative rank can be represented both in caste and in age. And as an inversion, this code-switch does seem to have a psychological function attributed to it by Kolenda: it gives the Harijans a prideful claim to former precedence, despite their present low status.

The first myth is the most widely known account of the origin of the Paraiyans; virtually every Harijan can quote its central rhyming line, "*Paraiyaa, maraiyaade*" (though the alternate etymology of the caste name, "one who plays the *parai*," is also universally known). The second Harijan myth

123

takes up where M_1 leaves off, and reiterates the theme of the good intentions of the original Paraiyan. Here, however, the stupidity of the original Paraiyan is more clearly stated, in conjunction with a new theme—trickery by the higher castes:

M_2 *The trickery of the Original Paraiyan*

Even after the separation of the brothers, the original Paraiyan worked hard in the fields, and became an expert in agriculture. Siva gave him a golden plow, golden bullocks, and everything else necessary to agriculture made of gold. As he was carrying them away, a Reddi and a Vellelar said, "since you are close to him, why don't you give us these things and go back to Siva." Gullibly he agreed. He gave the things away, and went back to Iswaran for more boons. Siva became furious with him, and told him, "you are useless for anything. Go and suck the penises of those two."

This myth quietly asserts that the Paraiyan is a hardworking agriculturalist (contrary to a high-caste stereotype of Untouchables as lazy and irresponsible), and that he is basically open and generous, here to the Reddi and the Vellalar. But he is also foolish, and his foolishness results in the curse of the god. Taken together, the first two myths complete a cycle. In the first, the gods set up the trial; in the second, a god effects the final degradation of the Paraiyan. In the first, the Paraiyan is spatially distanced from other men; in the second, he is distanced from the god Siva (for he is no longer "close to him" after the trickery) and he is made subservient to other men. And in the second myth, as in the first, there is no element of intentional deceit or wrongdoing in the Paraiyan's actions; due only to his stupidity, the consequences of his actions are fated to be disastrous for him.

Uur myths of the origin of the Paraiyans share many basic themes with the two Harijan myths, but they differ in the intention imputed to the original Paraiyan. In these *uur* myths, the original Paraiyan acts out of greed, not out of good intentions. In common with the Harijan images, how-

124

ever, the original Paraiyan also acts foolishly. The first of the *uur* versions again involves the god Siva:

M_3 *The Origin of the Paraiyans* (*uur* variant$_1$)

Once the "Scheduled Caste" people went and asked Siva for a boon. He told them they could help at his temple—help with bathing the stone, blowing the conch shell, and acting as watchmen. Siva also at that time divided up other duties for other kinds of people and animals. There are eighty-four lahks of kinds of life.

Still the Harijan was not satisfied with his lot. He went to Siva and said, "I want something more." Siva said, "Oh, is that so?" He had a donkey approach, and asked the Harijan, "what is it?" The Harijan said, "it is a donkey," and it died. Siva then told the Harijan to bury it in a place three hundred yards away. The man, thinking Siva would soon disappear, buried the donkey hurriedly, only just covering the body with sand. Siva then asked him, "who are you?" The Harijan replied, "I am *TooTTi* ["the digger," literally]." Siva told him to go look after the temple again, but out of frustration, the Harijan replied, "*een tambi pappaan*" ("my younger brother will watch it"). Siva told him, "yes, your younger brother is Brahmin (*paappaan*) and you are Paraiyan."

This myth turns on verbal play more elaborate than M_1. The key pun centers on the ambiguity *paarppaan—paappaan*; the former means "he will watch," the latter is a common term for Brahmins.[4] Other naming occurs. The Harijan

---

[4] Kenneth David has collected a similar but still more elaborate myth for Paraiyans in eastern Ceylon: "Two brothers were the *pusaris* [priests] in a Mariamman temple. The elder brother decided to fast and to observe a vow of silence. He wanted his younger brother to watch over the temple. So he said to the people '*Nan parrayan, tampi parpar*': 'I will be silent (*parrayan*), my younger brother will watch.' But the people misunderstood him and thought he said, '*Nan paraiyan, tampi parpar*': 'I am the drum person,' (*parai* = funeral drum; *an* = person) 'younger brother is the priest' (*tampi* = younger brother; *parpar*, from *par*, to see = seer, wise one,

names the donkey and it dies (a sign of the inauspiciousness of his language?). He carries out what is now Paraiyan *toRil* and buries the carcass, and then describes himself as *TooTTi*, which literally means "digger" but is also the most stigmatized term for those Paraiyans who serve as cremation ground attendants.

Like the Harijan myths, this *uur* myth describes a fall, though it is not so far as the fall described in the first myth. Like the first myth, this myth represents the original Brahmin as the younger brother of the original Paraiyan (for in a version of M_1 one of the younger brothers became the first Brahmin), and it implicitly refers to the same inversion from age-coded status to caste-coded status. Like the second Harijan myth, this *uur* myth relates the Paraiyan's degradation to a bad action that has angered Siva. But here—unlike the Harijans' versions—the fall is motivated by the original Paraiyan's bad intentions, by his inability to be satisfied with the god's boon, and by his sloppy performance of his "digger" duty.

A second high-caste myth of the origin of the Paraiyans turns as clearly on the theme of greed and, even more clearly than M_3, links the Paraiyan and his death duties:

M_4 *The Origin of the Low Position of the Colony People* (*uur* variant$_2$)

The goddess Kali made the first differences. In those days, the Colony people were higher in caste. Therefore Kali gave them the right to announce, to beat the drums, and to honor the dead. The *uur* people had to pay them a fee for this, so they had both honor and income in those days.

One day, Kali asked a Colony person to beat the drums and to declare: "Let the unripe and let the ripe fall" [that is, let the young and the old die]. The Harijan added two

---

priest)." (David 1972:18). This myth is clearly Harijan in its point of view, for in it, the original Paraiyan's only mistake is being misunderstood. His intention is the best: to undertake a vow and a fast to the deity.

or three more phrases: "let the bud and let the flower fall" [that is, let the unborn and let small children die]. He did this in order to get even more income. Kali became angry with him and said, "since you have changed my pronouncement, you are hereafter lower castes." Since then others have looked down on them as low, because they attempted to increase their income in this crude way.

Taken together, all four myths of the origin of the Paraiyans—Harijan and *uur* caste variants alike—form a mutually consistent transformation set, the messages of one supplementing the messages of another. All four describe a primordial fall, and all four attribute this fall to bad conduct on the part of the original Paraiyans. Gods figure in all four as the determinants or the judges of the fall. And one by one, the myths generate most of the present features of Harijan identity: beef scavenger and beefeater (M_1), watchman (for a temple) (M_3), death specialist (M_1, M_4), agricultural laborer, (M_2), announcer and drummer (M_4), person separated from other men and from gods (M_1, M_3, M_4), and extreme subordinate to the higher castes (M_2).

Given these commonalities, it cannot be said that there is in these myths any disjunctive mythic consciousness between high and low castes concerning the generation of the Paraiyans. If the theme of the precipitous fall is in these myths because it is psychologically comforting to the low castes, it must by the same token be psychologically discomforting for the higher castes to think of their original nonprecedence —for the same theme is in their versions of the myth. There are two differences between the Harijan versions and the high-caste versions: the fall is not so extreme in the high-caste versions, and the Paraiyan's intentions are better (but his actions are no better) in the low-caste versions. We could read these differences as examples of a minor "subcultural" disjunction, but they are better read as attitudinal differences keyed to relative perspective. That is, in these myths the *uur* castes are looking down at inferiors whom they consider to

127

thoroughly deserve their status. The Harijans, on the other hand, are looking at themselves. They may as ultimately deserve their status because of their stupidity and gullibility —but, they add, how near was the balance between these negative traits and their positive traits, their openness and good intentions. And when the Harijans themselves look down, they imply as clearly as the *uur* castes that those below them fully deserve to be low.

The Harijans of Endavur often represent themselves as foolish and naive, images in accord with those in the myths. Or, more exactly, Harijans who consider themselves a bit advanced deplore the general level of the community from which they have risen. One Harijan remarked that "these people" [his own caste] were so "uncivilized" that they could not even tell a lie properly: "they go on repeating an obvious lie instead of making it more complicated." Another Harijan, known in the caste for his low character, claimed that he often manipulated this mask of stupidity; he could always fool those *uur* people, he said, for they always underestimated him. And a third turned the image of naiveté around, and pointed to the openness that is part of the Harijans' stereotypic simplicity. Harijans, he said, were more likely to become possessed by deities because of their openness. *Uur* people had "worshiping minds," but they were secretive in their religion. Harijans, on the other hand, did things "brightly" and unsecretively, and therefore the gods were more likely to honor them by "coming down" into them, for "the gods are pleased with open worship."

The Harijans of Endavur also articulated self-images of crudity and lowness:

> My people are so uncivilized that even when they wear a loin cloth, their genitals will hang out.

> We do not know how to eat. We stuff large handfuls of rice in our faces.

> Our people are just like crows. We will gather raucously around anything we want.

128

Yet, as with stupidity and openness, there is a slight twist of the low and crude self-image in which the Harijans can take pride: "We were born of the *asuras* [the primordial anti-gods]. The *asuras* were strong enough to inflict pain even on gods and goddesses. Like them, we are ferocious and fear-less. A Harijan will catch a tiger; a Reddiyar fears to kill even a snake."

The Harijan who made this last claim was the best edu-cated man in the Colony, a young schoolteacher with some familiarity with the cultural revisionism of Ambedkar's neo-Buddhist movement. His claim is interesting, for it amounts to a conscious identification with antigods or the demons, an identification comparable to the Brahmins' link with the high gods, and an identification partially implicit in the Harijans' *toRil* of mediating downward toward the *peey*. But the *asuras* are not the *peey*; the *peey* are minor agents of evil, easily controlled by the higher gods. Nor are seeds of ideo-logical revision like this one widespread in the Endavur Col-ony. They are not widespread theoretically, and they are rarely brought into action. Even the young schoolteacher, despite his occasional ideological radicalism, worships not the *peey* or the *asuras*, but a conventional set of higher Hindu deities.

In their definition of their own identity and its lowness in *toRil* and myth, then, the Harijans of Endavur are in funda-mental consensus with the higher castes. They define them-selves as low for the same reasons as the higher castes do, and they agree with the evaluation that persons with their characteristics should be low. The Harijans are not entirely pleased that they themselves must continue to perform ac-tions that generate such lowness, but they agree with the fundamental social assumption that someone must perform these actions, and they are aware that the higher castes will probably prevent them from attempting to abandon the ac-tions, in the absence of others willing to take them up. Nor are Harijan origins and roles entirely dishonorable; there are features of pride in all of them, and there are material rewards for the *toRils* that we shall analyze in more detail in the next chapter. At this point, one further issue relating to rank and to self-image remains at the level of the Harijan caste as a whole, the issue of subcaste.

In the 1891 Census of India, 348 "subdivisions" were returned under "Paraiyan" for the whole of the Madras Presidency (which then included all of Tamilnadu and parts of Andhra Pradesh and Kerala). Today, there is among the Harijans of Endavur very little awareness of subcaste.[5] Only the old Harijan who told origin myth M_1 could recall the subcaste marker of the local Harijans: "we are *Sangu Paraiyan*, born of the conch [*sangu*] shell. We are Samba community." He went on to mention three lower-ranking Paraiyan subcastes, in rank order, with the following attributes:

1. *Karum Paraiyan*: "Their only fault is that they were born dark."
2. *PaLLa Paraiyan*: "They eat frogs. We eat beef and pork, but how can anyone eat frogs? They're not eatable."
3. *ViNNamagalattan Paraiyan*: "They committed adultery and did not obey the laws of our caste. We outcast them."

None of these subcastes is found in the Endavur area, and no subcaste distinction is presently related to Harijan mar-

---

[5] "Subcaste" is an inadequately understood feature of south Indian social structure. Literally, a subcaste can be defined as the empirically bounded unit of marriage and of relative rank. In this sense, all the "castes" described here are really "subcastes." But a given caste does not articulate its subcaste identity unless it is confronted with members of another subcaste; and, as in central India (Mayer 1960), in south India different subcastes of the same caste are not always found in the same village hierarchy (though their co-occurance is not particularly rare, either). Whether subcaste awareness is generally breaking down, whether subcaste boundaries are being ignored and marriages increasingly permitted by caste alone, are issues that have not been resolved for contemporary village India. The answer probably varies with caste,

riage, commensality, or rank in Endavur. As with the Valluvar Pandarams' subcastes, however, these subcastes are interesting for their cultural discriminations, whatever their social reality. For this Harijan is articulating many criteria of lowness used by the higher castes to inferiorize his own caste. The *Karum Paraiyans* rank below his caste, he says, due to an attribute often mentioned by the higher castes for the Paraiyans in general: inborn darkness of skin. The *Palla Paraiyans* rank below the local Harijans due to a food, or an eaten nonfood, even more unthinkable than beef and pork. And the *ViNNamagalattan Paraiyans* represent, in this old Harijan's account, an ideal of outcasting as solid among the Harijans as among the higher castes. To be a *Sangu Paraiyan* is to observe the Sangu caste "laws." To break these laws is to lose status as unequivocally here as higher in the system. Nor is outcasting merely an ideal in the Endavur Colony; witness its temporary enactment in the case of the Harijan-Valluvar Pandaram intercaste marriage.

THE HARIJAN VANNAN CASTE

The tiny Harijan Vannan caste is the third-ranking Untouchable caste of Endavur, and it replicates for the Untouchable castes above it the *toRil* performed by the *uur* Vannan for the higher *uur* castes, the *toRil* of washerman. The Harijan Vannans accept from the Harijans and from the Valluvar Pandarams menstrual cloths—said to be *tittu* ("extremely impure")—and other impure clothing, and they thus rank unambiguously below the latter two castes. The term *tittu* also marks the impurity of the death-polluted substances that the Harijans accept from the higher castes. The Harijan Vannans are then "acceptors of *tittu* substances from the acceptors of *tittu* substances," and thus doubly impure

---

with region, and with urbanization. For the record, in the Pudukottai region Harijans were more aware of subcaste than were Harijans in the Endavur region.

transactionally. It was this caste that was reported to be "Unseeable" as well as Untouchable in the far south of Tamilnadu fifty years ago; the Harijan Vannans, also known as the *Pudara VaNNans*, could only come out at night, for the sight of them during the day was polluting to members of the higher castes (Hutton 1963: 81).

The Harijan Vannans are not Unseeable in Endavur, but the Harijans consider them almost Untouchable. Many Harijans, who pay the Harijan Vannans for their services partly in cooked rice and leftovers from their meals, do not allow Harijan Vannans into their houses. The Harijans have not excluded the Harijan Vannans, however, for they presently live in the same social space with the Harijans (the Colony), and they worship at the Colony Mariyamman temple.

The Harijan Vannans do more for the Harijans than washerman *toRil*, however; they conflate into one *toRil* aspects of the *toRils* performed separately in the *uur* by the Vannan washerman, the Ambattan barber, and the Vettai-karan *pucari*. Conflation represents a simplification in the replicatory subsystem of the Untouchables, but it is a structurally consistent simplification in which the key relations of rank are maintained. For just as the Vannans, the Ambattans, and the Vettiakarans rank below most of the castes they serve, so too the Harijan Vannans rank below the Harijans. The Harijan Vannans are actors whose rank is already low due to Vannan *toRil*; they therefore concede little additional rank by accepting additional *toRils* of the Ambattan and the Vettaikaran. Conversely, by having below them a set of actors willing to perform these lowering *toRils*, the Harijans and the Valluvar Pandarams are able to maintain certain levels of purity, and are able to worship divinity in an orthodox fashion, despite their Untouchability in the larger system.

As Vannans to the Harijans, the Harijan Vannans work actively as personal household washermen. Each of the two households of the caste has a "share" (*pangu*) of about twenty Harijan patron households in the Colony, whom it is their right to serve on a regular basis. The poorer Harijan households do not employ the Harijan Vannans regularly, but all Harijans use the ritual services of the Harijan Vannans. One set of these services exactly replicates the services of the *uur* washerman in the life cycle of the higher castes, and can be outlined as follows:

Harijan Vannan ritual services that replicate uur *Vannan ritual services*:

1. At a Harijan girl's coming-of-age ceremony: washing out the first menstrual cloth of the girl. Constructing and decorating with clean clothes a mud ceremonial platform (a *manai*) for the ninth-day ceremony at which the girl is purified.

2. At a Harijan marriage: accompanying the bride's party to the groom's Colony, and receiving a gift from the groom's party. Decorating the marriage pavilion (*pandal*) with clean clothes. Making and decorating a ceremonial mud platform (*manai*). Tending three lamps during the marriage ceremony. Participating in a ceremony where pots of water are brought in from the fields.

3. At a Harijan funeral: making and decorating the funeral bier.

Many of these ritual services are connected with cloth and with its purification, and are thus linked to the regular service of the Vannans. As in the regular washing services, here also the Vannan purifies the subject of the ritual by accepting from the subject impure bodily substance—again, as it adheres to the cloth, for the clean cloths supplied to these rituals by the Vannan must be taken by him afterwards and repurified. In all these services, it is important that the Vannan be a subservient and less pure actor, one who is willing to serve the patron in this manner, but he cannot be

133

Untouchable relative to the patron—for an Untouchable's presence would be too inauspicious in these mostly auspicious contexts (excepting perhaps the funeral).

A second set of ritual services performed by the Harijan Vannan replicates those of the *uur* Ambattan barber for the *uur* castes. The Ambattan service that is not replicated in the Colony is barbering itself; the Harijan Vannan does not cut hair for his patrons (nor do the women of the caste serve as midwives), perhaps because this involves the direct acceptance of more impure bodily substance (and the concession of more rank) than the Harijan Vannans are willing to make. Harijans have their hair cut by close relatives, who cannot be polluted by the act since they already share bodily substance with the subject; or, they say proudly, they go to "hair-cutting saloons" in the town of Madurantakam, where their caste is not known. It is not known who serves as Harijan midwife. But the life-cycle ritual assistance provided to higher castes by the *uur* Ambattan is among the Untouchables provided by the Harijan Vannan. These services all center on the funeral, and they are as follows:

Harijan Vannan ritual services that replicate uur *Ambattan roles*:

1. At a Harijan funeral: leading the chief mourner in the funeral procession. Following the chief mourner in his three circumambulations of the body at the funeral ground; making holes in the water-filled mud pot that the chief mourner carries over his shoulder. In a burial, outlining a symbolic funeral pyre on the ground. Roles in the second-day ceremony ("cooling the cremation ground") and the sixteenth-day *karumadi* end-of-mourning ceremony.

These are the services labeled "funeral priest" by A. M. Hocart (Hocart 1950). The funeral is the most bivalent of the life-cycle rituals, for on the one hand, death and its strong impurities have touched the subject and the close relatives of the subject, and other humans risk the *tittu* of death by contact or interaction with the mourners of the body. On the other hand, the funeral ritual is intended eventually to restore the mourners to their normal states of purity, and at the same time to free the spirit of the deceased so that it can go to a higher world of the gods (see Moffatt 1968). The relation of the Harijans and of their *toRil* to negative pole of the ritual, to death and its *tittu*, have already been analyzed. Due to this negative pole, the Brahmin *purohit* (and the Valluvar *purohit* among the Untouchables) will not officiate during the mourning period of the funeral. Who then carries out the actions that accomplish the eventually auspicious outcome of the ritual?

One answer is the eldest son, in a kind of code-switching within the immediate family of the deceased. The necessity for a son to perform the death ritual of the father is a fundamental orthodox reason for having at least one male child in every family. Another answer is the "funeral priest," who is appropriately of a low but not Untouchable caste with respect to the subject of the ritual. Such a rank is consistent with the interplay of the two poles of the ritual; and an assistant who ranked much lower than the barber would be incapable of the enhancing actions needed for the successful outcome of the funeral. Hence in the *uur*, the barber's role; hence in the Colony, the replicatory Harijan Vannan's role.

An Ambattan ritual service that the Harijan Vannans delete in the replicatory subsystem among the Untouchables is that of *tavul-nadeswaram* band, the auspicious band that in the *uur* stands closer to the ritual focus than does the Harijans' inauspicious *parai* band, and which is provided to the *uur* by a separate subcaste of Ambattans. Among the Untouchables, the service of "auspicious band" is not performed due to simple lack of skill: both the *tavul* (a double-ended, barrel-shaped drum played with the hand and with a stick) and the *nadeswaram* (a large double-reeded wind instrument) are difficult instruments with complex repertoires, and both require a long musical apprenticeship to master. The Harijan Vannans do not have the time for this apprentice-

135

ship, and here again—as with the non-Sanskritic ritualism of the Valluvar Pandaram—Untouchability constitutes a real communications barrier. For it is unlikely that an *uur* Ambattan would accept an Untouchable apprentice and teach him these skills. There is a replicatory response to the lack of a *tavul-nadeswaram* band among the Untouchables, however, which we will identify in the next chapter.

A third set of *toRils* conflated into the services of the Harijan Vannans in the Colony are those of *pucari,* "the puja-person" or temple servant service performed in the *uur* by a member of the Vettaikaran caste. The *pucari* roles all center around possession by the goddess, around her physical presence as a low and bloodthirsty being:

Harijan Vannan ritual services that replicate uur *Pucari (Vettaikarar) services:*

1. At the annual goddess festival (and at some other occasions of goddess possession); evoking the goddess by singing songs of praise to her; playing the instruments (the *bambai, uDukkai,* and *silambu*) which "bring her down" into a devotee. Managing the possessed devotee when the violent signs of possession occur. Carrying out the bloody sacrifice demanded by the goddess in her possessed form.

These services are all low because the goddess (who is identical to the goddess handled by the *uur pucaris*) is a low being. In this form the goddess often demands a "life." The *pucaris* send it to her, in sacrifice, and are themselves left with the blood and the corpse of the sacrificed animal. The animal is eventually cooked and eaten by the Harijan devotees, but its killing is a lowering act, appropriately performed by specialists of a lower caste than the main body of devotees. And the *pucari* role, like the ritual roles of the barber and the washerman, is also best performed by actors who are not too low, who are not Untouchable to the main body of devotees, for the ritual occasion is ultimately an auspicious one.

136

Let us note that in the Colony, as in the *uur*, the role of *purohit* in worship is rigorously distinguished from the role of *pucari*. And, as in the *uur*, the former is given to a high-caste actor and the latter is given to a low-caste actor.[6] The Harijan Vannans, like the *uur* castes whose lowering *toRils* they are replicating, will not perform their services for the castes below them in the village hierarchy, here the Chak-kiliyans and the Kurivikarans. These two lowermost castes are thus cut off from all the replicatory services which, to this point, we have outlined for the three higher Untouchable castes.

The two male heads of the Harijan Vannan households are interesting character types, a type sometimes denigrated in the anthropological literature as an empirically nonexistent stereotype for the low castes. These men are mildly defer-ential to the Harijans and to outsiders, but they do not dis-play a type of cringing deference sometimes shown by the very low—a defensive type of deference. Their position in the system is secure, and they seem to have accepted its lowness in exchange for its security. In some ways, they seem

[6] The widespread distribution of this replicatory distinction is sug-gested by data from the Pudukottai area, two hundred miles south of Endavur. Here, according to a Harijan respondent, the following life-cycle rituals or *sadangus* are observed by the Harijan caste, and each has the following ritual officiant:

1. Name-giving *sadangu*: Valluvar Pandaram
2. Ear-piercing *sadangu*: Valluvar Pandaram
3. Girl's coming-of-age *sadangu: Pudara VaNNan* (Harijan Van-nan)
4. Marriage *sadangu*: Valluvar Pandaram
5. Death *sadangu: Pudara VaNNan*
6. End-of-death *sadangu*: Valluvar Pandaram

As in Endavur, the Valluvar Pandaram officiates in ritual occasions where there is little reference to the inauspicious or the impure (*sa-dangus* 1, 2, 4, and 6). The Harijan Vannan, on the other hand, of-ficiates where there is such impure reference—in the girl's puberty ritual (marking her first menstruation) and in the death-pollution period of the funeral (*sadangus* 3 and 5).

more Harijan than the Harijans themselves. As servants to the Harijans, the Harijan Vannans are knowledgeable about their patrons' caste, and they have an objectivity about the larger caste that goes with their nonmembership in it. The fact that the Harijan Vannans comprise a tiny caste still actively engaged in the nearly full-time performance of their traditional *toRil* is probably related to their character types. Brenda Beck has noted the same conservative and accepting personality types in the *uur* barbers and washermen of Coimbatore, in members of low castes who remain in economic relations to their patrons that are "a means of maximizing subsistence security in an unpredictable environment" (Beck, personal communication; 1972a: 192-93).

The Harijan Vannans of the Endavur Colony, like the Valluvar Pandarams, are too tiny to have a complex internal social structure. The two households are lineal relatives who worship in common the lineage god Muniswaram. The households have divided in two from an earlier joint household in terms of their washerman services to the Colony and their household goods, but they still work in common a small landholding of .65 acres of dry land. They find their marriage partners within their own caste over a wide region; most of the larger Colonies of villages around Endavur have two or three households of Harijan Vannans attached to them, many living in streets that are still territorially separate from the main Colony (and that are further from the *uur* than the main Colony). The Harijan Vannans report no formal caste organization, no caste council, at an extravillage level. Within Endavur, they are in fact commanded most directly by the decisions of the Harijan caste council, but they have the right to carry any disputes to the Reddiyars. They report no subcaste divisions for their caste.

As for *toRils* on their own behalf, the Harijan Vannans are not cut off from above, for the Valluvar Pandarams will serve the Harijan Vannans as *purohits*. The Harijan Vannans are cut off from below, however; as the Valluvar Pandarams are squeezed by their position at the top of this Untouchable

138

subsystem, so too the Harijan Vannans are squeezed at the bottom. For no one below them is willing to act as *pucari* or as death-removing Untouchable for them. The Harijan Vannans might be expected to code-switch into an age code, and have these lowering services performed by younger members of their own caste. Such a code-switch downward violates the cultural logic of rank and of exchange, however, as we shall see below. Therefore, here, near the bottom, replication begins to collapse, not for reason of change in values, but due to a simple lack of human personnel who are willing to serve as replicators. The Harijan Vannans then perform the lowering *toRils* for themselves, by themselves.[7]

The set of services performed for one another by the three higher Untouchable castes of Endavur (the Valluvar Pandarams, the Harijans, and the Harijan Vannans) form a nearly perfect and entirely closed replicatory subsystem near the bottom of the village caste order. This replication is not perfect, because it apparently lacks persons in the relation of Untouchable to the Untouchables—persons who are excluded by the Untouchables, as are the Untouchables by the higher castes, and persons who will perform the extremely lowering services for the Untouchables that the Untouchables perform for the higher castes.

[7] My data here are not as good as they should be. When I conducted fieldwork, I had the basic idea of replication, but I saw it as an absolute kind of thing that would emerge only with respect to the largest Untouchable caste, the Harijans, not as a continuous property of the system that would operate egocentrically for any actor regardless of his position in the system. I therefore did not ask enough questions about replication among the very low. I think it is possible that the Harijans of Endavur play their *paṛai* drums for the Harijan Vannans, and I suspect that if a cow died in the Harijan Vannan street, the Harijans would take it away—perhaps after having the Harijan Vannans drag it out of the street for them. I think it is less likely that the Harijans would act as cremation ground attendants for the Harijan Vannans. And I am quite sure that no one below the Harijan Vannans serves as *pucari*, washerman, or barber to them, that the Chakkiliyans and the Kurivikarans perform none of the *toRils* of Untouchables for the Harijan Vannans.

It develops, however, that from the point of view of the Harijans of Endavur, both sorts of Untouchables exist, although both are not combined in the same persons. For the Untouchables whom the Harijans have excluded are the Chakkiliyans and the Kurivikarans, while those who play for the Harijans the roles of Untouchables to the *uur* are found within their own caste, among the members of the lowest of the internal grades of the caste. Structurally, this amounts to the opposite of conflation: among the Untouchables, low functions that are combined in one set of actors higher in the system (the functions of the Harijans themselves) are differentiated among a number of distinct actors. Differentiation then represents a kind of complication of the replicatory subsystem of the Untouchables, but like conflation, it is a process that preserves most of the important relations of relative rank. For those who are excluded as Untouchables by the Harijans are lower than the Harijans in caste rank, while those who perform for the Harijans the lowering *toRils* of Harijans toward the *uur* are the lowest among themselves in grade rank. We will deal with the second aspect of this differentiation in the following chapter. Let us now consider those who are to the Harijans (as well as to the Valluvar Pandarams and the Harijan Vannans) Untouchables by exclusion—the Chakkiliyans and the Kurivikarans.

THE CHAKKILIYAN CASTE

Members of the fourth-ranking Untouchable caste of Endavur, the three-household Chakkiliyan caste, are or have been "Untouchable" to the higher Untouchable castes of the Colony. Up to a generation ago, the Chakkiliyan "street" was a separate *ceeri* that the Harijans did not enter for fear of polluting themselves. The *toRil* of the Chakkiliyans is more intimately related to the "death of cows" than is Harijan *toRil*; the Chakkiliyans not only accept dead cows from the higher castes, but they work their *toRil* directly on the

140

products of these carcasses, which they then sell back to the villagers as leather goods. The Chakkiliyans rank below the Harijans because, just as the Harijans take dead cows from the *uur*, so too the Chakkiliyans take the skin and bones of these cows from the Harijans, for cash payment. Therefore, due to the lowness of their *toRil,* and the low acceptances that their *toRil* involves, the Chakkiliyans were at one time excluded from habitation in the Colony, just as the higher Untouchables are excluded from habitation in the *uur*.

The Chakkiliyans' reaction to this exclusion is interesting, for rather than accepting all the implications of their lowness and, for example, agreeing to play roles of extreme lowness to the Harijans, the Chakkiliyans have maintained with lessening success a policy of noninteraction with the Harijans. A generation ago, they refused to accept cooked food or water from the Harijans, just as the Harijans refused the same transactions from them. Although this did not make them equal to Harijans—for they still took leather from them—it did change the relations at the bottom. One of the Harijan Vannans analyzed the rank situation near the bottom in precise transactional terms, making the surprising claim that his own caste ranked bottommost in the entire system: "The Chakkiliyans will not take food from the Harijans, but we will. Therefore the Chakkiliyans are above us. But the Chakkiliyans are workers for the Colony, so they are between us and the Harijans. The Harijans come first, the Chakkiliyans come second, and we are last."

The eldest male of the Endavur Chakkiliyans made a similar claim, though his was stronger—a claim that rank was irrelevant to the relation of his caste to the Harijans: "My caste is entirely different from those other castes [in the Colony]. I only allow my own relatives here. I don't have anything to do with those [Harijans]. It is not a matter of who is higher or lower." The Chakkiliyan elder's statement amounts to an exact transactional analysis of the logical result of no relations or interactions between two castes, in the absence of unequal transactional relations with the

141

larger system: separate and therefore not unequal (see Marriott 1968: 149). The Chakkiliyans have thus attempted a "minimizing strategy" with respect to the Harijans, a strategy that is found between status rivals at all levels of the caste system (see Marriott 1968, 1974). But the elder's claim is inaccurate, for it ignores the Chakkiliyans' acceptance of leather from the Harijans, a factor of which all the other castes in the village are aware, and which has given the Chakkiliyans a clear consensual rank below the Harijans in the total hierarchy of Endavur for the past several generations.

Furthermore, the Chakkiliyans have in this generation ended their minimizing strategy toward the Harijans. The adult sons of the Chakkiliyan elder now accept cooked food and water from the Harijans. And while the Harijans continue to refuse cooked food and water from the Chakkiliyans, they have lessened their exclusion of them in some ways. First, the boundaries of the Colony now include the Chakkiliyan street; and second, though the Chakkiliyans are still not served by the Valluvar Pandarams and the Harijan Vannans, they are protected by the powers of the Colony goddess Mariyamman. The result of this recent transactional adjustment is that the Chakkiliyans today rank unambiguously below the other three Untouchable castes of Endavur, save only the Kurivikarans. The Chakkiliyan elder was well aware of this new order, though he did not like admitting to it. Just after producing his statement on the irrelevance of rank between Harijan and Chakkiliyan, he was asked to rank the other Untouchable castes of the Colony, without regard for his own. He replied, "first Valluvar, then Talaiyari, then Vettiyan, then Pannaikkar [the three Harijan grades], then Harijan Vannan, then Chakk . . . "—and he literally stopped in the middle of pronouncing the name of his own caste as lowest among the residential Untouchable castes of the village. Thus both the Harijan Vannan above and the Chakkiliyan elder here have made claims to bottommost status among the residential Untouchable castes—the Harijan Vannan's claim being correct a generation ago, and the Chakkiliyan elder's admission being correct at present.

The growing prosperity of the local Harijan caste may be behind the decision of the younger males of the Chakkiliyan caste to concede rank to the Harijans in the present generation. For the concession makes it possible for the much poorer Chakkiliyans (whose three households own no land) to benefit from the prosperity of the Harijans. Before the concession, it is doubtful that the wealthier Harijans would have employed Chakkiliyans as daily *kuli* laborers on their land (as they do now), nor could the Chakkiliyans have accepted from the Harijans one of the customary payments for this labor under the old relationship, a cooked meal at midday. The Chakkiliyans' concession has had its limits, however. For the Chakkiliyans have not started acting as cremation ground attendants, nor as any other specialists of death, for the Harijans. As for their exclusion as Untouchables relative to the Harijans, this is now clearly more qualified than is the Harijans' exclusion relative to the *uur*, for the Colony now includes the Chakkiliyan "street" within its boundaries. Still, many Harijans today will not go into the Chakkiliyan street, complaining of its "bad smell," and many Harijans still claim that the Chakkiliyans pollute them by touch.

The internal organization of the Chakkiliyan caste is as simple as that of the Valluvar Pandarams and the Harijan Vannans. Like these other small Untouchable castes of Endavur, the Chakkiliyans are basically a single kin group who worship a common lineage deity, Maduraiviran. The three families have gone through a household division but still practice their leatherworking *toRil* collectively. Like the other small Untouchable castes, the Chakkiliyans also admit to no formal caste organization outside the village. They give their subcaste name as Arundadi Chakkiliyan, and say they are distinguished from "another" Chakkiliyan subcaste in that they do not sell lime and in that they are bilingual in Telugu and Tamil (while the other subcaste sells lime and

143

is monolingual in Tamil). There is no rank difference between the two subcastes, they say. As for *toRil* on their own
behalf, the Chakkiliyans of Endavur are cut off both from the
top and the bottom, and must turn entirely inward for their
ritual performants. Like the Valluvar Pandarams, they code-
switch into age to replicate the higher *purohit* function; their
own elders, they say, who have no special title but who are
"educated and knowledgeable," perform their marriages.
Like the Harijan Vannans, the Chakkiliyans apparently perform the lower functions of washerman and the rest reflexively, either within the kin group, or possibly between relatives by marriage.

THE KURIVIKARAN CASTE

The fifth and lowest Untouchable caste of Endavur, the
Kurivikarans (literally, "small-bird catchers," by connota-
tion "crow catchers") are without any reservation Untouchables to the Untouchables, polluting by touch to everyone
in the Colony (as well as to everyone in the village). The
Kurivikarans are ranked lowest in the Endavur due to their
suspected diet of crow (since the crow scavenges on every
other animal, its flesh is very impure), due to their acceptance of food leftovers from everyone, Brahmin to Chakkiliyan, and due to the fact that they "have no place." For
they are wanderers who travel continually through a specific
range of villages practicing their *toRil*, with a home base in
a village five miles east of Endavur. The wandering radius
of the two families of Kurivikarans who visit Endavur is
about ten miles; in Endavur, they stay in a "stopping place"
south of the *uur* for about ten days every six months.

Kurivikarans are peripheral to Endavur and to the local
Untouchable castes in every way. Their relations with the
other Untouchable castes are intermittent and of little importance to the other Untouchables. If the Kurivikarans are
in the village during Untouchable life-cycle rituals or the
Colony goddess festival, they will take cooked food handouts

from the lowest castes (or even leftovers from meals), and thus replicate with respect to the Untouchables a role played by the Untouchables in the *uur*—that of "the poor," who are willing to be fed on auspicious occasions to win merit for the feeder. The Harijans mock the Kurivikarans for their immoral way of life, replicating in a sense a higher caste attitude toward the Untouchables: in a dance which the Harijans perform to raise money for the Colony goddess festival, the Harijans act out a sexually fickle Kurivi wife and an amusingly helpless Kurivi husband. Otherwise, the Kurivikarans are rarely referred to by the other Untouchables of the village. A possible tactic for avoiding admission to bottommost status in the local hierachy—for everyone to assert that they are at least higher than the Kurivikarans—was never enacted in our presence.

The Kurivikarans' self-presentation in Endavur is very distinctive. Their dress is colorful and non-Tamil. Their roots are in north India, and they still speak a form of Marathi among themselves. Their reaction to the anthropologist was boisterous, less deferential, and more obviously manipulative than that of the average Untouchable. The Kurivis are beggars and fortunetellers in the village, and they also have a reputation as tricksters. According to a common tale, a Kurivi will shoot nine crows and one quail in the bush, pluck the nine crows and leave the quail unplucked, and sell all ten birds to higher-caste meat eaters as pure quail flesh.

Little research was conducted with the Kurivikarans, and it was not possible to learn much about the internal social organization of the caste. The Kurivikarans do have their own lineage god, whose "silver" image they leave behind them with a local Reddiyar in their home village. Interestingly, this deity is a form of the territorial goddess Mariyamman, from whose powers the Kurivis have been excluded both by the *uur* and the Colony, and whom they might therefore be replicating internally. Though the Kurivis retain some Marathi kin terms, the structure of these terms is common to other bilateral Dravidian terminologies, and the

145

Kurivikarans practice a standard type of south Indian "cross-cousin marriage" among themselves. Thurston's account of the Kurivikarans suggests that they are very low everywhere in Tamilnadu, that they are rarely provided with ritual services by any other castes, and that they have little in the way of internal ritual specialization (1909, 4: 181-87).

The Kurivikarans of Endavur, then, like the Chakkiliyans just above them, have been forced to turn totally in on themselves. The Chakkiliyans have responded to their turning-in with an orthodox village Tamil adaptation; in general lifestyle, the Chakkiliyans are indistinguishable from any other poor Tamil villagers. The Kurivikarans have responded in a different way, by accentuating their ethnic distinctiveness and by manipulating the system for every handout that it will give them. We might say we have finally reached some cultural distinctiveness at the very bottom of the Endavur hierarchy. It is a manipulated type of distinctiveness, however, and it is vested in a tiny and often absent group whose general significance to the eighteen residential castes of Endavur is very minor indeed. The Kurivikarans are only incidental to the structure of caste in Endavur.

Caste and Its Acceptance among the Untouchables of Endavur

The general point of the present chapter should be clear. The replicatory social structure internal to the bloc of Untouchable castes in Endavur—that structure which orders relations between the five lowest castes of the village—indicates the existence of no major cultural disjunctions between the higher castes of the *uur* and the Untouchables. No systematic subcultural break corresponds to the physical and social break between *uur* and Colony. Two genuine cases of blocked communication have been identified: the non-Sanskritic ritualism of the Valluvar Pandaram, and the nonexistence of a distinct auspicious band among the Untouchables. Both of these cultural exclusions are a result of the

146

fact that both are defensible skills among their higher-caste performers, for both require closely supervised and lengthy apprenticeships. Yet the Untouchables attempt to replace these exclusions to the best of their ability, with Tamil *mantrams* in the case of the Valluvar *purohit*, with a type of code-switching by the *parai* band and by another band that we will describe in the next chapter. The Untouchables do not lack the Sanskrit of the Brahmins or the auspicious music of the Ambattans because they do not value them. They lack them only because they are effectively denied access to them.

As for their "acceptance" of their position, the Harijans' mythic attitude toward their lowness can be summed up as an attitude of "yes, but. . ." "Yes," they say, they are low and deservedly low because of bad actions. "But," they say, they were once higher, and the generation of their lowness was a near thing. And when the Harijans look at groups below themselves—at other subcastes of Paraiyans, at Harijan Vannans, Chakkiliyans, and Kurivikarans—the "but" drops off their attitude entirely. From the point of view of the Harijans, these groups deserve their lowness as thoroughly as do the Harijans from the point of view of the higher castes.

The Harijans of Endavur are, like Indian actors at every other level of caste, concerned about their position in a consensually defined hierarchical system. They deplore their loss of former precedence, they would like to improve on their present status, and they are concerned that no one below them gain status at their expense. There is in this attitude virtually no criticism of the legitimacy of the system as such. Which is not to say that the Harijans of Endavur could not be brought to a critical awareness of caste as a system, but only that such an awareness is almost totally absent among them at present.

Nor is acceptance of lowermost status entirely untenable to Untouchables in Endavur. The Harijan Vannan seems to have achieved this acceptance willingly, and the Chakkiliyan elder has also reached it, though less willingly. Such acceptance does, however, require other rewards, and we can be a

147

bit more explicit about the structure at the bottom if we examine its system of rewards more carefully.

What we have as we work down through the caste hierarchy of Endavur is a series of exclusions and replications. The exclusion of the Untouchables as a bloc is only the most visible of these exclusions; others operate both higher and lower in the system. The response of an excluded group to its exclusion is replication—evidence of cultural consensus. If possible, an excluded caste replicates in a caste-code: it convinces other small castes to attach themselves to it (or possibly differentiates these smaller service castes out of itself) as enhancers of purity and as removers of impurity. But such replication requires collective resources, an ability for dominance within the excluded subset which, in Endavur, we find among the Harijans. When replication in a caste-code breaks down, it does not do so for reason of a sudden change in values or in consciousness near the bottom; it does so for reason of an exhaustion of material resources, of low humans able to pay others to serve them and of other humans willing to so serve. This exhaustion occurs in Endavur among the Chakkiliyans, but the progressive unfolding of these structures of exclusion and replication can proceed further among Untouchable castes.

N. S. Reddy's survey ethnography of the "depressed castes" of Andhra Pradesh, for example, suggests that a second-order replication can occur among Untouchables who are excluded by other Untouchables, given sufficient material resources. One large Untouchable caste of Andhra is the *Malas*, a Paraiyan-like caste excluded by the higher castes of Andhra as Untouchables. The Malas have reacted to their exclusion with a replicatory subsystem virtually identical to that of the Harijans of Endavur: they have above them a caste of *"Dasari" purohits*, and below them their own washermen. The Malas have in turn excluded the *Madigas*, the other large Untouchable caste in the region, who are Chakkiliyan-like leatherworking Untouchables. But in Reddy's ethnography, the Madigas are often present in

sufficient numbers to respond to this exclusion by the excluded by replicating the system once again among themselves. The Madigas' second-order replicatory subsystem
also includes higher-ranking *purohits* and lower-ranking
pucaris and "pipers" (the washermen services may be shared
among these), and, incredibly enough, yet another level of
exclusion—that of the *Dakkalis*, an ultimately low group
who beg from the Madigas, and are not permitted inside
the Madiga hamlets (see Reddy 1952). The Dakkalis are
thus excluded by the excluded by the excluded. Theoretically, a ranked system like this, based as it is on pervasive
cultural consensus, could continue to unfold endlessly. Its
only limits, as we have noted, are set by the material resources at the bottom of the system.

Among the Untouchables, as among the higher castes,
delicate tradeoffs are continually being made between rank
and material resources. An Untouchable caste the size of
the Harijans of Endavur has the resources to attach to it two
smaller castes, actors willing to make the rank concessions
necessary to serve the Harijans. The Chakkiliyans of Endavur, on the other hand, do not have the human numbers
(nor the material resources) to so attach to themselves
members of other castes, and they must therefore code-
switch into age in order to replicate. Why do the Valluvars
and the Harijan Vannans not also serve the Chakkiliyans?
Because to do so would be to concede more rank, in return
for minor additional material benefits. More seriously, the
Valluvars and the Harijan Vannans would probably lose
their Harijan patrons if they began serving the Chakkiliyans,
so they would lose both rank and material resources by these
service adjustments.

Why then do the Chakkiliyans not take the material benefits that would come to them if they agreed to be true Untouchables to the Untouchables, if they agreed to take death-
polluted substances from the Harijans? The answer here is
trickier, but its elements include the fact that there already
exist among the Harijans those who will take these sub-

149

stances from other Harijans. Also, the Chakkiliyans concede less rank by taking leather from the Harijans than they would if they also served as their Untouchables, and they have apparently chosen not to be so low. And the Chakkiliyans already have their *toRil*, one that is defined relative to the village as a whole and not just relative to the Harijans. Finally, the Chakkiliyans *have* made a rank concession to the Harijans in recent years (accepting cooked food), and it was probably a concession calculated to win them a share of the Harijans' recent material prosperity (employment as laborers to the Harijans).

One problem remains with regard to code-switching among the lowest castes of the village, among the Harijan Vannans, the Chakkiliyans, and the Kurivikarans. Code-switching into an age-code works for the purity-enhancing functions of the *purohit*; an orthodox elder in a given caste is a fit actor for mediating upward. An age-code switch does not work for downward mediation, however. For to give impure bodily substance to a younger member of one's own kin group does not remove it from the kin group; in substance terms, such a transaction is a transaction with oneself. We unfortunately do not know how the lowest castes in Endavur deal with this dilemma (see note 7). Perhaps downward mediation is simply impossible for them, and this part of the replicatory response to their lowness finally collapses at this point in the system.

There is a solution to the dilemma at the bottom, however, a particularly elegant solution. Aiyappan describes it for the *Nayadis*, an absolutely low begging caste of Kerala. The Nayadis have a ritual functionary called *"inangan"* (which Aiyappan translates as "chum") who accepts death pollution from them—who helps with the burial, who cooks for the mourners when they are in mourning, and who cuts the mourners' hair on the last day of death pollution. Since there is no one who ranks lower than a Nayadi, who could play this role? The answer is a "relative-by-marriage," a cross-relation who does not share bodily substance with the

150

subjects of the death ritual, and who can therefore genuinely accept impure substance from these subjects (Aiyappan 1937: 34, 35). Presumably, if A serves as *inangan* for B at a funeral of B's kin group, B will reciprocate the service for A. The Nayadi solution then is reciprocal downward mediation; just as cross-relatives are those who have exchanged women in marriage, so too here they exchange death substance at death.

Unlike the lowermost Nayadis of Kerala, however, the Harijans of Endavur do have lower humans below them and among them to mediate downward on their behalf. To recapitulate the structural analysis to this point, the Harijans have been included by the higher castes in the ritual services of the Pandaram florist and the Acari carpenter, as well as in a range of other nonritual services. They have therefore not had to replicate these services internally. The Harijans have been excluded by the higher castes from the *toRils* of the Brahmin *purohit*, the Vettaikaran *pucari*, the Vannan washerman and ritual assistant, the Ambattan barber, midwife, ritual assistant, and auspicious drummer; and from the *toRils* of themselves, the Harijans (from relations with persons lower than themselves, to whom they can give death substances, who can mediate downward against the *peey* for them, and whom they can exclude). The Harijans have responded to these exclusions by replicating some of these ranked relations with members of other Untouchable castes. These replications are thus in a code of caste, and they include the *toRils* of *purohit* (with the Valluvar Pandarams), of *pucari* (with the Harijan Vannans), of washerman and Vannan ritual assistant (with the Harijan Vannans), of Ambattan ritual assistant (with the Harijan Vannans), and of Harijan-as-the-excluded (with the Chakkiliyans and the Kurivikarans).

In formal structural terms, this replication represents an isomorphic transformation, a "mapping," in Pierre Maranda's terminology, of one structure onto another. In this transformation, the same relations (rank) are mapped in

151

the same code (caste). Some aspects of the isomorphic transformation represent what Maranda calls a one-to-one mapping. Thus the *purohit* role, which belongs to a single high caste at the level of the *uur*, also belongs to a single high caste at the level of the Colony. Other aspects of the transformation represent a many-to-one mapping. Thus the *pucari*, washerman, and barber roles, which belong to three distinct low castes at the level of the *uur*, are "conflated" into the role of a single low caste at the level of the Colony. Still other aspects of the transformation will soon represent a one-to-many mapping. Thus a set of roles vested in a single low caste at the level of the *uur*, those of the Harijan, will in the Colony be divided or differentiated among a number of distinct low actors, actors ranked low relative to the Harijans both in a code of caste and in a code of grade (cf. Maranda 1972). In these formal terms, it cannot be said that the replicatory Harijan structure represents a simplification of the *uur* structure. Or, if the many-to-one mapping is taken as making the structure transformationally more simple, the one-to-many mapping must by the same token be taken as making it more complex (see Table 4-2).

The exclusionary *uur* roles that are not replicated among the Untouchables in a code of caste are those mostly lowering *toRils* of the Ambattan barber, midwife, and auspicious drummer, and of the Harijan-as-acceptor-of-death-substances. The first two, barber and midwife, are entirely deleted from the Untouchable subsystem in Endavur, and thus represent the only real structural simplification in the Untouchable subsystem.[8] The last two are not deleted, however, and the last in particular directs us to the next and most microscopic level of the present analysis, to the internal structure of the Harijan caste itself. For as we have suggested above, it is among the grades of the Harijan caste

---

[8] Replication of barber *toRil* is not always deleted, however. Harijans in a Colony larger than Endavur's, in a village ten miles south of Endavur, reported receiving the services of a touring caste barber who ranked below them, though the code of his rank was not clear.

TABLE 4-2. The Isomorphic Transformation between the *Uur* Structure of Ranked Services and the Harijan Structure of Ranked Services

Uur *Structure*		*Nature of Mapping*	Harijan *Structure*	
PoRil	Caste of performer		Caste of performer	ToRil
Purohit	Brahmin	one-to-one	Valluvar Pandaram	*Purohit*
(Dominance)	Reddiyar	one-to-one	Harijan	(Dominance)
Pucari	Vettaikaran		Harijan Vannan	*Pucari*
Washerman, Vannan ritual assistant	Vannan	many-to-one	Harijan Vannan	Washerman, Vannan ritual assistant
Ambattan ritual assistant	Ambattan		Harijan Vannan	Ambattan ritual assistant
Auspicious drummer		replication in another code		
Barber	Ambattan	X (deletion)		
Midwife	Ambattan	X (deletion)		
Acceptor of death substances, intermediary with the *peey*	Harijan	one-to-many	Harijan, second and lowest grade	Acceptor of death substances, intermediary with the *peey*
"The excluded"	Harijan		Chakkiliyan, Kurivikaran	"The excluded"

that the final features of structural replication unfold. It is at this internal level that we obtain the most convincing evidence on Harijan definitions and evaluations of their own low identity, by answering the question, who acts as Harijan to the Harijans?

153

CHAPTER V

The Internal Structure of the Harijan Caste

THE Harijan caste of Endavur is a local segment of a larger endogamous subcaste that spreads horizontally through the bottom of the caste hierarchies of a number of surrounding villages. The boundaries of this horizontal unit are not known. No local Harijan would articulate them, and their empirical determination would have been a very time-consuming matter. In all probability, the unit extends over a region at least fifteen miles from Endavur in all directions. The local Harijans make all their marriages within this distance (or with Harijans who have emigrated from this general region to towns and cities). Assuming that no other subcastes of Harijans exist within the same territory, it is not necessary for a local Harijan to think of either subcaste or of boundaries when he contracts a marriage. He rather thinks of *moṟai*, individual "relationship" calculated according to past marriages; or he contracts a "new" marriage with a Harijan family that is not too far away, and that is therefore in the same unnamed subcaste. Subcaste markers may become more important near the boundaries of the region, or in the cities, unless subcaste is indeed "breaking down" (see note 5, Chapter IV). The endogamous unit of the Endavur Harijans may correspond to the "*Sangu Paṟaiyan*" subcaste remembered by the old Harijan above (p. 130).[1]

[1] Present survey work suggests that south Indian castes are empirically bounded endogamous units, that they do not "fade" at the boundaries. Brenda Beck has traced the marriage network of the *OkesaaNTi PaNDaarams* of Coimbatore, and found it to form a closed inmarrying set of about three thousand people, distributed over 105 villages in central Coimbatore (Beck 1972b). And Edward Montgomery has similarly worked through the membership of the

It is also possible that the endogamous territory of the Endavur Harijans corresponds to an area that was once under the jurisdiction of a distinct caste of *"Desa Chettis,"* who lived in a village two miles north of Madurantakam (ten miles from Endavur) and who had authority over Harijans within a twenty-mile radius. These authorities, known to the Endavur Harijans as "our *gurukkals*" (an honorific term that is also applied to Brahmins who serve as temple priests), came periodically to Endavur and acted as a court of appeal to the local Harijans. The *gurukkals* had the power to appoint or to depose local Harijan headmen, and to settle disputes between Colonies that the local headmen had not been able to settle. They have not come to Endavur for the last thirty years, however, according to older Harijans.[2]

Whatever the general spread of the Harijan subcaste, the Harijans of Endavur are very much a distinct territorial unit

---

Yelnadu Reddis of northern North Arcot district, and found them to comprise a closed population of 4,522 persons concentrated in thirty-six clustered villages (Montgomery 1977). If the Endavur Paraiyan subcaste is similarly bounded, I would guess that its population exceeds both of these figures.

[2] We made several unsuccessful attempts to locate this caste in its home village. The local Harijans were unclear as to whether it was a higher but still Untouchable caste, or a much higher representative of dominant authority in the region. Evidence for the latter is found in Thurston, who mentions for North Arcot a role called *Deesaayi* ["territorial"?] *Chatti*, a high-caste officiant who belonged to the Kavarai Naidu or the Baliga caste, and who had peace-keeping authority over the eighteen "right-hand" castes within a certain *taluk*. The details of Thurston's description are close to what is remembered by the Endavur Harijans (though there are no traces in contemporary Endavur of the "right-hand/left-hand" caste distinction). The official toured a region and adjudicated within it, and his village representatives in each caste were called *Periyatanakaarans*, a title still used by a Harijan headman in a neighboring Colony, though no one there knew its significance. Also congruent with Thurston's description is the fact that the "head village" of the local *Desa Chettis* was the old *taluk* headquarters for Endavur under the Muslims, before the British reestablished it in Madurantakam in the early nineteenth century (cf. Thurston 1909, 2:121-24).

within this subcaste. The territorial unity of the ninety-eight Harijan households of Endavur is expressed in two ways: all worship in common the deity of the local territory, the Colony goddess Mariyamman, and all are commonly under the authority of the local Harijan caste council, a group of five Harijan headmen. The internal organization of this territorial unit is too complex for marriage ties to correspond to the unit in any simple way. The majority of local Harijans cannot marry with one another either because they have "parallel" brother-like relations with one another, or because they belong to the separate quasi-endogamous grades within the caste. These Harijans therefore find their marriage partners among their cross-relations in neighboring Colonies (the cross/parallel distinction will be glossed below), and the marriages they make with them are mostly patrilocal or virilocal. A large minority of local Harijans, however, are the descendents of matrilocal or uxorilocal marriages made in the last two generations, marriages in which the husband has settled with the wife's family in Endavur. Descendents of these marriages are able to marry with other Harijans in Endavur. There is thus a considerable incidence of intra-Colony marriage among the Endavur Harijans, though it is lower than the incidence of extra-Colony marriage.

To be a Harijan in Endavur (and anywhere else) is, firstly, to be the product of an endogamous marriage between two Harijans. Like the members of any other caste, Harijans cannot change their birth-defined identity in their lifetimes, except in a negative direction, by being outcast. To be a Harijan, secondly, is to belong to the caste (*jaaDi*) that performs the caste-definitive *toRils* that have been treated above: *parai* drumming and the rest. Not every Harijan does or even can perform these *toRils* in actuality, but co-caste membership with persons who do is enough to give one Harijan identity. For the *toRils* are themselves lowering, and to share food and bodily substance (by marriage exchange or by common descent) with those who do this *toRil* is to share in their low identity. As the *uur* people say, all the Harijans "move together in the Colony," therefore internal distinctions among them are not that important. The *uur* people are correct in that internal distinctions among the Harijans do not modify their fundamental Harijanness, and in that these distinctions do not matter much in relations with *uur* people. The internal distinctions do matter tremendously to the Harijans, however.

For among the Harijans, the *toRils* that commonly define Harijan identity externally have been internally differentiated, and serve to mark three ranked divisions or "grades" within the caste. The highest ranking of these grades are the Talaiyaris, who as assistants to the village policeman (*munsif*) do none of the basic lowering *toRils* of the Harijan caste. Second ranking of the Harijan grades are the Pannaikkars, who have a titular claim to the position of headman among the Harijans, and who perform only one role in Harijan *toRil*, that of *varayan* announcer. And the third and lowest grade in the caste are the Vettiyans, the "true people" of the Colony, who perform four of the five caste-definitive roles in Harijan *toRil: parai* drummer, cremation ground attendant, cattle scavenger, and village watchman.

These three grades, called *vagaiyaras* (literally, "etcetera," connotatively, "division") in Tamil, have caste-like properties. They have a degree of endogamy (though they are by no means perfectly endogamous), they transact asymmetrically with one another in food, they are associated with distinct *toRils*, and they are differentially ranked according to relative purity and impurity. The grades also differ in putative lifestyle. For example, beefeating, like the performance of *toRil*, is also internally segmented among the Harijans. The highest-ranking Talaiyaris are said to be non-beefeaters, the Pannaikkars are said to be eaters of freshly killed beef, and the Vettiyans are said to be eaters of carrion beef.

In general terms, the grade divisions of the Harijan caste represent the existence of strongly held hierarchical values at a level of the system where the power of the higher castes

157

does not operate. More specifically, an examination of these grade divisions answers most of the remaining questions about replication with respect to the Untouchable Harijans. For what these divisions mean is that, among themselves, the Harijans have taken the lowering *toRils* that define them as Harijans to the village, and turned these actions inward to create rank. Thus Harijans serve as Harijans to other Harijans, but it is the lowest of Harijans who do so. Otherwise stated, in order to find their acceptors of death-polluted substances and their intermediaries with the *peeys*, services that they can convince no separate lower caste to perform for them, the Harijans code-switch from a caste-code of rank into a grade-code of rank, and assign most of the lowering roles to the lowest of their grades. The solution is not a perfect one, for in intercaste relations all Harijans share in the identity of these lowest Harijans. Among themselves, however, there are degrees of sharing, and within the caste each higher grade of the caste shares less in the identity of the lowermost Vettiyans.

There are two other units of social organization besides "grade" within the Harijan caste of Endavur: *kottu*, "lineage" or "sublineage," and *kuDumbam*, "family." Each of these units is smaller in scale, and each is encompassed by the next higher unit. Thus each grade is composed of a number of lineal units, and each of these lineal units is composed of a number of families. When we move from grade to lineage, ranking finally becomes almost irrelevant to Harijan social structure, and we enter a domain of purer "kinship." Birth precedence can still create rank at this level of the system, but by and large, the constituent lineages of a grade and the constituent families of a lineage do not differ from one another in rank, in relative purity, or in transactional relations. We have finally reached a level of "oneness" among the Harijans, a level of solidarity found similarly among higher south Indian castes, for it is based on common, shared bodily substance (see Dumont 1966, Inden and Nicholas 1972).

158

Though the three grades of the Harijan caste each break down internally into lineal groups and families, they each do so in rather different ways. Likewise, the relations between the grades is a complex matter, involving an intricate set of marriage exchanges and a finely tuned system of tradeoffs between rank and material rewards—tradeoffs similar to those we have discerned among the bottom five castes of Endavur, above. Let us therefore approach the complexities in the ranked structure of the Harijan caste of Endavur grade by grade, working from the first-ranking Talaiyaris to the second-ranking Pannaikkars to the fundamentally low, third-ranking Vettiyans.

THE TALAIYARI GRADE

The term *Talaiyaari* literally means "head person" or "chief person," from *talai*, "head." The service involved is that of assistant to the village policeman, the *munsif*, a role that in turn is generally vested in a member of a high caste. In Endavur, the *munsif* is a Sengundar Mudaliyar. The Harijan who serves as Talaiyaari helps the *munsif* to collect land tax and to restrain acts of physical violence in the village. His *toRil* has one link with death, for it is part of the Talaiyari's duty to watch over the body of a suicide until its relatives come for it (recall that death by suicide is one means by which the *peeys* are created). But this link with death is a weak one, and the Talaiyari does not take death-polluted substances in the performance of his *toRil*. He is not low to the same degree that other Harijans are, due to their more polluting *toRils*.

Consistent with this fact, Talaiyari *toRil* is not invariably assigned to members of Untouchable castes in Tamil villages. There is in western Chingleput a low *uur* caste that makes simultaneous claim to the titles "*Talaiyaari*" and "*Naidu*," and Thurston mentions a non-Untouchable caste distributed through northern Tamilnadu and southern Andhra, the *Muttarajas*, said to have originated as military camp followers of

159

the Vijayanagar armies, who in 1900 served as village Talai-yars (Thurston 1909, 5: 127-31).

In Endavur, Talaiyari *toRil* is a prerogative of one grade within the Harijan caste, and its relatively nonpolluting nature marks the members of this grade, the Talaiyaris, as higher in rank than the rest of the Harijans. The ten "true" families of the Talaiyari grade live in a distinct territorial cluster in the southeast quadrant of the old Colony (see Map 4-1). They represent themselves as the common descendants of a single male ancestor, who had six sons by two wives; these sons in turn founded the six "old families" of the current grade. Figure 5-1 shows a current collective genealogy of the

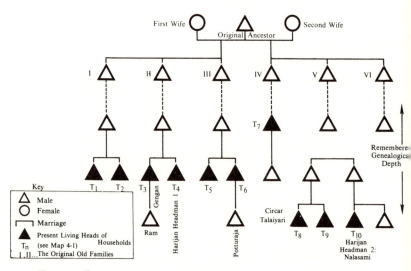

FIGURE 5-1. Genealogy of the Talaiyari Grade of the Harijan Caste

Talaiyari grade. The "remembered depth" (the generational distance to which personal names are continuously applied to male ancestors) of this genealogy is, as with all Harijan genealogies, very shallow, two or three generations. The generational distance from the oldest remembered specific

160

ancestor to the sons of the original ancestor (represented by a dotted vertical line in Figure 5-1) is not known to the Talaiyaris.

The Talaiyaris do not apply the term *kottu* (literally, "bunch," approximately, "lineage" or "sublineage") to the lineal groupings within their grade, as do members of the other two grades. Rather, the Talaiyaris say that they were once "one family," that they later differentiated into "six old families" (marked I, II, etc. on Figure 5-1), and that they are now "ten families." The term *kuDumbam* is applied to all these levels of "family."

In its most restricted sense, *kuDumbam* labels (for everyone in Endavur, Untouchable or non-Untouchable) a single household, marked off from other households by separate residence, separate cooking hearth, separate property ownership, and a separate household deity (*viiTTu devam*). The other households that a restricted *kuDumbam* has differentiated from are its *pangalis*, literally its "sharers"— those with whom it shares descent from a common ancestor. A *"pangali* split" is for the Harijans, as for all the other castes, a well-defined and crucial event. The *pangali* split of the two Reddiyar families two generations ago has been noted above; it literally bifurcated the entire village. Among the Harijans, a *pangali* split generally occurs between two brothers soon after their father's death (if it hasn't occurred before); there are thus few collateral joint families among the Harijans. The split is made in front of the soon-to-be-divided image of the household deity, and it is presided over by at least one of the Harijan headmen. *Pangali* splits must, among all castes, be equal ones. It is thus at this level of the system that "equality" (here, of male siblings) first appears.

The ten present households of the Talaiyari grade are said to have resulted from a succession of *pangali* splits from the time of the original ancestor. Those who have so divided from one another, however, remain in the relation of *pangalis* or "sharers." From the point of view of Talaiyari household T_1, for example, family T_2 is a "first leg sharer," families T_3 and T_4 are "second leg sharers," and family T_{10} is a "third leg sharer." What these families still share in, besides patrilineal descent, is land; each has a "share" (a *pangu*) of the *maniyam* land, which is the right of the Talaiyari in exchange for his service to the village. Twelve acres of this land remain unalienated in Endavur (nine acres dry and three wet), and cultivation rights to it have been divided along the lines of the successive *pangali* splits. The resulting "shares" are not equal, family to family, for some of the present families are the result of more splits than others (thus T_7 has one-sixth of the original *maniyam*, while T_8 has only one-twenty-fourth of it). Nor is the land presently held in particularly useful portions by most of the Talaiyari families. The *maniyam* land is more important symbolically than economically, for it is with respect to shares in this land (however large or small) that "true" identity as an Endavur Talaiyari is determined. Thus an eleventh Talaiyari family in the Endavur Colony, T_{11} on Map 4-1, living at the far end of the new Colony, is not a "true Talaiyari" in Endavur, for it has married into the Colony and it possesses no *maniyam* land here. It is a "true Talaiyari" in its home Colony two miles away, however.

As for the actual performance of Talaiyari *toRil* in Endavur, this position is handed down from father to son in the fifth "old family" of the Talaiyari grade (V on Figure 5-1), and it is presently filled by the head of family T_8. The exact title of the position is *circar* Talaiyari ("government Talaiyari"), and its performer is paid seventy-two rupees a month by the local government at the *taluk* level. As a steady monetary income in a position that leaves time for additional agricultural earnings, the salary is substantial for a Harijan. By analogy with other Colonies, Endavur probably also had at one time a separate position of *uur* Talaiyari, an older pre-British position that was also the "right" of the Talaiyari grade. In other Colonies, the *uur* Talaiyari is paid not in money by the government, but in grain by the higher castes of the village, at a certain rate per *uur* household. The *circar*

Talaiyari post was probably created and funded by the British sometime in the nineteenth century (see p. 47, above), and perhaps assigned to the junior wing of the Talaiyari grade (the descendents of the "second wife" of the original ancestor) to balance the right of the senior wing to act as *uur* Talaiyari. Since then, for reasons not remembered in Endavur, the *uur* Talaiyari position has become defunct. These speculative historical facts are not, however, particularly important to members of the Talaiyari grade in Endavur. Though male members of five of the six "old families" of the grade can never act as Talaiyari, their preeminent grade identity within the caste is established by two facts: one, that they are "sharers" with the individual who does act as Talaiyari, and two, that they are sharers in the *maniyam* land that goes with Talaiyari *toRil* in Endavur.

Another prerogative of the Endavur Talaiyaris, besides their rights to Talaiyari *toRil*, is to provide two members of the local five-man council of Harijan headmen. After they are chosen, these headmen are said to operate at the level of the caste as whole, without preferential ties to the grade from which they are drawn. A Talaiyari grade member might take a problem either to one of the two Talaiyari headmen or to the other three non-Talaiyari headmen, and the headmen represent the caste externally irrespective of its internal divisions. Among themselves, the Talaiyaris assign these two headmen by loose genealogical criteria; Figure 5-1 indicates the present Talaiyaris who are Harijan headmen, the heads of households T_4 and T_{10}. There is a tendency to hand this position down from father to son, but it is unanimously agreed among Harijans that a man must also be fit for the position, that he must have "good character," and have a personality suited to negotiating grievances. If the proper lineal relative does not have these qualities, the post will go to another man in the same general descent line, to a brother or to a father's brother's son.

As *pangalis* or sharers of common patrilineal descent, the Talaiyaris of Endavur are a *kulam* (a "lineage" or a "com-

163

munity") who commonly worship the lineage god (*kula devam*) Periyandavar, whose image is in a ruined temple northeast of the Harijan Vannan street outside the new Colony. The Talaiyaris report worshipping at the Periyandavar temple on a family basis before marriage, on the day of an end-of-funeral ceremony, and at individual life crises. In these crises, a vow is made to the god of a penance or payment to be made to him in return for the removal of a disease, of infertility, or of a curse. The Talaiyaris also say that they worship Periyandavar collectively in February or March, and that at one time they practiced for him a ritual called "looting the cremation ground." This ritual probably expressed the control of Periyandavar over the maleficent *peey*; it is said by the Talaiyaris to have had the result of protecting their children from the attacks of these beings. The ritual included a group visitation to the cremation ground, and possession and pig sacrifice there.[3] The Talaiyaris of Endavur are now ashamed of "looting the cremation ground," calling it "uncivilized" (without "*naagari-gam*"), and they say they have discontinued the ritual for the last twenty years. Talaiyaris in a poorer neighboring Colony (one that the Endavur Harijans define as "less civilized" than their own) admitted to performing it at present. There is no simple correlation between the apparent lowness of the lineage god Periyandavar and the lowness of the Talaiyaris as Harijans, however, as we shall see in Chapter VI.

Among themselves, the Talaiyaris of Endavur are most

[3] Thurston describes the ritual "looting the burning ground" as practiced by Sembadavan Fishermen (a low but not Untouchable caste) with the help of Valluvars and Paraiyans, in the context of a festival to the goddess Ankalamman. Acts included bloody sacrifice in the graveyard and the possession there of many of the devotees: "hundreds of persons are said to become possessed, eat the ashes of the corpses, and bite any human bones, which they may come across. The ashes and earth are much prized, as they are supposed to drive away evil spirits, and secure offspring to barren women" (Thurston 1909, 6:357).

emphatic about their precedence vis-à-vis the other two grades in the Colony. They see themselves as purer (more *suttam*) than the Pannaikkars or the Vettiyans, and they link this purity to their "*saivam*" diet. In most village contexts, "*saivam*" marks the distinction between vegetarian and meat-eating diets. Here it marks the distinction between nonbeefeating and beefeating diets. For the Talaiyaris claim to have been, two generations ago, strictly nonbeefeating. They also claim at that time to have been strictly grade-endogamous, going outside the Colony to the Talaiyaris of neighboring Colonies for their brides. As a result, they say, "at that time" grade distinctions within the Colony were more extreme than they are today; in the time of their fathers' fathers, for example, Vettiyans were not let into Talaiyari households, and no food transactions were accepted from Vettiyans. More recently, however, the Talaiyaris have made marriage alliances with some Pannaikkar families within the Colony, and their non-Talaiyari wives have introduced beefeating into their households. Their *saivam* has thus decreased somewhat, they say, but not so much that they have lost relative rank within the Colony. For they still avoid intergrade marriages with the local Vettiyans, and they still refuse to take cooked food or water from the hands of a Vettiyan or from a Pannaikkar who is not a relation by marriage.

The actual marriage choices indicated by local Talaiyari genealogies are mostly in agreement with the Talaiyaris' general status claims. In a sample of twenty-one recent Talaiyari marriages, thirteen (62 percent) have been grade-endogamous, mostly with Talaiyaris from other Colonies. The remaining eight have been with Pannaikkars, mostly from inside the Colony. The Talaiyari genealogies show no Talaiyari-Vettiyan intermarriages within the Colony in the last three generations. One Talaiyari marriage claim is not substantiated statistically, however. The Talaiyaris claim that when they do make intergrade marriages with the Pannaikkars, they do so only hypergamously; they only "take women" from the Pannaikkars. In the sample marriages, however, they have in fact given five women to Pannaikkar families in marriage, and taken only three. But the hypergamous claim remains interesting as an ideal, as a status claim congruent with status claims at other levels of the system.

As a grade, the "true" Talaiyaris of Endavur are on the average the most prosperous Harijans in the Endavur Colony. The mean landownership of the ten households is 4.2 adjusted acres per household. None of the true Talaiyari households is landless; the range of ownership is 7.1 adjusted acres to 1.0 adjusted acres per family. The Talaiyaris attribute their present prosperity to a kinsman who traveled to Kerala two generations ago, disguised his caste, and apprenticed himself to a higher-caste mason. He then returned to Endavur and taught his *pangali* relatives masonry and other house-building techniques. At present half a dozen Talaiyaris are active in the trade, contracting independently in Endavur and in neighboring *uurs* and Colonies. The Talaiyaris have reinvested the earnings from this trade in land, and due to their masonry and their landownership, they are, of all the Endavur Harijans, the most independent of vertical economic ties with the Reddiyars. Their independence is still heavily qualified, however. Many of them supplement their own incomes with *kuli* labor to the Reddiyars, and all the Talaiyari families are still very much aware of which Reddiyar family they "belong" to.

Note that the economic precedence of the Harijan Talaiyaris is a recent event, while their grade precedence is in all probability a much older fact. The Talaiyaris did not have better opportunities than other Harijans to learn masonry because of their high-grade status in Endavur, nor did they increase their differences from the other grades after they had learned these skills. They decreased them, in fact. Neither the grade system nor the position of the Talaiyaris can then be interpreted as a simple historical product of recent economic changes within the Harijan caste. There are looser connections between economic position and rank, however.

For if the Talaiyaris were on the whole much poorer than lower-ranking Pannaikkars and Vettiyans, they would probably by now have made more extreme status concessions to the other grades in order to share in their prosperity. They have done this in a limited way, in fact, with respect to the Pannaikkars (for reasons we will analyze when we come to the Pannaikkars). Here then, at other levels of the system, tradeoffs can be made between rank and prosperity, but one does not in any simple way determine the other.

Compared to the other Harijans, the Talaiyaris are not unduly affluent. The Talaiyari section of the Colony is uniformly mud-and-thatch in construction, with no electrified houses, and if it differs in any way from other sections of the Colony, it does so only in that its huts are in more uniformly good repair than are those of other sections of the Colony. The average economic level of the Talaiyari households is higher than the caste average, but the two most visibly prosperous members of the caste are not Talaiyaris.

The range of adult male personalities within the Talaiyari grade is of some interest. Nalasami (T_{10} on Map 4-1 and Figure 5-1) and Gengan (T_3) typify two males of an older generation. Nalasami is a dignified elder in his late sixties, a knowledgeable caste headman who can expound for hours on the precise sequence of ritual acts in every ceremony at which a Harijan headman's presence is required. Nalasami's family is one of the few in the Colony that has not gone through a *pangali* split after the father's death; Nalasami and his brother have kept the family together with a division of labor, the brother working at the nearby leprosy hospital, Nalasami managing the family's 6.2 adjusted acres of land. Gengan is a younger member of the senior generation, a hard-working agriculturalist in his late forties who owns 5 acres of dry land and his own electric pumpset. Gengan is quiet and straightforward, perhaps the most reliable Harijan with whom we dealt in the Endavur Colony. Of a dozen or so Harijans whom we asked to estimate their own economic levels, Gengan was the most precise, neither inflating his

167

holdings to make an impression, nor deflating them out of fear. In seeming contradiction to his otherwise unflamboyant personality, Gengan becomes wildly and impressively possessed by the Colony goddess Mariyamman once a year. Though there are other Harijans whose accounts of their subjective experiences under possession had to be taken cautiously, Gengan's accounts of possession were more difficult to discount, given his simple honesty elsewhere in life.

Poturaja (T_6) and Ram (T_3) are notable among the Talaiyari men of the younger generation. Each is in his late twenties and each still lives in an undivided household with his father, mother, wife, and young children. Poturaja is the Harijan who made the intercaste marriage with a Valluvar Pandaram woman (pp. 107-108 above). He is a capable mason who was able to be self-supporting during the four difficult years of his outcasting, and, perhaps as a result of this experience, he has the most detached view of the Colony of any Harijan in it. On our first meeting with him, he volunteered a clear and succinct model of the grade structure of the caste, one that our next eight months of fieldwork served mostly to confirm and expand. Ram has an outsider's view of another sort: he is the most educated man in the Colony, who had the opportunity to become educated due to his father Gengan's agricultural prosperity. He presently works as a schoolteacher in a Harijan Welfare school about five miles from Endavur, and he is the source of the few radical political ideas that come into the Colony. He is the first to admit, however, that he himself finds it impossible to act on these ideas, and that they have little effect on others in the Colony. At one time, he attempted to found an "Ambedkar association" in the Colony, but it folded for lack of interest. And though he is attracted to Ambedkar's neo-Buddhism, he goes on worshiping a conventional set of Hindu gods, for, he says, "despite the horrors we have suffered, we must have a god," and the Buddhist "gods" are not available in the south.

Each of these Talaiyari men is somewhat exceptional for

a Harijan; each has a quality of openness and self-confidence
not usually found in Harijans who are more directly tied to
the local dominant castes in daily economic terms. Yet each
of these men remains very much a Harijan, fully aware of
the realities of being a Harijan; and each participates in the
replication of his own Harijanness. Nalasami and Gengan
are important ritual actors in the system; Poturaja has re-
belled only in very personal terms and has now been readmitted to his caste; and Ram, despite his prestigious position
as a teacher, lives as a Harijan in the village. Only Ram approaches a state of intellectual alienation, for only he has
really considered an alternate point of view on the system.
But these ideas are both too unintegrated in Ram's mind, and
too irrelevant to the village as it actually exists, to have much
power, even for Ram.

THE PANNAIKKAR GRADE

The second-ranking internal collectivity in the Harijan
caste of Endavur is the Pannaikkar grade—the largest, the
most internally diverse, and the most problematic definitionally of the three Harijan grades. Its grade title *PaNNaikkaar*
is in itself a paradox, for this is also the honorific term applied to the five Harijan headmen of the caste, but none of
these headmen is in Endavur drawn from the Pannaikkar
grade. The Pannaikkars of the Endavur Colony are anomalous in a number of other ways: they are outsiders who have
originated as immigrants from a number of different Colonies,
they perform only one of the five basic lowering *toRils* of
the Harijans, they are not a single descent group but a com-
plexly organized set of descent groups, and they can marry
both among themselves and with the grades above and below
them in the Endavur Colony. When all these anomalies are
analyzed together, however, the position of the Pannaikkars
in Endavur begins to clarify itself.

Let us begin with the title. The term *PaNNaikkaar* means
"field man" or "paddy man," and may derive from a role

that Harijan headmen have in other Colonies (but not in Endavur): as leaders of the Harijans, they are the agents through whom anyone from an *uur* caste must work in order to engage Harijan field laborers. In some neighboring Colonies, Harijan headmen are drawn preferentially from a Pannaikkar grade, a grade ranked as in Endavur between the higher-ranking Talaiyaris and the lower-ranking Vettiyans. In these Colonies, the Pannaikkar grade has no *maniyam* land, for its members do no *toRil* for the village as a whole. But its rights in the village are recognized ritually by a third share that it receives in a food distribution to the Harijans at the end of the village goddess festival. The *toRil* of the Pannaikkar grade in these Colonies is internal to the Harijan caste; it stands between the Talaiyaris and the Vettiyans, and it mediates their disputes. As the "center" (*matti*, as in the axle of a wheel) of the Colony, the grade appropriately ranks second, between those for whom it mediates. It also appropriately ranks second in terms of the logic of avoidance of basic Harijan *toRil*. In this logic, the Talaiyaris have first rank because they do relatively nonpolluting work for the village. The Vettiyans have third rank because they do distinctly polluting work for the village. As nonworkers for the village (in terms of *toRil*, not of daily labor), the Pannaikkars thus fall between the positively marked Talaiyaris and the negatively marked Vettiyans, or second.

Endavur differs from these Colonies in that no member of the *PaNNaikkaar* grade is a *PaNNaikkaar* headman. It has in common with these Colonies the fact that its Pannaikkar grade ranks second. How do we account for this anomaly?

One place to start is back in the neighboring Colonies, where there exists a fourth category of Harijans. These are the "outsiders," families like the eleventh, "not true," Talaiyari family in Endavur, who have settled in the wife's Colony and are thus away from their home villages, where they have their *maniyam* land, to which their "true" grade identity is referred. This fourth category has no definite identity in these Colonies, and as a category called people "without address," or "anonymous people," it ranks diffusely lower than the members of the three true grades—the local Talaiyaris, Pannaikkars, and Vettiyans, each of whom has either its *maniyam* land or its share of the temple food distribution. The "anonymous people" in these Colonies have little in the way of internal organization, for they usually come from a number of outside Colonies and thus have no lineal ties with one another. Their living sites are generally peripheral to the main Colony, and transactionally they are treated in lowering ways by members of the three main grades.

If we carry this category back to the Endavur Colony, the situation of the Pannaikkars who are not Pannaikkars becomes still more paradoxical, for the Endavur Pannaikkars are the descendents of people who have come from perhaps six distinct Colonies in the last two or three generations. Since they are outsiders, without rights in Endavur, they should thus be people "without address" here, ranking below the Vettiyans, with no claim whatsoever to the honorific title "*PaNNaikkaar*."

The solution to the paradox is complex, and it requires some historical reconstruction in which not all the facts are known exactly. The solution amounts to the proposition that the first Pannaikkars came to Endavur as allies (in both a kinship sense and in a political-economic sense) of the first-ranking Talaiyaris. They may have been from any grade in their home Colonies (there are rumors of their Vettiyan origins), but they avoided lowermost rank in Endavur by making and emphasizing important marriage ties with the Endavur Talaiyaris from the beginning. The most important of these ties were with the family of the Talaiyaris Gengan and Ram (T_3), who (contrary to the hypergamous ideal of the Talaiyari grade) gave one woman in marriage to one of these outside "Pannaikkar" families in the generation of Gengan's grandfather, and another to a separate group in the generation of Gengan's father.

The Talaiyaris' motives for making these alliances are not known, but they can be inferred. In all probability, the im-

171

migrating Pannaikkars had economic and political resources that the Talaiyaris needed. The present male heads of the two Pannaikkar families with whom marriage was made are presently the two most prosperous men in the Colony. One, Adimelem (P_5 on Map 4-1 above and Figure 5-2) is a road inspector for the local Block headquarters; and the other, Nagamalai (P_9), is the most active mason in the Endavur Colony. Though these Pannaikkar families were probably not as prosperous two generations ago, they may still have had resources that the Talaiyaris needed—money for the purchase of land, for example, or additional masonry skills. Since among the Harijans the family of the bride receives a bride-price rather than paying a dowry, the gift of two women to two prosperous outside families could then have been financially motivated, and might have constituted the basis of Talaiyari family T_3's present prosperity. This, then, is the other side of the small rank concession that the Talaiyaris have made within the Colony, a concession that has meant a slight loss in the Talaiyaris' *saivam* but at the same time a slight compensatory gain in the Talaiyaris' material prosperity.

At the time of the Pannaikkars' first migrations into Endavur, there was also a political conflict of some sort developing between the local Talaiyaris and the local Vettiyans. Since the Talaiyaris were outnumbered three to one by the Vettiyans, the Talaiyaris probably brought the Pannaikkars into the Colony as their political allies as well as their kinship allies. One Talaiyari respondent, attempting to resolve the paradox of Pannaikkars who do not serve as Pannaikkars, told us that there had once been a quarrel between the "original people" of the Endavur Colony (the Talaiyaris and the Vettiyans), "so we called in these people [the Pannaikkars] to be between us." "These people" were generally, if not specifically, in a mediating position, the respondent continued, "therefore they have a right to be called *PaNNaikkaars.*"

The Pannaikkars on their own side have made material

172

and perhaps status gains by immigrating to Endavur. Two generations ago, Endavur was beginning to develop economically; so was the local strength of the Harijans. Endavur was thus probably already a better place to be a Harijan than were the home villages of the original Pannaikkars. The Pannaikkars risked status loss by their immigration, for they might have moved downward from their "original" position in their home Colonies (probably Pannaikkar or Vettiyan) to the lowermost status of "anonymous people" in Endavur. They did not suffer this loss, however; they have, if anything, gained in status.

In the end, what has most fundamentally allowed the Endavur Pannaikkars to avoid the label of "anonymous people" is their marriage ties with the Endavur Talaiyaris. The Endavur Vettiyans have their own view of things here, and they delight in pointing to the outside "nameless" origins of the Pannaikkars. But they cannot deny the implications of the fact that the Endavur Pannaikkars have intermarried with the Endavur Talaiyaris, and they have not. In most cases, the Vettiyans grant to the Pannaikkar grade the honorific title *"PaNNaikkaar."* This title in itself represents the basically successful nature of the local Pannaikkars' attempt to avoid their potential identification as "anonymous people." What they have not been successful at, however, is gaining the right to provide one or more of the *PaNNaikkaar* headmen from their ranks. These positions were apparently allocated to members of the "original" Talaiyau and Vettiyan grades before the advent of the Pannaikkar grade in Endavur, and this allocation has not changed in two generations.

The present internal social organization of the Endavur Pannaikkars reflects the mixed history of the grade. Most of the forty-eight Pannaikkar households in the Endavur Harijan caste can be grouped into six lineages—*kottus* ("bunches") —each probably originating in a different outside Colony. Three of these are major lineages, large and relatively prosperous aggregations; three are minor, smaller, and less prosperous among their membership. Even this classification leaves eight Pannaikkar households unaccounted for, how-ever. These eight are said by the other Pannaikkars to be "our distant brothers, but we don't know how"; they fall, of all the Endavur Pannaikkars, closest to the status of "nameless people."

To understand the interrelations of the Pannaikkar lin-eages, we must digress briefly into the complex matter of Dravidian kinship categories. The Dravidian kin terminology, whose basic structure is shared by most groups in south India, the Endavur Harijans included, divides all kin into two major categories, which we can term analytically "parallel relations" and "cross relations." Cross relations are relations of and for marriage; their analytic term is taken from the fact that the so-called cross-cousin, the mother's brother's daughter or the father's sister's daughter, is in these systems included in the category of those whom it is best for a man to marry. But there are many other persons in this category as well. Parallel relations are persons related as "brother" and "sister," with whom marriage is strictly prohibited.

A simple way to grasp the structure of the Dravidian terminology is to see it as the logical correlate of the direct reciprocal exchange of women in marriage between two groups of men. If the men of group A give their sisters and daughters in marriage to the men of group B in exchange for the women of group B, and if the men of each group are lineal or parallel relations who consider themselves "brothers," then within two generations a man in either group will automatically be marrying from a category of women in the other group that includes his mother's brother's daughter and his father's sister's daughter. If this category of women is then named, and if simple additional categorical distinctions are made between senior and junior men and women of one's own group and the "cross" group that gives and takes women from one's own group, then most of the categorical terms of the Dravidian terminology will be created. Thus, for example, *mamaan*, a Tamil term that in-cludes the mother's brother, the wife's father, and the sister's husband's father, really means (in these exchange terms) "senior male of a cross group." For by the exchange logic above, this category (*mamaan*) includes the man who gave mother to one's own group a generation ago, the man who gives his daughter to one's own group in this generation, and the man whose son receives a woman from one's own group in this generation. It is possible but not necessary in south Indian marriage systems for these three men to be a single person.[4]

Among the Endavur Harijans, the logic of this Dravidian terminology is followed very exactly, and certain transformation rules are applied to preserve the system through the tangle of its actual marriages. Obviously, the Endavur Harijans do not all simply marry between group A and group B. But they do make their marriage calculations by these strict reciprocal principles, which means that they must sort out all actual known lineages into two groups, those with whom they can marry and those with whom they cannot. Two general transformation rules are applied for this purpose, more or less consciously. The first is that parallel relationships are transitive. If lineages A and B are related "as brothers" (literally as "elder brother/younger brother," *aNNan-tambi* in Tamil) due to common descent from a common ancestor,[5] and if lineages B and C are also related "as brothers," A and C must therefore also be related "as brothers" or as parallel relatives—and must therefore be unable to exchange women in marriage. In more indigenous Harijan terms, "the *aNNan-*

---

[4] This discussion is intended only to help the novice grasp the logic of the Dravidian terminology. It is not meant to imply that the Dravidian terminology developed historically out of this exchange situation, nor that androcentricity and patriliny are necessary concomitants to it, nor that it only occurs where there is in fact direct bilateral exchange of women between kin groups. For further technical literature on the Dravidian terminology and its variations, see Dumont 1957c, Yalman 1967, Beck 1972a, and Barnett 1976.

[5] They can be *pangalis* only if the ancestor is traceable and if they are still actually "sharers" in a common lineage and a common lineage god.

tambis of our *aNNan-tambis* are also our *aNNan-tambis*, and we cannot give and take [women] with them."

The second Harijan transformation rule is that cross relations have a "double-negative" property. By this property, if lineages A and B have each exchanged women in marriage with lineage C, they cannot then exchange women with one another. Even if A and B have no prior relationship to one another, they become by these common cross relations with C "like brothers" with one another. In indigenous Harijan terms, "the *mamaan-machans* [cross-relations] of our *mamaam-machans* are our *aNNan-tambis*."[6]

Given this kinship logic and these transformation rules, the social organization of the Pannaikkar grade of Endavur can then be sketched as follows. Though the three major lineages of the Pannaikkars probably originated in separate Colonies, they are all presently related "as brothers" by means of the transformation rules. Figure 5-2 shows the present relations of the three major lineages, and Map 5-1 shows the spatial distributions of all six Pannaikkar lineages in the Colony. We can see, on comparing the two figures, that Pannaikkar lineage I is central in several ways. It is central spatially, with a residential site on the *uur* side of the old Colony, just across the street from its Talaiyari allies—closer to the Talaiyaris spatially than are the local Vettiyans. And it is central genealogically, for the other two major Pannaikkar lineages are related to one another through lineage I.

These interrelations can all be referred to the transformation rules. Thus lineage II is related to lineage I in that the same Talaiyari family, T_3, has given both lineages women in

---

[6] Many higher and dominant south Indian castes do not follow this logic so strictly. Thus among the Gavarai Naidus of the Endavur region, among the Kavundars of Coimbatore (see Beck 1972a: 221), and among most Brahmins, a very distant woman in a parallel, "sister" relationship can be married, as long as she is not a member of one's own descent group. These deviations among the higher castes may be related to the exigencies of territorial dominance, where widely ramifying descent groups become more important than they are among the lower castes.

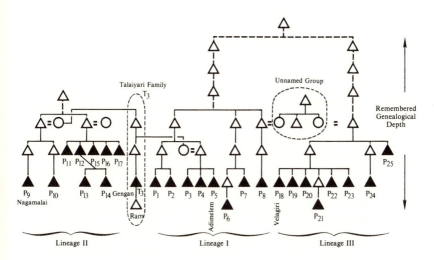

FIGURE 5-2. Relationships between the Three Major Lineages of the Pannaikkar Grade

marriage. By the double-negative rule, lineages II and I are therefore in a parallel, "elder brother/younger brother" relation to one another. The third major Pannaikkar lineage, III, is in turn related to lineage I by the fact that both have taken women in marriage from a third, unremembered group (or possibly from one that is well but not proudly remembered, a local Vettiyan group), and is once again "brother" to I by the double-negative principle. These two lineages also say that they may be parallel relatives by a very distant *pangali* tie of common descent. Finally, lineages III and II are related to one another through the transitive rule of parallel relations; since both are "brothers" to lineage I, they are therefore "brothers" to each other. In short, Pannaikkar lineages I, II, and III are all in *aNNan-tambi*, "brother," relations to one another, despite their heterogenous origins.

The "brother" relation of the three major lineages of Endavur Pannaikkars has some important consequences for

177

them. Most basically, the relation binds them together in the same collective identity. Though they are not "one" by common descent, as are *pangali* relations, they are by their "brother" relation seen as bound up in a common marriage network; their transactional status with respect to the giving and receiving of women should be identical. If we look at the spatial distributions in the Colony (Map 5-1), we can speculate that lineages I and III came into the Colony as close allies of the Talaiyaris (for twenty years ago lineage III was, like lineage I today, still entirely located in the old Colony), while Pannaikkar lineage II was originally made to live outside the Colony, slightly beyond the then separate street of the Harijan Vannans (for the new Colony had not developed two generations ago). Thus lineage II might have come in originally with a lower status, like that of the "nameless people" of other Colonies. Yet as "brothers" to lineages I and III, lineage II has benefited from the same status claims made by these other two. Its members have as strong a right to the title "*PaNNaikkaar*" as do members of the other two lineages.

The three minor lineages of the Pannaikkar grade constitute a stronger strain on the major lineages' status claims than did II at one time. Lineage IV is in a cross relation with the other three, and three of its households (P_{26}, P_{27}, P_{28}) have intermarried downward with the Vettiyans. What is worse, one of the younger males in household P_{26} actually acts as "government Vettiyan" until the time when one of his Vettiyan wife's brothers becomes old enough to qualify for the position. Since one of their *pangalis* is acting as a Vettiyan, members of lineage IV are therefore "almost Vettiyans" collectively. Yet lineage IV is also the link group between Pannaikkar lineages III and V, who are "brothers" to one another because they have both "given and taken" women with lineage IV. Pannaikkar lineage V is also therefore, by the transitive principle, "brother" to the three major lineages.

Finally, Pannaikkar lineage VI, living at the back of the Pannaikkar section in the old Colony, is said to be "brother"

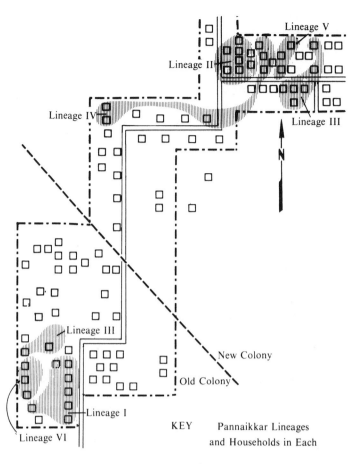

Lineage V

Lineage II

Lineage IV

Lineage III

N

New Colony

Old Colony

Lineage III

Lineage I

Lineage VI

KEY   Pannaikkar Lineages
and Households in Each

Lineage Number	Household Numbers
I	1-8
II	9-17
III	18-25
IV	26-33
V	34-36
VI	37-39
Unclassified by Lineage	40-48

MAP 5-1. Distribution of Six Pannaikkar Lineages, Endavur Colony

179

to the brother groups I, II, III, and V, "but we don't know how." This lineage is the biggest embarrassment to the major Pannaikkar groups of Endavur, for one of its members acts as *varayan* announcer for the village as a whole. *Varayan* is the only basic Harijan *toRil* not performed by the lowermost Vettiyans, and it is a *toRil* that its performer must play for all the Harijans—including the Vettiyans—as well as for all the higher castes. Like the other basic Harijan *toRils*, *varayan* is marked as low by its association with death, for it is the duty of the "announcer" to carry the news of a death in any caste to all the appropriate relatives of the deceased. More seriously still, the *varayan* accepts from the family of the deceased death-polluted food immediately after a burial or cremation. By this acceptance of death-polluted substances, he then becomes as low as the lowermost Vettiyans.

In most Colonies, *varayan toRil* is conducted by the Vettiyans, along with their other four lowering functions. Why a Pannaikkar here agreed to do announcing is not known, but probably this particular lineage was much poorer on its entry into the Colony than the major Pannaikkar lineages, and it had to make a bad bargain to gain entry into the Colony. Or perhaps it simply needed the small material gains that came with *varayan* service, and the Vettiyans decided to renounce these in order to embarrass the Pannaikkars collectively. In any case, the Vettiyans delight in pointing to the fact that a Pannaikkar here serves as *varayan*, and that he serves them, the Vettiyans, among others. "He is our servant," they say of the Pannaikkar announcer, "we can tell him when to come and go." And therefore, according to these same Vettiyans, because of the *varayan* role and because of the "brother" interrelations of five of the six Pannaikkar lineages of Endavur, *all* the Pannaikkars are really servants to the whole Colony and should rank collectively below the Vettiyans.

The Pannaikkars of the major lineages reply to these accusations of the Vettiyans in three ways. They stress their relations of marriage with the Talaiyaris, saying that they are the "children of Talaiyaris." They minimize their relations with members of the minor Pannaikkar lineages. And they point out that they are not as strongly and continuously engaged in low actions as are the Vettiyans. They must therefore rank above the Vettiyans. The Pannaikkar Adimelem (P_5), a member of Pannaikkar lineage I, stated his view of the ensuing relation between the three Harijan grades in a carefully segmented culinary code. In private, Adimelem divided up the Harijan caste into four categories: Talaiyaris, "clean" Pannaikkars, "dirty" Pannaikkars, and Vettiyans. The Talaiyaris, he said, were nonbeefeating. His own category, the "clean" Pannaikkars, ate beef "occasionally," while the "dirty" Pannaikkars ate it regularly. All Pannaikkars ate only "freshly butchered beef," however, while the lowermost Vettiyans ate the carrion beef that they got as cattle scavengers in the village.

Adimelem's discriminations amount to a feature hierarchy, in which the general negative action of "beefeating" has been internally segmented three times to generate four ranked groups (see Figure 5-3). In this hierarchy, which is entirely congruent with the attitudes of the non-Untouchable castes toward beefeating, nonbeefeating is better than beefeating. Within beefeating, occasional beefeating is not as bad as regular beefeating. And within regular beefeating, the eating of freshly killed beef is less polluting than the eating of carrion beef, for the polluting agents of death have had more time to intrude into the last form of the meat. As for the dividing line between the "clean" Pannaikkars and the "dirty" Pannaikkars, Adimelem said that the "clean" Pannaikkars comprised all the families in his own lineage and a few of the "better" families of lineages II, III, and V. The rest of the Pannaikkars, with whom Adimelem claimed he did not interdine, were "dirty." These included, in particular, the entire memberships of lineages IV and VI, the lineages whose members serve as temporary Vettiyan and as *varayan*.

In the end, the Pannaikkar grade remains something of an anomaly in the Endavur Colony. But the ways in which its anomalous status are conceptualized are in agreement with

181

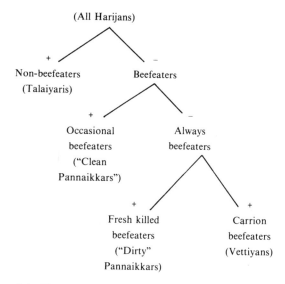

FIGURE 5-3. Feature Hierarchy of Adimelem's Discriminations with Respect to Beefeating

the major argument here—with the argument for internal consensus among the Untouchables about the symbolic markers of status in the system. When Adimelem claims his near equality to the Talaiyaris, he does so by the internal segmentation of an action that stands for Harijanness in the *uur*, beefeating. When the Vettiyans claim that the Pannaik-kars as a whole are inferior to their own grade, they do so by stating that anyone who acts like a Harijan toward them (that is, who announces for them) must be lower than them. Both sides of the argument are one-sided, though in the end the balance of the argument goes to the Pannaikkars. But the controversy is only about how a certain group of people should be placed in a ranked system; it is not about the cri-teria either of the system, or of being a Harijan. On these criteria, the Harijan disputants are in perfect agreement both with one another and with those well above them in caste.

182

Other attributes of the Pannaikkar grade in Endavur reflect its social heterogeneity. Given the complexity of the grade's internal organization, the total grade endogamy figures are almost meaningless; but, for the record, the forty-five Pannaikkar marriages that were sampled for grade identity are about thirty-six percent grade-endogamous. The figures are more interesting when internal discriminations are examined. Thus for the major Pannaikkar lineages, I and II in particular, most grade exogamy within the Colony is directed upward, toward the Talaiyaris. Adimelem's genealogy shows four intermarriages with the Talaiyaris in the last three generations, and Nagamalai's (family P_9, lineage II) shows seven. The grade-exogamous marriages of the other Pannaikkar lineages, on the other hand, particularly those in Adimelem's "dirty" Pannaikkar category, are directed downward, toward the Vettiyans. Another significant distinction appears when we look at Pannaikkar marriages with Harijans outside the Endavur Colony. Here, in a sample of twenty-eight marriages, only one has been made upward, with outside Talaiyaris; the rest have been made with other outside Pannaikkars (16) or with outside Vettiyans (11). This concurs with the suspicion that, outside the Colony, the Pannaikkars may be known to belong to a lower grade—that their status claim operates at present only within the Endavur Colony.

The gods of the Endavur Pannaikkars are also heterogeneous. Since the Pannaikkars are not a single descent group, they do not have a single *kula devam*. Rather, each lineage worships its own lineage god, but not all of these gods are found in Endavur, and some of the Pannaikkars are unusually reticent about them. It is probable that many Pannaikkars still return to their home Colonies to worship their lineage gods, and the gods that they return to may indicate their "true" grade in these Colonies—hence the reticence. Members of Pannaikkar lineages I and III do say that they worship a lineage god named Kateri in Endavur, but this god has no permanent image here; it is worshipped once

a year in a temporary mud image, in the fields. One Pannaikkar *kula devam* is spectacularly prominent in Endavur, however. This is the goddess Periyapallaiyattar, the lineage god
of Pannaikkar lineage VI, who possesses a devotee in the
Colony twice a week—to whom anyone may come for "foretelling" or for exorcism (see Chapter VI).

Finally, the landholdings of the Endavur Pannaikkars are
very unevenly distributed within the grade. Only sixteen of
the forty-eight Pannaikkar households have any land at all,
but these possess a respectable 2.4 adjusted acres per household. Furthermore, the landed households are dispropor-
tionately distributed in the major lineages of the grade.
Table 5-1 shows this disproportionate distribution of land.

TABLE 5-1. Landholdings by Lineage and Household, Pannaikkar Grade

Lineage	Number landed households	Number landless households	Total households in lineage	Household and its in- dividual holding (adjusted acres)	Total holdings in lineage (adjusted acres)
I	7	1	8	P_5 . . . 5.8	12.1
				P_3 . . . 1.3	
				P_4 . . . 1.4	
				P_1 . . . 1.1	
				P_2 . . . 1.0	
				P_7 9	
				P_6 6	
II	2	7	9	P_9 . . . 6.0	8.6
				P_{11} . . . 2.6	
III	2	6	8	P_{18} . . . 5.7	8.6
				P_{19} . . . 2.9	
IV	1	7	8	P_{32} . . . 5.7	5.7
V	1	2	3	P_{35} . . . 1.0	
VI	0	3	3	none	0
Residual Pannaikkars ($P_{40} - P_{48}$)	0	9	9	none	0

Lineages I, II, and III are clearly dominant in their land-holdings, owning 83 percent of the total land possessed by members of the grade. Though we know little about when this land was acquired, the figures support the supposition that families from lineages I and II might have been able to make their initial and subsequent marriage alliances with the Talaiyaris because of their relative economic prosperity.

There are two distinct Pannaikkar residential concentrations, and probably at least two Pannaikkar factions, in the Endavur Colony. One of these centers around the house of the road inspector Adimelem, in the old Colony close to the Talaiyari section (household P_5). The other centers on the house of Nagamalai (P_9), who is the main contractor for masonry work in Endavur, in the new Colony. Both houses are only thatched (prosperous Harijans in other Colonies sometimes indicate their status with tiled roofs), but both are electrified and are the largest structures on their streets. People are gathered around each at all hours of the day; but Nagamalai's house has the edge over Adimelem's, since it often has a radio playing, and the *uur* Chettiyar's tiny shop is in an outer room of the house. Both Pannaikkar sections show about the same range of material prosperity. Adimelem's section contains his own well-kept house and that of his brothers and of the Pannaikkar elder Veligiri, and the much poorer section of lineage VI and of some of the "extra" Pannaikkars in its back street. Nagamalai's section has as its showpieces Nagamalai's own house, that of household P_{11} in the same lineage, and the electrified house of the only landed family in lineage V, P_{34} (its head is also a mason). The rest of this new Colony section, including that into which households from lineage III moved twenty years ago, is visibly very poor.

The personalities of the leading males of the Endavur Pannaikkar grade show some interesting contrasts. The road inspector Adimelem, a man in his mid-fifties, is perhaps the best known Harijan in the Colony, and the most self-important. He has over the years invested his substantial salary

(270 rupees a month in 1972) in land, and he plays the role of the dominant landowner, paying his poorer Harijan relatives to cultivate the land while he sits in prominent leisure on the veranda of his house in the evenings. The only time we saw him in a field was when we had gone out to take pictures of some unidentified Harijans, who turned out to be "his" *kuli* laborers, plowing. When Adimelem saw what we were up to, he displaced one of the plowmen in order to be in the photograph. Adimelem always made sure that he held center stage when he received us on his veranda, and he would permit few contradictions from onlookers to the information which he gave us, hours at a time, about the caste and about the village. His accounts were basically correct, but they contained a constant thread of exaggeration and self-aggrandization. Adimelem was full of stories about early days in the Depressed Classes League, about his many meetings with prominent state and even national level politicians, and how he and the big Reddiyar settled the road case in the Colony ten years ago, about his continual work for "his" people. We always had the feeling that anything he did for his people he would also be doing very much for himself. The Talaiyari schoolteacher Ram is Adimelem's sister's son, and he treats his older uncle with a certain respect. Ram's father Gengan, on the other hand, despises his brother-in-law quite openly for his "braggardly" character.

The Pannaikkar Nagamalai (P_9), the "leader" of lineage II, is a younger and quieter type. Like Adimelem, he derives his influence in the caste both from his landed prosperity and from his contacts outside the village, for as a masonry contractor he works in a region of perhaps ten miles radius around Endavur. Nagamalai is knowledgeable about village politics, for he has been a Harijan member of the local panchayat in past years. He was part of the anti-Reddiyar coalition that briefly upset a village election in 1963. By and large, Nagamalai seems a contented and pragmatic man, with some appreciation of the relative "strength" of the Harijan caste in Endavur, but with no desire to challenge the system in any fundamental way.

Veligiri (P_{18}), the senior and most respected male in lineage III, is an older type of Harijan, one whose prestige in the grade and in the caste does not derive from his connections outside the village, but from his exemplary character within the caste. He is a diligent farmer known for his religious piety. He often appears in the evenings freshly bathed, with Saivite marks in cowdung ash on the upper half of his body, and he was the man to whom most Harijans would refer us for "stories" about the local gods. As a neighbor and a near *pangali* of Adimelem, Veligiri got on better with Adimelem than did most of the other influential males in the caste. But he alone would carefully and forcefully overrule Adimelem's accounts of the caste when these claims became too far-fetched.

THE VETTIYAN GRADE

With the third and lowest-ranking grade in the Endavur Harijan caste, the Vettiyans, we come at last to the "true people" of the Colony. The Vettiyans call themselves the "true people," in distinction to the Pannaikkars and the Talaiyaris. For unlike the Pannaikkars, they do not have the stigma of outside origins, and unlike the Talaiyaris, they are "really Harijans"; it is members of the Vettiyan grade who actually do most of the lowering *toRils* by which the identity of the caste as a whole is defined. We have discussed in detail the cultural attributes of "being a Harijan" (see pp. 111-30). These attributes apply most directly to the Vettiyans. From the *uur* point of view, the attributes apply equally strongly to the Pannaikkars and the Talaiyaris; from the Harijan point of view, they apply differentially, for though a Pannaikkar or a Talaiyari cannot deny his essential Harijan caste identity outside the caste, he can and does claim superiority to the lowermost Vettiyans inside the caste.

187

The Vettiyan grade is low within the Harijan caste for two related reasons. First, it is persons of this grade who are most directly involved in the lowering acceptances that constitute basic Harijan identity in the village as a whole. Second, it is members of this grade who act as Harijans for other Harijans, for the Vettiyans make their lowering acceptances not only from the higher castes of the village, but from the higher grades of the Harijan caste. Here the last details of the replicatory structures among the Endavur Untouchables appear. To find their own Harijans, the Harijans have code-switched from caste to grade. This replication finally and inevitably collapses among the lowermost grade, for within the Vettiyan grade, acceptance of impure death substances must be done reflexively; it can no longer create rank. But this replication has not collapsed for the majority of the Harijan caste population in Endavur; it operates quite satisfactorily for the Talaiyaris and the Pannaikkars.

The term "*VeTTiyan*" is the preferred term of self-reference for members of this lowest grade in Endavur. The meaning of the term is not known to the Vettiyans, but it may denote "chopper" or "cutter" (*veTTi* = "to cut or chop"), and it may once have referred to some action in agricultural field labor. *TooTTi* is an alternate term for the grade; its known meaning is "digger," and refers directly to the Vettiyan role of gravedigger at the burial ground. In the Endavur Colony, *TooTTi* is distinctly perjorative, and is used more often by members of the higher grades to disparage the Vettiyans than it is within the grade. The same grade in a Colony ten miles to the south, however, prefers the title "*TooTTi*" to "*VeTTiyan*."

The internal social organization of the Vettiyan grade of Endavur resembles the Talaiyaris' in being predicated on common descent from a single ancestor, and from an ancestor "original" to Endavur. But it also resembles the Pannaikkars' organization in that these lineal descendents are organized into distinct *kottus* or "bunches," here four in number. Technically, however, *kottu* among the Vettiyans does not designate "lineage"; it designates "sublineage," for members of all four *kottus* of Vettiyans are related to one another as *pangali* "sharers" by descent from a single common ancestor. Hence, unlike the Pannaikkars' *kottus*, the Vettiyan *kottus* are not separate marriage groups with separate lineage deities and complex interrelations; here, they all form a single *kulam* or "lineage." Each of the four Vettiyan sublineages is named for one of four brothers, sons of the original ancestor, whose name is not known. Figure 5-4 shows the basically simple genealogy of the Endavur Vettiyans. As with the genealogies of the other Harijans, the remembered depth in this genealogy is only two or three generations, and as with the Talaiyari genealogy, the distance from the last immediate ancestor to the founding brother in each lineage is indefinite.

As a whole, the Vettiyan genealogy gives most Vettiyans in the Colony an equal claim to the identity of "true Vettiyan" in Endavur.[7] The *maniyam* land attached to Vettiyan *toRil* is about the same as that attached to Talaiyari *toRil*, four acres of wet land and eight acres of dry. But in this grade even more than among the Talaiyaris, the *maniyam* land is more important for its representation of "true" Vettiyan identity than it is economically, after its division among thirty-three separate households.

The Vettiyan households of the Harijan caste are solidly clustered in the northern half of the old Colony, with some spread into the new Colony (see Map 4-1). The four sublineages are not particularly clustered within this territorial aggregation, though recently divided close *pangalis* often remain adjacent. Households of all four Vettiyan sublineages are mixed together at the core of the old Colony, and house-

---

[7] There is a total of thirty-nine Vettiyan households in the Endavur Colony, and the genealogy accounts for thirty-three as "true Vettiyans." The remaining six Vettiyan families are "outsiders" who have settled with the wife's family in Endavur. The importance of these families here is minor, except as local representatives of the fourth category of "nameless people."

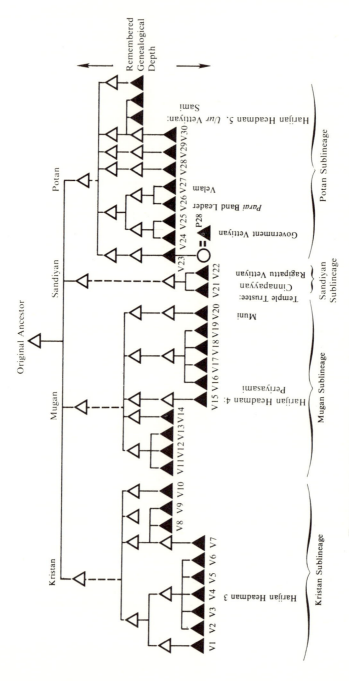

FIGURE 5-4. Genealogy of the Vettiyan Grade of the Harijan Caste

holds from three of the four sublineages also live in what was probably the earliest expansion of the new Colony, to the northeast. All four sublineages shown in Figure 5-4 are extant in Endavur, though the Sandiyan sublineage is small. Most of the Sandiyan Vettiyans have migrated to Madras city, but they retain rights to the *maniyam* land, to Vettiyan *toRil*, and to their "true Vettiyan" identity in Endavur.

The division of the Vettiyan genealogy into four sublineages or *kottus* organizes two rights of the Vettiyan grade with respect to the village and to the Harijan caste: Vettiyan rights to provide Harijan headmen to the Harijan caste council, and Vettiyan rights to the actual positions of *VeTTiyan*. Three of the four sublineages appoint a Harijan headman; the present headmen are indicated on Figure 5-4 (V_3, V_{15}, and V_{30}). It is not known whether the Sandiyan sublineage also once had a right to a headman, which it lost after most of its members left the Colony. Rights to headmanship in the Vettiyan lineages follow the same weak hereditary principle that they do among the Talaiyaris: a man passes the position on to one of his sons if the son has the proper character and temperament. If not, the position goes to another man in the same sublineage. And as with the Talaiyari-appointed headmen, a Vettiyan who once becomes a headman functions for the caste as a whole, not for the Vettiyans alone.

As for the actual positions of "*VeTTiyan*," there are in Endavur three of these. One is called "government Vettiyan" (*circar VeTTiyan*), and is a salaried post that pays seventy-two rupees per month and entails assistance to the village *munsif* and regulation of the water of a large reservoir just west of the *uur*. Like the position of government Talaiyari, the position of government Vettiyan was probably created or renovated by the British sometime in the nineteenth century. And like the Talaiyari position, this position also passes from father to son in one line, here in the eldest branch of the Potan sublineage (family V_{23}). The man who actually serves as government Vettiyan is the Pannaikkar from Pannaikkar lineage IV (P_{28}) mentioned above, who is "almost a Vettiyan." He will turn the position back to one of his wife's younger brothers when they come of age.

The other two Vettiyan positions in Endavur are the older positions that define the grade, positions analogous to one that has become defunct among the Talaiyaris: the positions of *uur VeTTiyan*, "*VeTTiyans* to the *uur*." There are two of these positions because there were once two *uurs* in the village of Endavur. The other *uur*, besides the main caste hamlet described earlier, is a hamlet called Ragipatti. It is located to the southeast of the main *uur*, and it is presently inhabited by a residual population of twelve Vettaikaran families and one poor Reddiyar family; these families, who own no land, have not been counted in the village totals above. One of the two *uur* Vettiyans among the Harijans is called "Ragipatti Vettiyan," and was formerly assigned to Ragipatti exclusively. Now, however, both *uur* Vettiyans divide the much larger duties of the main *uur* of Endavur between them, and each is in fact assigned to one of the two Reddiyar families, for whom each does most of his actual guardianship.

The role of *uur* Vettiyan differs from the government Vettiyan in two ways: payment for it is in raw rice, at a certain rate per *uur* household (most of these payments, however, come from the Reddiyars), rather than in cash; and every adult male in the grade has a chance to act as *uur* Vettiyan, as is not the case with the lineally descending position of government Vettiyan (or of government Talaiyari). Rights to this enactment are determined by an eight-year cycle of each position through the four sublineages. That is, the first *uur* Vettiyan position is filled for two years by a member of Kristan sublineage, then for two years by a member of Mugan sublineage, followed by two-year performances by members of Sandiyan and Potan sublineages, and then back to Mugan. The rotation of the second *uur* position (Ragipatti Vettiyan) follows the first cycle with a delay of two years. This means that each sublineage of Vettiyans has one of the two positions to fill every other four years. Within each sublineage, the performer is selected by a consensus of the male heads of household. There is no regular rotation within the sublineage, the Vettiyans say; they pay attention to need, and to the right of every family to serve as Vettiyan at least once a generation. The present *uur* Vettiyans are indicated on Figure 5-4—the households V_{22} in Sandiyan sublineage and V_{32} in Potan sublineage.

The men who play the role of *uur* Vettiyan in the Harijan caste are the specific link between the higher castes and the lowness of the Harijan caste as a whole. It is they who act as cattle scavengers, cremation ground attendants, and village watchmen; and they arrange in the *uur* for performances of the *parai* band, which is almost uniformly played by members of the Vettiyan grade alone. We have discussed the general cultural meaning of these lowering Harijan *toRils*— their associations with death substances and with the death-generated *peey* (pp. 111-18). Let us consider these *toRils* in more detail here: their specific allocation within the Harijan caste, the exact behavior that they entail, their material and cultural rewards, and the sanctions that ultimately enforce their performance.

To begin with cattle scavenging, the *uur* Vettiyan has the responsibility of removing from the *uur* or the Colony the carcass of any cow, bullock, or water buffalo that has died in these territories, presumably of natural causes. He skins and cuts away the meat and bones of this carcass, and sells the skin and bones either to the local Chakkiliyans or to Muslims in the town of Madurantakam. If the cow has died in the *uur*, the Vettiyan may keep the money he receives for its products; if it has died in the Colony, he divides the receipts with the animal's Harijan owner. According to some members of the Vettiyan grade, the *uur* Vettiyan buries the flesh of carrion cattle; according to other Vettiyans and to all non-Vettiyans, he often divides this beef with his *pangalis* and they cook and eat it.

Beefeating was done very covertly by the Endavur Hari-

193

jans, further evidence for the Harijans' consensus with a culture that defines this practice as very low.[8] According to a reliable Harijan informant, however, the Vettiyans and other Harijans certainly ate fresh beef regularly, whatever their use of carrion beef. Every month or so, according to this Harijan, several members of the Vettiyan grade bought a cow and butchered it themselves. They then sold pieces of it through the Colony, household by household, to anyone who wished to buy it. On this basis, thirty to fifty households of Endavur Harijans were eating fresh beef at least once a month, a minimum estimate that ignores their other sources of beef. The Harijans are motivated to eat beef by the fact that the higher castes would define them as beefeaters even if they didn't (unless they stopped cattle scavenging as well, which the higher castes would prevent), by their belief in its strengthening properties, and by its low cost. Since perhaps eighty percent of the rural population of Tamilnadu is non-beefeating, beef is the cheapest meat when it is available on the town or village market (when the Harijans don't butcher a cow directly, they get beef from Muslim butchers in the towns).

The second low role performed directly by the *uur* Vetti-yan is that of cremation ground attendant—the lowest role of the lot. As cremation ground attendant, the Vettiyan

---

[8] I never succeeded in convincing village Harijans in Tamilnadu to include me in their beefeating, though I was fed regularly by Hari-jans both in the Pudukottai area and in Endavur. In Pudukottai, I tried a gambit that Owen Lynch said had worked among the Un-touchable Jatavs of Agra. I told a Harijan man in the family that fed me regularly that beefeating was my own custom, that it was in fact a national custom in America, and that I personally "relished" the meat. I was rewarded with the reciprocal confession that my inter-locuter's family also "took beef" occasionally, but I was asked not to let the other Harijans of the same settlement know this. And the same family continued to serve me mutton, chicken, and fish, but never beef. In Endavur, I ate cooked food less regularly with the Harijans; when I did, it was prestigious wedding food, such as lamb *biriyani*.

handles the bodies of the human dead, deals implicitly with the *peey*, and takes both death-polluted food and death-polluted cloth from the family of the deceased. The *uur* Vettiyan is in his death function assisted by the Pannaikkar *varayan* announcer—and thus in this lowering function the Pannaikkars are also touched by the lowness of death acceptance.

In the case of a death in the Harijan caste or in any of the fifteen village castes above the Harijans, the *varayan* announcer first informs all close lineal relatives of the deceased in the village or in surrounding villages. After the body has been washed and covered with a single burial cloth by the close relatives at the house of death, the *uur* Vettiyan, together with the *parai* band, leads the funeral procession from the house of death to the *suuDu kaaDu* outside the village boundaries, the "hot ground" or burning ground, where, more often than not, a burial is performed as a cheaper substitute for cremation. At the boundary of the burning ground is a stone dedicated to *Arichandiran*, and here the Vettiyan pauses and chants to the higher-caste mourners:

I was the first born	*Munda pirandavan naan*
I first wore the sacred thread	*Mudanaal puunaal tarittavan*
I am Sangu Paraiyan	*Sangup paraiyan naan*
Samba kulam is superior to all castes.	*Ellajaadikku usanta sambak kulam*
Arichandran was our slave	*Arissandiran aDimaikoNDavandaan*
He minds his own business;	*Avan paaTTukku avan irukkiran*
I mind my own business.	*Naan paaTTukku naan irukkireen.*

The first four lines of the chant refer to the initial precedence of the Paraiyans, as described in Paraiyan origin myth M_1. The *uur* man who told Paraiyan origin myth M_4

195

referred to the important Harijan task here of "honoring the dead," and said that in recognition of this service, higher-caste people give the Harijans some respect at this point in the ritual; here "we must nod our heads to these Harijans." Arichandaran is a mythic figure known throughout India, a king whose virtue was tested by the gods. The gods subjected Arichandran to a series of Job-like trials, the worst of which reduced him to the slave of a "Candala" funeral ground attendant and forced him to collect death fees from his own wife for the cremation of his son. In the Endavur Harijan version of the story, Arichandran is the slave of the *uur* Vettiyan, who buys him without knowing his background, and who cannot figure out why he is so incompetent at his simple tasks. Arichandran in this chant is a further claim for the formal precedence of the Harijans; this caste, according to the chant, once had a great king for a slave. The meaning of the last line of the chant is obscure; it may refer to Arichandran continuing to serve in his low function for the Harijans, or it may be a vaguer reference to the separation of the higher castes and the Harijans after the Harijans' mythic fall from their original precedence.

After the halt at the Arichandran stone, the Vettiyan leads the funeral procession on into the burning ground. In the case of burial, the *uur* Vettiyan has already dug the grave, and he places the body in it now, and eventually covers it with earth. In the rarer cases of cremation, the Vettiyan is in charge of the body while it is on the pyre. Here his contact with the body can be particularly gruesome, according to informants, for the body's muscles may contract with the heat of the fire, and the Vettiyan has to physically restrain its involuntary movements. The Vettiyan receives a cash payment for his grave digging or for his cremation assistance, and he also receives the extremely impure cloth shroud that has covered the otherwise naked body. At the conclusion of the funeral, the family of the deceased makes another cash payment to the Vettiyan and additional cash payments to other Harijan assistants—the *parai* drummer, the *varayan*, and one or two Harijan headmen, who attend to supervise the Harijan specialists. This family also feeds cooked food to the Vettiyan and to the Harijan *varayan*. By this last transaction, of food from a family under the extreme pollution of death (*tittu*), the Vettiyan and the *varayan* are particularly lowered.

The third service performed by the Harijan *uur* Vettiyan is the least low of his actions for the higher castes, that of village watchman. Here the Vettiyan operates during a time when the *peey* are active, but he takes no particularly lowering substances from the higher castes as part of this *toRil*. A title for the Vettiyan working as night watchmen is *kambu kuTiyan*, "one who carries the *kambu kuTi* stick." The *kambu kuTi* is a heavy wooden stick that the Vettiyan has the right to carry as his weapon and as a symbol of this watchman position, and he displays it proudly.

The fourth low service of Harijan *toRil*, *parai* drumming, is arranged but not done by the *uur* Vettiyan. It is, like the other aspects of the Vettiyan's *toRil*, a prerogative of the Vettiyan grade. The local "leader" of the *parai* band is the male head of family V_{26}, who says that drumming has been a tradition (*parambarai*) in his family, and that it is a task that he takes seriously: "Suppose I have already got agricultural work tomorrow, but this evening I am told to play the *parai* band at the same time tomorrow. I will go do the drumming, leaving the agricultural work aside. For my family has been engaged in this work since the days of my grandfather, and I must honor the word of the *uur* Vettiyan who has summoned me."

Parai drumming is not an exclusive right of this family or lineage, however; men within the Vettiyan grade take it up according to personal inclination. Of the nine Harijans in the Colony who serve regularly as drummers, eight are Vettiyans and the ninth, a Pannaikkar of household P_{47}, is the exception who proves the rule. P_{47} is a "very distant brother" to the other Pannaikkars, "we don't know how," and the main Pannaikkar lineages are very vague about his social identity.

197

The Vettiyans are not vague about P_{47}, however. They say that his father married a local Vettiyan, and that since he also does "Vettiyan *toRil*" (that is, plays the *parai*), he is in fact "three-quarters Vettiyan." P_{47} is then like the male of family P_{28}—changing from Pannaikkar to Vettiyan identity by marriage transactions with the Vettiyans and by taking up their status-definitive *toRil*. Both men have probably acted in this way in order to get the payments that come with these actions. P_{47} is also aware of the downward mobility that his actions entail. He minimizes his *parai* drum playing, and claims—in contrast to V_{26}'s serious attitude toward drumming—that there is really nothing to it as a skill or a tradition: "What is there to learn about it? It comes with two days of practice. I myself learned without any teacher." The Vettiyans counter P_{47}'s disparagement of their drumming by claiming that they only call on him when they are "short of drummers."

The *parai* band in Endavur generally consists of five drummers, four playing *parai* and one playing *satti*, a small bowl-shaped drum held horizontally and hit with two sticks. The *parai* is a larger, one-sided, tamborine-like drum, held vertically and played with one stick and one hand. The head "must" be made with the skin of a calf, which is bought from the *uur* Vettiyan and given to the Harijan Vannan D_2, who constructs the drum for another fee. This drum making is apparently an individual skill of the Harijan Vannan, though it could also be consistently linked to the lower caste of the Harijan Vannans, and to the fact that the Harijan Vannans as *pucaris* themselves play several drums. When the *parai* drum plays, the four *parais* keep a common rhythmic beat appropriate to the occasion, while the *satti* taps out the tempo in rapid even beats. The *parai* heads must have a particular tension to sound as they should, and the band stops every fifteen or twenty minutes, particularly on cool mornings, to heat the drums over a small fire and to restore the correct tautness to the heads.

198

The Vettiyan *parai* band plays at least nine different beats, a distinct beat for each distinct ritual occasion. The Harijans sometimes call these beats *talams*, a term also used for the complex forms that underlie classical Carnatic music; but among the Harijans, there is no more to this ethnomusicology that the division of these nine *talums* into five "good beats" and four beats that are "not for good things." The five "good beats" are played at the village Selliyamman festival, at the *uur* and Colony Mariyamman festivals, and at Harijan marriages and other auspicious life-cycle rituals. The four bad beats are played for more inauspicious forms of the goddess (Gangaiyamman and Villiyamman), for a dance in which the Harijans make fun of the Kurivikarans, and—the most inauspicious beat of all—for funerals of *uur* and higher Colony castes, when the rhythm is called *saavu meelem*, "death drum."

Another division can be made of the "beats" and of the ritual contexts of the *parai* band. In the *uur*, among the higher castes to whom the auspicious *uur* Ambattan band provides its services, the *parai* band is a strictly inauspicious band. It is, as noted earlier, always farther from the focus of the ritual than is the auspicious band of the Ambattan barbers, and it is most prominent in occasions to which the evil *peey* might be attracted: goddess possessions, processions through places inhabited by the *peey*, bloody sacrifices, and death. The *parai* band is in the *uur* a part of the Harijans' function of mediating downward to these low and inauspicious beings, the *peey*.

The *parai* band also plays in the Colony, however, and while it on the one hand replicates here the same low functions that it performs in the *uur*—reinforcing the lowness of the Vettiyans relative to the other Harijan grades—it also picks up a new set of functions in the Colony. For here it also plays "good beats" not used in the *uur*—for Harijan marriages, for the relatively auspicious ceremony marking the seventh month of a woman's pregnancy (*seemandham*), for a girl's coming-of-age ceremony, and for the occasion on which a woman leaves her home Colony to marry into another Colony (*nalangu*).

We have noted before that the auspicious band of the *uur* barbers refuses to provide its services to the Untouchables, that this refusal results in an apparent deletion in the replicatory order at the bottom of the system. We now see that there is, within the musical repertoire of the *parai* band, a replicatory response to this apparent deletion. To stretch our structural language slightly, we can say that here the Harijans have code-switched from a code of caste to a code of music. High and low forms for music, which in the system as a whole are performed by members of higher and lower castes, are here replicated by a single set of musicians playing "good" and "bad" beats, separated from one another only in time.

As with other replications that require code-switching, this one is not perfect; it is only as good as circumstances will allow. For even when the *parai* band is playing its good beats in the Colony, it carries with it some of its more fundamental inauspiciousness. Whereas the auspicious band of the *uur* barbers plays its music under the marriage pavilion in a high-caste marriage, the *parai* band must at an Untouchable marriage remain at some distance when it plays its good beats, outside the marriage pavilion. Some of the more prosperous Talaiyari households in the Endavur Colony (Gengan's, for example) have solved this problem of inadequate replication by convincing an *uur* Ambattan barber band to serve them. This Ambattan band is not the same band that serves the higher castes in Endavur; it comes, for a substantial fee, from a village about ten miles south of the village. But its presence in these Harijan marriages serves the replicatory purposes of the Harijans much better than does the code-switching *parai* band, and these Harijan households have therefore entirely eliminated the *parai* band from their marriage ceremonies (though they still use the band, after the fashion of the *uur*, in their funerals).

200

The definitively low *toRils* performed by the *uur* Vettiyan, by other Vettiyans, and by the Pannaikkar *varayan* announcer, all have their material and cultural compensations. All are done for monetary payments. Most of these payments range between one and two rupees, a half to one day's wage in agricultural labor, and though the payments may seem very small and very irregular, they are not inconsequential for work that is less physically taxing than field labor, and among people as poor as the Harijans. The attractiveness of these payments is in any case testified to by Pannaikkars P_{28} and P_{47} (and possibly by the *varayan*), who are willing to trade their higher grade status for these small material rewards. The rewards in rice and in free or cheap beef are also significant to the Harijans.

The cultural compensations for Harijan *toRil* have been noted above. There is in most of these functions some factor for pride: pride in the responsibility of drumming, in the low but ritually important task of "honoring the dead," and in the less low service of village watchman. These services are truly complementary for the system as a whole: they are necessary to the higher castes, and the lower the services are, the more the higher castes are dependent on the Harijans. Hence the higher castes' willingness to listen to the Harijan myth of inversion at the edge of the burning ground. Yet to say that the Harijans can take pride in these low tasks is not to say that they themselves can entirely deny their lowness. This the Harijans do not do; rather, they betray their consensus with a culture that defines these tasks as low by assigning most of them to the lowest of their grade.

The Vettiyans indicate both directly and obliquely an accurate awareness of their position in the Harijan caste. They admit that the Talaiyaris are, or at least have been, more *saivam* than themselves, and that they are also more "civilized" (they have more *nagarigam*, literally "qualities of the city"). The term *nagarigam*, incidentally, is the term that members of the local Harijan caste in general use to differentiate themselves from the Harijans of other, less prosperous Colonies; "we Endavur Harijans," they say, are more "civilized" than the Harijans of other Colonies. The Vettiyans occasionally make a statement like that of the Chakkiliyan elder, claiming that they are only separate from the Talaiyaris, and therefore not unequal: "We don't take brides from the Talaiyari *vagaiyara* [grade]. We are different, they are different." Some Vettiyans claim that they make decisions about interdining and intermarrying not on the basis of grade, but on the basis of household. They judge the "civilization," the purity (*suttam*), and the prosperity of families case by case, and then decide whether to exchange women or food with them. Statements like this accurately reflect the fact that Vettiyan families in Endavur do have some marriage ties with local Pannaikkars (mostly with those of Adimelem's "dirty Pannaikkar" category, but also with some Pannaikkars of sublineages I and II), but it disguises the fact that no local Talaiyari family will take cooked food, or women in marriage, from the local Vettiyans.

The Vettiyans also make claims for local precedence over the Pannaikkars, based on the "outsider" status of the Pannaikkars and on the fact that the *varayan* (who serves them, the Vettiyans) is a Pannaikkar. But it is difficult for the Vettiyans to ignore the fact that they themselves have made no marriage transactions with the more *saivam* Talaiyaris, while the Pannaikkars have. Nor is it easy for the Vettiyans to deny that if the Pannaikkars are once inferiorized by serving the Vettiyans as *varayans*, the Vettiyans must be four times inferiorized by serving the Pannaikkars as *paṛai* drummers, cremation ground attendants, cattle scavengers and village watchmen.

The Vettiyans also have stories about the origins of the grade differences, which, though they are briefer and more historical in effect than the Paraiyan origin myths, replicate some of the themes of myths M_1 through M_4 at the level of grade differences. One was told by two educated Vettiyan schoolboys who had just started college in Madras:

M_5 *The Origin of the Grade Differences*

In the early days, we *TooTTis* were not in the majority, but we had some money. While we watched the fields at night, we had a chance to steal things. We didn't use our money wisely, however; we stored our paddy in large pots, and gave it away freely to all who asked for it. We were very gullible. When the Pannaikkars and Talaiyaris, who were more educated than us, asked to borrow money from us, we innocently obliged. In due course, those two [grades] became more powerful and we lost ground.

As in the Harijan versions of the Paraiyan origin myths, this story tells of a group that lost its original precedence due to its generosity, its gullibility, and its good intentions. The gullibility of the Vettiyans or the *TooTTis* is very specifically contextualized in this story, however. Toward the higher castes of the *uur*, the story seems to say, the Vettiyans were sneaky, clever, and underhanded, stealing things at night in the fields while they did their *toRil* as village watchmen. Toward their own people, on the other hand, they were open, generous and stupid, giving paddy and money away to all who asked for them.

Another account of the grade differences, that of the Vettiyan elder Periyasami (V_{15}), deals more specifically with the rise of the Pannaikkars:

M_6 *The Rise of the Pannaikkars*

Those Pannaikkars are really outsiders, "nameless people." They are really only our servants. We Vettiyans are the first ones. Adimelem's family came from a village ten miles away, two generations ago, and married with the Vettiyans and the Talaiyaris here. They were very poor. Because we Vettiyans and the Talaiyaris were engaged in our village *toRil* and in agricultural work, we left the Pannaikkars to "do panchayat." Also, they were free to get some education. During M. C. Raja's time [a prom-

inent Untouchable politician of the early twentieth century]
he saw to it that twenty-five Harijans got government jobs
[in the state]. Then, even though Adimelem had only a
fifth-standard education, he got his job as road inspector.

Though this story is the most factual sounding of all the
myths here, some of its facts are dubious. It is doubtful that
Adimelem's family was all that poor a generation ago, for a
Harijan child can be educated only when its family can
afford to forego the economic contribution of the child as a
field laborer. Also, Adimelem's two brothers own 1.5 acres
of land each, suggesting that the family might have had about
4.5 acres of land when it divided into its present three families. Nor is the story particularly logical in accounting for
the free time of the Pannaikkars: the Talaiyaris and the Vettiyans do not put that many actual man-hours into the performance of their *toRil*. Nor do the Pannaikkars in fact "do
panchayat" (operate the caste council) in the Endavur
Colony.

What story M_6 admits, despite its denigrating tone, is that
the Pannaikkars have somehow gained over the Vettiyans in
Endavur, that though they really ought to be servants to the
Vettiyans, they are no longer in fact in this lower relation to
the Vettiyans. Like story M_5, this story stresses "education"
as the operator of the Pannaikkars' upward mobility, though
it is less explicit than the other stories in attributing gullibility
to the group that has lost precedence, to the Vettiyans. Periyasami is attempting to make a status claim for the Vettiyans
by grouping them together with the Talaiyaris ("we Vettiyans and Talaiyaris") as "true people," versus the outsider
Pannaikkars. Significantly, Periyasami does not comment directly on the relation *between* the true people of Endavur,
between the Talaiyaris and the Vettiyans. He does make one
indirect allusion to Vettiyan precedence, however: "we Vettiyans are the first ones." This theme constitutes a quiet under-
current to Vettiyan self-identity—an idea that even before
there were Talaiyaris in the Endavur Colony, there were

Vettiyans, that Vettiyans are the original Paraiyans, just as Paraiyans were the "original" people.

Periyasami is very proud of his family's marriage transactions with Talaiyaris outside the Colony, however, an oblique admission to the relative lowness of his own grade versus the Talaiyaris. His genealogy shows nineteen marriages over three generations with a Talaiyari lineage in a Colony ten miles southeast of Endavur—thirteen Vettiyan women given in marriage and six Talaiyari women taken. Periyasami's pride in these upward marriages outside the Colony constitutes a kind of counterclaim to the status implications of the Pannaikkars' upward marriages within the Colony, but it is not a strong enough counterclaim to win him rank vis-à-vis the Pannaikkars. For the unit within which grade rank is maintained in the Harijan caste is a single Colony; only on a Colony-by-Colony basis are the distinctive features of grade identity assigned—rights to *toRil* and to *maniyam*. Here the Vettiyans win over the Pannaikkars in having *toRil* and *maniyam*, but they lose to them in serving the Pannaikkars in their *toRil*-based actions.

The overall grade endogamy of the Vettiyans is as unimpressive as that of the Pannaikkars: only thirty-six percent of seventy-three Vettiyan marriages sampled are with other Vettiyans. This low figure is in part a function of two facts: the number of intermarriages between local Vettiyans and poorer local Pannaikkars (eleven in this sample), and the number of outside Talaiyari intermarriages on the genealogy of Periyasami alone. If we subtract these two figures from the total, however, the percentage of grade-endogamy still only rises to sixty percent. But one statistic does remain constant: there are in none of the Vettiyan genealogies sampled any cases of intermarriage with the local Talaiyaris.

Like the true Talaiyaris of Endavur, the true Vettiyans of the Colony worship a common *kula devam*, Kudiraikaran, "horseman." As with the Talaiyaris, this common worship among the Vettiyans is a function of their *pangali* social organization, of the fact that they are all putatively descended from a common ancestor. The Vettiyans' worship of Kudirai-karan also constitutes part of their claim to the status of "original" people of the Colony. Kudiraikaran was the only *kula devam* of the Colony for whom an origin myth was forthcoming. Ironically, it was told not by a Vettiyan, but by the Pannaikkar elder Velagiri (P_{18}). The story is as follows:

M_7 *The Story of Kudiraikaran* (told by the Pannaikkar Velagiri)

This place [the Endavur Colony] has some importance in the Kudiraikaran story. Long ago, there was only one person here, a single Vettiyan. One day, a young boy came by. The boy was pleasant and active, and the Vettiyan said to him, "you don't have any permanent place. I am alone. You stay here and I will adopt you as a son." The boy agreed, and lived with the man as a son.

One night the two of them were by the place near the coconut tree [a particular spot on the northern boundary of the old Colony]. The Vettiyan told the boy to go to sleep, while he went back to his house to get food for the boy. While the boy was sleeping, the seven sisters (*KaNNiamma*) came by with their whole entourage of servants, chariots, and horses. When they saw that the boy had seen them, they warned him not to tell anyone what he had seen, or his head would fly into a hundred pieces. The boy managed to keep quiet for three days, but finally he told his father, "goddess [*Amman*] visited me three nights ago." His head flew into a hundred pieces, he died and was buried by the tree.

After that, the boy came to the Vettiyan in a dream and told him, "I am a horseman in the stable of the seven sisters. They are taking very good care of me here. Since I am now in god's place, please raise a stone up after me, and name it Kudiraikaran ("horseman"). I will save you from suffering and bring you prosperity." After this dream, a horseman was seen roaming around the area. So the stone was erected and worshipped as Kudiraikaran.

Kudiraikaran has in this story similarities both to Aiyanar and to Karuppan, male village deities who are more important further south in Tamilnadu. Like Aiyanar, Kudiraikaran rides a horse and guards a boundary (the Colony) at night. Like Karuppan, he is a servant to the goddess (cf. Dumont 1959). The important social feature of myth M_7 for the Endavur grade structure, however, is its message that the Vettiyans are the first people of the Colony. For in the beginning, the myth says, the only man in the Colony was a Vettiyan.

The Vettiyans of Endavur report conducting the same sort of group and individual household worship to their *kula devam* Kudiraikaran as do the Talaiyaris to Periyandavar—a collective yearly festival, and individual household worship before life-cycle ceremonies, and at life crises. There is for Kudiraikaran, however, no equivalent to the now-abandoned "looting the cremation ground" for Periyandavar. Like Periyandavar, Kudiraikaran helps to protect the health of small children in the group that worships him. He is also associated with human fertility and, among Vettiyans and non-Vettiyans alike, with the bringing of rain: "do puja to Kudiraikaran, and rain will come in three days," the Endavur Harijans say. Non-Vettiyan Harijans pay respect to Kudiraikaran more often than do Harijans for other *kula devams* to whose primary group of worship they do not belong. In the annual festival to the Colony Mariyamman, for example, all Harijan devotees make three ritual circumambulations of the Kudiraikaran stone on their way to the Mariyamman temple. "We must pay some special attention to the god of the Vettiyans," says a non-Vettiyan Harijan somewhat cryptically in accounting for these circumambulations.

A member of the Vettiyan grade currently plays one other significant ritual role in the Colony, that of "temple trustee" to the Colony goddess Mariyamman, here performed by Cinnapayyan, V_{21}. The temple trustee (*dharmastarbanam*) is the treasurer of the Colony temple, a man supposedly trusted by all in the Colony to keep the accounts for the temple and to arrange the finances for the goddess's yearly festival. Cinnapayyan does more than just temple trustee work for the Colony Mariyamman, however. For two other roles to the goddess have in the Endavur Colony been abdicated by those who are supposed to perform them: daily *purohit*, a function that the Valluvar *purohit* once played, before a dispute over his payments; and temple servant, a function supposedly performed by the *varayan* announcer, but here avoided by the Pannaikkar *varayan* for reasons that are not known (but are probably related to the local Pannaikkars' status claims over the Vettiyans). Cinnapayyan plays these two additional roles as well, going to the Mariyamman temple most mornings and evenings, cleaning the temple, awakening and dressing the goddess, and performing daily puja to her.

It is not inappropriate for a sincere devotee to do all these things for a deity, and Cinnapayyan sees himself as such a devotee to the Colony Mariyamman. Likewise, though the temple trustee role is not a prerogative of the Vettiyan grade in the Endavur Colony (the trustee before Cinnapayyan was a Talaiyari), the fact that a Vettiyan is now doing all these services for the Colony Mariyamman is a factor of pride for all the Vettiyans in the Colony. It means that they have a particular closeness to the goddess of the local territory, for they are the ones who really care for her, despite their relative poverty. The more prosperous Pannaikkar and Talaiyaris families have no comparable devotion to the Colony Mariyamman, say the Vettiyans.

Thirteen of the thirty-nine Vettiyan households in the Endavur Colony own land, with an average landownership among the landed families of 2.3 acres per household, ranging from 5.6 acres per household to 0.5. As a grade, then, the Vettiyans are only marginally poorer than the local Pannaikkars. Distribution of land through the Vettiyan sublineages, however, is not as uneven as it is through the Pannaikkar lineages. Every Vettiyan sublineage has its landed families. But Potan sublineage is economically advantaged among the four sublineages: seven of the thirteen landed Vettiyan families belong to Potan sublineage, and thirteen of the thirty acres owned by Vettiyans belong to these families. Potan sublineage is not dominant within the Vettiyan grade to the same degree as are lineages I, II, and III among the Pannaikkars; Potan sublineage does not mark itself off from the other three sublineages of the Vettiyans as differentially higher and purer (it could not do so without abandoning its position in the rotation of *uur* Vettiyan *toRil*). Potan sublineage has used its prosperity to arrange a slightly superior marriage network, however. For it is with families of Potan lineage that lineage IV among the Pannaikkars—the Pannaikkar group that is "almost Vettiyan" by its performance of the government Vettiyan position—has intermarried. By marrying down, Pannaikkar lineage IV shares in the marginal prosperity of the Vettiyan Potan lineage; by marrying up, Potan lineage enjoys the marginal prestige of having Pannaikkar affines.

The Vettiyan residential concentration in the Endavur Colony is not split in two, like the Pannaikkars' living sites; it consists of the contiguous rear of the old Colony and front of the new Colony. Correlatively, the Vettiyan grade does not seem to be as clearly factionalized as does the Pannaikkar grade. There are fewer obviously prosperous households among the Vettiyans than in the other two grades. The majority of the Vettiyan households, combined with the poorer half of the Pannaikkar households, comprise together the poorer half of the Endavur Colony—a collection of small, run-down, poorly maintained mud huts, with more in common with the uniform poverty of surrounding Colonies than with the qualified prosperity of the wealthier Endavur Harijans.

Of the significant adult males of the Vettiyan grade, the elder Periyasami (V_{15}) has the most vivid personality. Periyasami is of the same generation as the Pannaikkar Adimelem, and he has similar stories about his political involvement in the old Depressed Classes League. But his personal style is in total contrast to Adimelem's self-important dignity. For Periyasami, who makes his living as a cattle trader in Endavur and in surrounding villages, is scruffy in dress, undistinguished in lifestyle, and spends most of his leisure time in the village toddy shop. He is also more direct and vulgar verbally than is Adimelem. An example of his style, and another example of a Harijan ideal of openness, is the following comment that he made on Adimelem's claims for his own clean diet: "I have to tell you something. Adimelem was bragging the other day about not eating pork. Whenever pork is available, Adimelem is the first man to send someone to get a large amount for his family. If we eat something, we should not hide it. We should be open. If a man fornicates with his mother, he must say that he fornicates with his mother. Whether it is right or wrong is a second matter."

Of the five Harijan headmen in the Colony, Periyasami is the acknowledged master of dispute settlement—either on the formal occasions when two or more brothers sit down equally to divide the property of a household, or on more informal occasions. "Who is better for settling quarrels than someone who quarrels so much?" as one of Periyasami's admirers said of him. His reputation here extends even to the *uur*. On one occasion, we witnessed a village Chettiyar coming into the Colony to seek out Periyasami's advice in his own *pangali* split. Periyasami himself claims that he does as much "headman work" for *uur* people as for Harijans, mostly at the village toddy shop.

Other Vettiyan males are less extroverted than Periyasami. The temple trustee Cinnapayyan (V_{21}) is a relatively young man in his middle twenties, serious about his work for the Colony goddess, and more thoughtful than most Harijans about ritual matters. Cinnapayyan attributes a dispute between himself and his younger brother (V_{22}) to hard feelings brought on by his service to the goddess. Because for one month he spent most of his time supervising the construction of a new temple car, he says, his younger brother decided he was not contributing sufficiently to the family income, which in this family comes mostly from field-labor earnings of the adults. A *pangali* division of the family resulted, which Cinnapayyan regrets.

Muni (V_{20}) is a man in his mid-forties who devotes himself to his 1.5 acres of wet land and 2 acres of dry land. Unlike some other prosperous Harijans, Muni has acquired his land without extravillage sources of income; his capital has come from field labor and the profits of tenant farming. He has sent one of his four sons through school, and the boy is now in college in Madras. This son, Muni says, has already gotten family wealth in the form of educational support. When the time comes for a *pangali* split in the family, the division will be made only among the three brothers who have remained on the land.

The headman Sami (V_{31}) is a strong and slightly disreputable man. Though his family has divided from that of his brother's son (V_{30}) and his younger brother (V_{32}), Sami acts very much as the authoritarian elder in this group of three close *pangalis*. There are grumblings about Sami elsewhere in the Vettiyan grade. Some accuse him of regularly "grabbing" the *uur* Vettiyan positions when they rotate into Potan sublineage, rather than allowing poorer members of the sublineage to perform them regularly (for Sami owns some land). Others accuse him of classificatory incest, saying he is having an affair with a woman in the Colony who is in a "sister" relation with him. Sami on his own behalf is proud of his headman position and of the temporary authority of being one of the village watchmen. But his services are used less often than those of the other Harijan headmen.

The last Vettiyan male worth mentioning here is Velam, the younger brother of the *parai* band leader, a man in his early twenties (V_{27}). Velam has spent some time as a college student in Madras, but he did not finish his degree. He says he returned voluntarily to the Endavur Colony to help "manage" the family, for his older brother was mismanaging his share of the land after their father's death. There were probably other reasons for his return, since the joint (but since

211

divided) land here is not much over an acre. Velam is the most fashionable of the younger men in the Colony, with a few synthetic shirts from Madras and a generally citified style of dress. Velam has flirted half-heartedly with communist ideology, talking about it to another young Vettiyan, and going secretly at night to the village tailor to have a communist flag made. But he and his friend subsequently burned the flag, for fear of its being discovered, and Velam's understanding of communism is rudimentary, amounting mostly to a belief that the communists would redistribute the land. Few others among the Harijans of Endavur have any interest in communism. As with the Talaiyari schoolteacher Das's extraneously learned Ambedkarism, Velam's communism is thin and confused in his own mind, and mostly irrelevant to the village as he experiences it.

The Caste and the Grades

The internal social structure of the Harijan caste of Endavur can be summed up by a hypothetical history. Suppose that the original two Harijans of the Colony were a Talaiyari male and a Vettiyan male, and that the former ranked over the latter by the superiority of his *toRil*. Suppose further that the male descendents of each of the original Harijans had remained a single *pangali* group of "brothers," residing together, sharing the ancestral *toRil*, worshiping a common god, and appointing common headmen. Suppose finally that neither of these local descent groups had intermarried, due to the superiority of the former, but that each had found its brides either among outsider groups of its own identity, or among a third group in the Colony who ranked between the two. If this third group were of mixed origin, and if it were internally split according to who had married up and who had married down with the original groups, the result would be a set of social relations much like those in the Endavur Harijan caste at present.

Endavur is not the result of an historical process quite

this simple, but the account does bring out some general features of the complex internal structure of the Harijan caste here. One feature is that, in terms of conventional kinship terminology, the two "true" grades of the Colony are in a sense simply two nonintermarrying lineages. Like other south Indian descent groups to which a standard definition of "lineage" has been applied (Beck 1972a: 3-4; Dumont 1957a: 167-68), the Talaiyaris and the Vettiyans of Endavur are each apparently attached to a given territory, and each group is corporate, named, unilineally organized, and exogamous. Yet to label the local grades as lineages is not to understand them fully, and there are problems even with the application of the standard definition. One is that the corporate heads of the Talaiyaris and the Vettiyans (the Harijan headmen) are not in fact leaders of the groups from which they come; they are leaders of the local caste segment as a whole. Another is that these two groups are not exogamous by name. For Talaiyaris do not marry outside a "Talaiyari lineage"; they marry other Talaiyaris by preference.

More important than the social-typological essence of these Harijan subunits is the structural relations between them. For each of the grades in the Endavur Colony takes its identity from its position in a ranked system of grades, and the grade structure in turn takes its form and meaning from the position of the Harijan caste in the local caste system as a whole. What more can we say of the Harijan grades from this structural point of view?

A first, almost purely ethnographic point, is that the distinctive features of grade identity are on the one hand very general, and on the other hand very local. That is, the general criteria that determine Talaiyari, Pannaikkar, and Vettiyan identity are widespread in northern Tamilnadu, and serve to differentiate Harijans one from another in most villages of the region.[9] The specific "rights" to grade identity,

[9] We verified the existence of distinct Harijan grades in Colonies up to twenty-five miles from Endavur, and a Harijan doctor we spoke with remembered the same divisions in the Paraiyan *ceeri* in

213

however, are strictly localized: a given Harijan's rights to a
particular grade identity exist only in a single village, and
the Harijan loses this "true" identity when he moves to another village. Village by village, then, Harijan grades have
the caste-like property of dividing a population into ranked
groups according to performance of *toRil*, but between villages, grades lack the territorial spread and boundedness of
true castes. With this property go the characteristics of intermarriage between the grades: strict endogamy among the
"true" grades of a given Colony, and far less attention to
grade endogamy in marriages between Colonies.[10]

A second feature of the microsociology of the Harijan

---

which he was raised, near Trichy, about two hundred miles to the
south.

[10] Similar internally ranked subdivisions of a single local subcaste
have been described for a subcaste much higher than the Harijans,
in a region not far from Endavur. *KoNDaikkaTTi VeeLaaLars* (or
KVs) of central Chingleput, a very high dominant caste with Brahmanic pretensions, divide themselves in each of their village clusters
into a number of unnamed grades or *vagaiyaras* (the same term used
for "grade" by the Endavur Harijans), said to differ from one another in innate blood purity and in strictness of collective conduct.
In the "56-village cluster," for example (a territorially bounded unit
of endogamy for the KVs, and thus a subcaste region), there are
five of these grades, each with 125 to 150 families each, each known
to the others, each largely endogamous. And the highest of these
grades has a disproportionate concentration of power and landed
wealth (Barnett 1970: 66-78; Barnett 1973). The KV grades differ
from the Harijan grades in their endogamous territorial spread
through a region of villages, a feature that may be linked to the
dominance of the KVs in these regions. The Harijan grades, on the
other hand, differ from the KV grades in that their identity in a
given village is linked to externally known and externally practiced
differences in *toRil*, while the existence of KV grades is purely internal in definition, and known only to the KVs. The existence of
grades in both castes, however, indicates that "grade" as a demon-
stration of a caste's concern with purity-linked internal ranking is
tied in no direct way to the rank of that caste in the overall system.
In these more general terms, both the high-ranking KVs and the
low-ranking Harijans are equally rank conscious.

grades is that both individual and collective grade identities can be changed. Cases of individual mobility have been noted above. As with changes of caste, changes of grade are easier in a downward than in an upward direction. The simplest change is made by moving away from the Colony of one's "true" identity and taking up in the new Colony the lower rank of a "nameless person." The particular Pannaikkars of Endavur who do Vettiyan *toRil* (P_{47} and P_{28}) have also moved downward, becoming "almost Vettiyans" by their actions as Vettiyans. Persons who successfully renounce Vettiyan *toRil*, on the other hand, have a chance to move up, as many of the Pannaikkars of Endavur may have done by leaving their home Colonies and intermarrying with the Endavur Talaiyaris. Each of these status actions has an equal and opposite reaction, however: the Endavur Talaiyaris have lost some absolute status in the Colony because of their marriage transactions with the incoming Pannaikkars. Ultimately, most of the upward and downward moves are motivated by tradeoffs between grade status and economic prosperity, which accounts for the loose correlation between the landedness and the rank of each of the three grades in the Endavur Colony. But this correlation is only loose, and the transactional interrelations that state the rank order at any given time are slow to change. As with caste, so too the status order of the grade system must accommodate itself to wealth, but the order is not determined by wealth. Nor is the grade order endlessly flexible. Its one constant is that there must be, in any given Colony, some Harijans willing to perform for the village the most basic lowering actions by which Harijan identity is defined.

A third feature of the Harijan grade structure has been amply emphasized above: it indicates in a most forceful manner the degree to which the Harijans are in consensus with a system that defines them as fundamentally low. We have located in the internal social structure of the Harijan caste the missing replicatory functions that we could not find in relations between distinct Untouchable castes in the last

215

chapter, the functions of auspicious drummer and of Harijans to the Harijans (see Table 4-2). The former function is reproduced by the "good beats" of the *paṛai* band. The latter functions are given mostly to the lowermost grade within the caste, though one low function, that of *varayan* announcer, is given to a higher-grade Pannaikkar performer—an allocation that the Harijans themselves see as productive of ambiguous status orderings. As noted above, however, this ambiguity is about the rank of certain individuals and groups, not about the lowering nature of these functions of Harijans to the Harijans. For all of the Harijans tacitly agree that to act like a Harijan with respect to themselves, the Harijans, is to be definitionally lower than themselves. All Harijans thus agree on the criteria by which their own lowness is defined in the system as a whole. The internal replicatory ordering of the Harijans, left incomplete in Table 4-2, can now be completed as shown in Table 5-2.

TABLE 5-2. Total Replicatory Order of the Harijans of Endavur

Service or function	Performer in Harijan subsystem	Code of status ranking
Purhoit	Valluvar Pandaram	Caste
(Dominance)	Harijan	Caste
Pucari, washerman, washerman ritual assistant, barber ritual assistant	Harijan Vannan	Caste
Auspicious drummer	Vettiyan band, "good beats"	Music, time, grade
Varayan announcer	Pannaikkar	Grade
Paṛai-drummer, cattle scavenger, cremation ground attendant, village watchman	Vettiyan	Grade
The excluded	Chakkiliyan, Kurivikaran	Caste

216

With this final unfolding of the replicatory subsystem among the Harijans, the basic social-structural argument of the present work is complete. Replication this thorough, we suggest, indicates a deep consensus among the lowest members of the caste order concerning the most fundamental principles of rank in the total system. The Harijans and the other four Untouchable castes of Endavur have recreated to the best of their materially limited abilities the functions and relations from which they have been excluded, and have found among themselves, again to the best of their abilities, groups and individuals who will consent to be lower than themselves. As is the case higher in the system, material dominance is necessary in order to induce poorer groups to play replicatory roles with respect to one's own group, and this dominance the Harijans of Endavur have to a degree. They have nothing like the Reddiyars' degree of dominance, however, and as a result, the Harijans have not managed to find a separate caste that will accept death substances from them—who will act as their own Harijans transactionally. Hence the Harijan grade system.

As a system internal to the Harijan caste, the grade system is a very strong social-structural indicator of the Harijans' own hierarchical values. Not surprisingly, such an internal structure also facilitates the Reddiyars' control of the Harijans. As we have noted above, the Reddiyars could control a Harijan threat to the total system by their economic domination of the Harijans. Thus if the Harijans stopped performing their *toRils*, the Reddiyars could stop giving them agricultural employment until Harijans took these *toRils* up again. But given the grade structure, it is doubtful that a challenge would get this far. For a cattle-scavenging boycott by the Vettiyans, for example, would threaten the status position of the Pannaikkars and the Talaiyaris more immediately and directly than it would the higher castes. Pressures against such action would thus be as strong within the Harijan caste as without.

Power has a clear and delimited role in caste as it is presently structured in Endavur. Power keeps certain people in

217

lowering positions that they might otherwise try to abandon; it is the ultimate sanction against movement in the system (or, conversely, in the case of an upwardly mobile, dominant caste, the principle operator for movement in the system). Power does not, however, explain either the specific structure of the system or much of its daily processual dynamics. Nor does power operate often in caste. Granted their knowledge of the power of the higher castes, the Untouchables are also motivated to stay in place by a number of other factors: by material rewards, by cultural rewards (the realization that all *toRils* are equally necessary if not equally ranked), and perhaps by psychological rewards (the much maligned "security" of knowing one's place in a stable, ranked system). Finally, Untouchables are motivated to stay low by their fundamental agreement with the postulates of a system that requires such low actors as themselves.

In delineating this consensus, we have worked up to this point mostly in the domain of social structure, in the relations of men to men, and we have worked analytically down from large to small elements of the system. Let us now shift the description to the domain of the religious system, to the relations of men to divine beings, and make the same fundamental argument for cultural consensus by working synthetically up from smaller units to larger ones—from the gods of the individual and the family up to the territorial gods of hamlet and village. If power has only a delimited role in explaining the social-structural replication of the Untouchables, its role in accounting for religious consensus among the Untouchables is even more restricted. Here we enter more directly a domain of belief; here, the Untouchables are even more openly the carriers of a conceptual system identical in all its basic principles to that of the higher castes.

CHAPTER VI

Replication and Complementarity
in Harijan Religion

THE religion of the Harijans, and of the other villagers of Endavur, will here be defined as the relation of these human actors to a category of divine beings, entities variously called *devams, saamis, ammans, devatas,* and *peey-pisasus,* loosely translatable as "gods," "goddesses," and "demons." As in a recently analyzed north Indian village religious system (Wadley 1975), the religious data from Endavur permit us to define these divine beings as entities whose distinctive feature is their *shakti,* their "power" relative to a given worshiper. The key structure of south Indian village religion is thus the relation of a worshiper to a god, a relation which resembles that between south Indian humans in being based on a ranked, unequal transaction. The worshiper gives the divine being devotion, honor, food, and gifts; the divine being in turn either uses its power beneficently on behalf of the worshiper, or fails to use it maleficently toward the worshiper (cf. Wadley 1975: 54-59).

The divine beings in Endavur can be ordered in two different ways, one purely cultural and the other more sociological in reference. Culturally, the gods of Endavur can be ordered according to their indigenously defined natures, powers, and interrelations. Some of them are high, pure, mostly beneficent beings, with wide-ranging, generally defined powers (for instance, over the world order). Others are intermediate beings, alternately pure and impure, beneficent and maleficent, with more specifically defined powers (such as over rain and human fertility). And a third general category of divine beings are very low, impure beings, almost entirely maleficent, with very narrow powers (such as

219

over a single human sufferer). Generally speaking, the higher divine beings control the lower divine beings, but lower beings (particularly the *peeys* or demons) can act independently on occasion, and certain ritual actions are directed at bringing these lower beings back under the control of higher divinities. There are more links in the divine hierarchy of Endavur than this simple threefold categorization suggests, as we shall see, and a given divine being can change its nature according to ritual context. But the general categories are stable and well structured (cf. Wadley 1975: 127-48; Babb 1975: 215-46).

As a number of analysts have noted, there is a homology or analogy between this divine hierarchy and the human hierarchy—the caste system—in south Indian culture (Dumont 1959, Harper 1959, 1964, Beck 1969a). The same principles order both hierarchies: purity and impurity, control and subordination. And the same threefold categorization can be loosely applied to each hierarchy: the relation of Brahmins to non-Brahmins to Untouchables is in many ways homologous to the relation between high gods, intermediate gods, and demons (see especially Harper 1964). This analogy is only a loose one, however, and it is deceptive on a number of culturally specific points. First, the analogy is sometimes taken to suggest that Brahmins worship only high gods, that non-Brahmins worship only intermediate gods, and that Untouchables worship the lowermost demons. This implication is emphatically untrue, as we shall show. Second, the analogy assumes a rigid cultural distinction between the human and the divine, a distinction equivalent to the Western dualistic dichotomy between the natural and the supernatural. Wadley's analysis of a north Indian village religion constitutes a fundamental attack on this quiet, perhaps ethnocentric assumption, and asserts to the contrary that there is no separate "supernatural" domain in Indian religious conceptions, that instead humans and divine beings interact in a single, continuously defined hierarchy of being (Wadley 1975: 54). We shall adopt Wadley's point of

view below, not as a paradigm that has been fully demonstrated for south Indian religious data, but as one that orders the present religious data from Endavur in a simple
and adequate manner.

The second, more sociological way of ordering divine beings and their worship in Endavur is in terms of communities
of worship. For every Harijan and every other villager in
Endavur has at least five distinct gods to whom he gives
regular devotion. The first of these is the "chosen god" (*ista
devam*), the divine being whom an individual worshiper
decides is paramount for himself or herself. The second and
third are the "household god" (*viiTTu devam*) and the "lineage god" (*kula devam*), divine beings shared by the worshiper with the kin of his immediate family (*kuDumbam*)
and of his patrilineage (*kulam*). And the fourth and fifth
are the "hamlet god" (*kooloni devata* or *uur devata*, depending on the worshiper's caste) and the "village god" (*kiraama
devata*), beings shared by the worshiper with those with
whom he or she has a common territory—hamlet or village.

The communities marked by this set of gods—person,
family, lineage, hamlet, and village—form a roughly ascending set; here, worship marks out the significant social groups
in a precise, Durkheimian fashion.[1] And this set defines very

[1] The Chinese-boxlike quality of this ascending scale is not perfect, however. The groups relevant to the first three levels of worship
are each larger than the last, and a number of lower-level groups
is nested in each larger group. Thus a chosen god is worshiped by a
single person; a number of kin, each with his own *ista devam*, worship a common household deity; and a number of households, each
with its own *viiTTu devams*, worship a common lineage deity. We
could then proceed to the fourth and fifth levels, and say that a number of lineages (both from common and different castes), each with
its own *kula devam*, worship a common hamlet god, and finally that
two hamlet collectivities, each with its *uur* or Colony deities, worship
a common village god. But the link between the kin groups and the
territorial groups is not a nested one, for a *kulam* or lineage can cut
across a number of local territories. My thanks to McKim Marriott
for pointing this out to me. The ascending scale is still useful here
for descriptive purposes, especially since the Harijan lineages rarely

221

exactly the contexts in which the lowness of the Harijans is relevant to their ability to worship. In brief, the Untouchability of the Endavur Harijans is entirely irrelevant to their choice of personal gods, and largely irrelevant to their worship of these divine beings. The Untouchability of the Harijans, moreover, is also entirely irrelevant to their worship of the kin gods; at this level, members of all castes, high to low, are equally cut off from one another. It is only in the worship of the third set of gods, the territorial gods, that Untouchability becomes relevant to religious practice. For as Untouchables, the Harijans are excluded from the *uur* and thus from the higher-caste cult of the *uur* goddess Mariyamman. Their response to this exclusion should by now be predictable: the Harijans, as the dominant group in the Colony, replicate for themselves an identical cult to a Colony Mariyamman, who exists as a separate image inside the Colony; and the Harijans employ in this cult a replicatory set of ranked specialists drawn from the Untouchable microcaste system sketched in the last two chapters. As Untouchables, however, the Harijans are not excluded from the village, and they are thus not excluded from the intercaste cult to the village goddess Selliyamman. The Harijans' response to their ritual inclusion is twofold. On their own behalf, the Harijans are the last among equals as worshipers of Selliyamman. And on the behalf of others above them, Harijans are mediators downward, between the goddess and the higher-caste worshipers on the one hand, and the lowest of the divine beings, the *peey*, on the other.

In this chapter, we will describe Harijan worship in the rough ascending order delineated by the communities of di-

---

do ramify beyond a single basic Colony. It seems possible, by the way, that these separate parameters of community worship—kin and territory—correlate with a cultural distinction that Ronald Inden sees as fundamental in the ethnosociology of Bengal. In Inden's terms, the first parameter corresponds to the shared bodily substance of the worshipers, and the second corresponds to the shared "territorial substance" of the worshipers (see Inden 1975: 11-48).

vine worship, in terms of the second, sociological order that we have outlined here. But we will refer constantly to the first, cultural order, as well, and we will continue to draw on Wadley's work for insights into divinity as it is indigenously understood in Endavur. It is important to bear in mind from the start that these two orders of divinity, the cultural and the social, cut across one another. At most levels of community worship, divine beings with a wide range of culturally defined ranks exist, either as objects of direct worship, or as beings referred to in establishing the divine credentials (what we will describe below as the "genealogy of control," following Wadley) of the deities being directly worshiped.

From this point follows another familiar point about the Harijans and cultural consensus. Religiously speaking, by replicating the *uur* territorial cult from which they are excluded as Untouchables, the Harijans have recreated for themselves the single specific divine being from whom the higher castes have cut them off. This deity's powers are thus available to them. More generally, in all of their various cults, the Harijans interact with divine beings whose cultural definitions are identical to those worshiped by the higher caste villagers, and whose range of natures (high to low, and so on) is as wide as is the range of those worshiped by the higher-caste villagers. In a word, the Harijans are not differentially oriented toward the bottom of the divine hierarchy because of their placement near the bottom of the human hierarchy.

Furthermore, Harijans and other Untouchables play toward this complete range of divine beings a complete set of ritual roles found in the *uur*: *purohit*, devotee, possessed dancer, *pucari*, and mediator downward. There is even a Harijan in the Endavur Colony whose actions approach those of an orthodox *sannyasin* renouncer. In short, with the exception of the Brahmin's Sanskritic words and the barber's auspicious music (both of which are imperfectly replicated among the Untouchables), there is nothing in the total re-

223

ligious system as it is defined and enacted by the higher castes of Endavur from which the Harijans are cut off for reason of their lowness. Let us look at this religious replication by the Endavur Harijans in more detail.

CHOSEN GODS: ISTA DEVAMS

The *ista devams* of the Endavur Harijans are as various as the term indicates. *Ista* denotes "desired" or "chosen." A given person decides that a given god is his chosen god by a strong personal experience with the god's power. In the case of sickness, for example, a person might exhaust the powers of available local gods, and be referred to the power of a new god, some distance away. If a vow to this god resulted in the alleviation of the sickness, the person might then decide that this new god was his own chosen god, a god who was for him in particular all-powerful. The same person could in theory make the same discovery about a more available local god, as well. But it appears that Endavur villagers do not take as their chosen gods a god who is also already their household or lineage god, or their hamlet or village god (with the possible exception of those persons who become possessed by one of these gods, in which case the god is "choosing" them).

Not all the Harijans of Endavur were surveyed systematically for their chosen gods, and it is possible that some Harijans do not maintain regular worship to such beings. Those who do, however, mention a range of chosen gods from *Muniswaran* (a very low guardian god) to the higher and more generally popular gods Ganapati and Murugan. Murugan was mentioned most often by Harijans as their chosen god. In the Pudukottai region, some Harijans also mentioned Siva and Vishnu as their chosen gods.

Various types of worship are carried out by Endavur Untouchables to their chosen gods. The Valluvar *purohit* maintains a "stone" for his chosen god Ganapati, just to the west of his dwelling, and he performs regular puja offerings to it.

In the Harijan section of the Colony, no stone images of particular chosen gods were discovered. Many Harijans say they go to temples outside the village to worship their chosen gods, through the intermediacy of other priests. Some believe that the village goddess Selliyamman of a village ten miles east of Endavur is particularly powerful for them, and go to her yearly festival (this particular goddess attracts worshipers of all castes from villages miles around her). The Talaiyari schoolteacher Ram (T_3) goes once a year to a Murugan temple one mile north of Madurantakam, where the priest is a Brahmin. When the priest does a puja to the god for Ram, he asks Ram his *kulam* (here euphemistically connoting caste), and Ram replies that he is an "Adi Dravida" ("original Dravidian"). Ram says that it would not have been possible for him to have gone to a temple served by a Brahmin several generations ago, but that now "times have changed and only the money [for the puja service] matters to the priest." And as far as Ram is concerned, "we don't care about these people [that is, about the Brahmin's piety]; we just have our faith in the god."

Ram's ability to worship at the Murugan temple, and the ability of other Harijans to worship at Siva and Vishnu temples in the south, is a legacy of the old temple-entry movement of the late nineteenth and early twentieth centuries, associated in its later years with Gandhi, but initiated at a grass-roots level by the Nadars of the far south. The larger temples of Tamilnadu have been legally open to Untouchables since 1939, but Ram would be far less likely to gain entry into a Murugan temple in the village of Endavur than in the town of Madurantakam. It is possible that two generations ago, Harijans had more difficulty maintaining relations of worship with particularly high chosen gods, but it is also possible that other forms of devotion to these gods were practiced: worship "in the mind," or worship from afar. Most Endavur Harijans are familiar with the story of the *bhakti* saint Nandan, an Untouchable of a thousand years ago whose legendary devotion to the god Siva at Chidam-

bram was eventually recognized by Siva himself. In one Endavur account, the god arranged that the stone image of his
Nandi (the bull, his "vehicle") be moved off center so that
Nandan, paying his respects from outside the temple walls,
could see directly into the central shrine. In another local
account, Nandan was absorbed directly into the god himself.

The Harijans of Endavur thus worship, and perhaps always have worshiped, a collection of chosen gods whose natures cover a full range of divine types, from the high gods
Siva and Vishnu, to regional gods like Murugan (a son of
Siva), to village goddesses like Selliyamman, to low guardian gods like Muniswaran. There is in their choice of these
divine beings no relation between the nature of the god and
the low nature imputed to Harijans by the higher castes; so
far as the Harijans are concerned, it is appropriate for them
to take as their *ista devams* any god, high or low, who personally demonstrates his or her power to them. Members of
the higher village castes of Endavur maintain a similar range
of chosen gods, according to a similar cultural logic. It is
possible that non-Untouchables need not go so far afield
from Endavur to find their chosen gods, since one mecha-
nism by which an Untouchable worships a high chosen god
is to do so in a location where his Untouchability is not well
known, a consideration not relevant to non-Untouchables.
Systematic data were not collected on this point, however.

Household Gods: VⅡTTu Devams

Every household in Endavur, Untouchable and non-Untouchable, has a family goddess, a deity whose definition and
worship is virtually identical regardless of the caste of the
family worshiping her. The family goddess, a being called
puuvaaDai,[2] is the spirit of a deceased woman in the family,
one who has died in an auspicious married state rather than

[2] There is no commonly given folk etymology in Endavur for the
term *puuvaaDai*. One Mudaliyar suggested that it derived from the
way the goddess was brought from a well in a flower pot: *puu* =
"flower" + *aDai* = "coming in contact with."

226

in an inauspicious widowed state. Such auspicious female ancestors are also called *mangalis*. The *puuvaaDai* is worshiped by all members of an undivided household (a *kuDumbam* or *viiDu*) with the eldest male officiating, on "good" family occasions such as marriage or the birth of a child, or on critical family occasions having to do with the health of the children in the family. She is thus strongly associated with the fertility of the family. The family goddess is worshiped in the form of a *kalasam* pot (a particular type of tall pot) inside the family's house, on the auspicious north or northeast side, and in the form of a stone near a well in the fields.

The particular being who is a given family's *viiTTu devam* is usually a near ancestor, and is generally known by name. The family goddess of the Harijan Talaiyari elder Nalasami (T$_{10}$), for example, is "Ayyamma," Nalasami's father's mother. According to Nalasami, every Harijan family renews its family goddess every one or two generations, in a ceremony identical to that by which the territorial goddesses of the *uur*, the Colony, and the village are installed in their temples at the beginning of their yearly festivals. After the death of a *mangali* woman, her family waits a year and then goes in procession to "the Ganges" (a well in the fields), evokes "Mother" (*Amman*) by playing the *bambai* and *uDukkai* drums for her, and causes her to possess a family member, usually a male. The new family goddess is then transferred from the well to her stone in the fields, and then to a ceremonial *karagam* pot. The *karagam* pot is carried in procession to the family household, where the goddess is transferred into the old *kalasam* pot of the former family goddess, where she can then be worshiped inside the household whenever necessary. This new being is the family goddess for the family for a generation or two, when another recently deceased auspicious woman will be so honored. When this occurs, the older family goddess loses her individual identity and merges with the new one: "all dead *mangali* women are *puuvaaDai*; all are one."

Social structurally, the worship of the family goddess

227

puuvaaDai marks the locus of a single undivided family as rigorously as does a common cooking hearth or undivided property. Among the Harijans, when a *"pangali* split" occurs in a formerly undivided family, the principal movable goods of the family are first placed in front of the goddess, and a small puja offering is made to her by the eldest male of the family. After the ceremony, the division of family goods and land is carried out under the supervision of one of the Harijan headman. One of the first acts in establishing the new household of the divided-off family (usually that of a younger brother) is the installation of a new *kalasam* pot to the family goddess. The identity of the goddess is not divided at this time, however; only after the death of an auspicious woman in the new household does the family go to the fields and evoke a new "mother."

Some Harijans in the Endavur Colony (and some non-Harijans as well) also possess a separate family goddess, Mariyattai,[3] who is worshiped on the same occasions as *puuvaaDai*, but who has a slightly different origin, character, and cult from the auspicious *puuvaaDai*. For Mariyattai is the spirit of a recently deceased woman in the family who has died in an inauspicious state, as a widow. Consistent with her inauspicious origin, she receives a lower form of worship than does *puuvaaDai*: *puuvaaDai* is given only vegetarian food offerings, while Mariyattai is offered chicken, mutton, fish, and even country liquor (toddy and arrack). The duality of *puuvaaDai* and *Mariyattai* inside the family replicates at this social-structural level a duality of the divine found even more systematically at the territorial level, and particularly associated with the goddess: a duality between

[3] Mariyattai is an alternate title of Mariyamman, the "goddess who changes," a being worshiped most prominently at the level of the hamlet. Mariyattai means literally "elder sister Mari," and *Mariyamman* means "Mother Mari." In the hamlet festival, the title Mariyattai is used for the goddess only when she is present in her relatively low, possessed form. This usage is consistent with the same usage in the family cult for the relatively inauspicious ancestor.

228

high, pure, and auspicious forms of god, and low, impure, and inauspicious forms of god. Here again, then, both for Harijans and for villagers, a range of forms of divinity is available to human actors in a given ritual context. In Dumontian terms, we can say that an opposed pair of two such forms—high and low, pure and impure—may constitute the minimum complementary set necessary for a ritual action of any sort.

LINEAGE GODS: (KULA DEVAMS) AND A HARIJAN POSSESSION CULT

The lineage gods or *kula devams* of the Harijans of Endavur have been noted above. All the true Talaiyaris of the Colony worship the lineal god Periyandavar, whose stone is in a half-ruined temple on the eastern edge of the Colony, and all the true Vettiyans worship the lineal god Kudiraikaran, whose stone is just north of the Mariyamman temple in the old Colony. Pannaikkar lineages still return to their old home Colonies to worship their *kula devams*, though lineages I and II report worshiping Katteri in a temporary form in Endavur, and lineage VI has brought a duplicate of its lineal goddess Periyapalaiyattar from its home Colony two miles to the west of Endavur.

Individuals and families in a given *kula devam*'s lineage worship their lineage god on much the same occasions and for much the same reasons as they worship their family gods: before family life-cycle rituals, and at family crises. And the lineage gods have much the same powers as the family gods: over the fertility of those who worship them and over the health of small children in the lineages. Each lineage also reports conducting a yearly collective festival for its lineage god, with the eldest male in each lineage acting as priest. As a group, the lineage gods are almost uniformly low in nature, the sorts of male guardian figures who rank below the goddesses, and stand between them and the lowest of divine beings, the *peey-pisasu* (though higher gods are also present

229

at their worship). Periyandavar's festival "looting the cremation ground" suggests such a low nature; he is probably a being who stands just above the *peey* of the cremation ground, and thus has power over them. And Kudiraikaran's origin myth (p. 206) places him in the role of servant to the goddess.

The lowness of these Harijan lineage gods, however, does not correlate with the general lowness of the Harijans. For many village castes reported *kula devams* with the same natures. Some of the Idaiyars of the *uur*, for example, mention the low beings Katteri and Muniswaran as their lineage gods, and village Kavundars and Villis say that they worship the low goddess Kanniyamma as a *kula devam*. Among the Untouchable castes the uppermost Valluvar Pandarams have Periyandavar as a lineage god, and the Harijan Vannans have Muniswaran. When members of two different castes mention the same divine being as a lineage god, by the way, they do not mean they are worshiping him at the same temple; each of these groups worships the god in a separate form and with separate cults. Though we do not have systematic data on all the lineage gods of Endavur, it is possible that most of these gods are, whatever the caste of those worshiping them, low beings who serve as alternative sources of aid in cases in which the powers of the family gods are either not sufficient or not appropriate.

The Harijan lineage deity with the most prominent cult in the Endavur Colony, and perhaps in Endavur village as a whole, is the goddess Periyapalaiyattar, the deity of Pannaikkar lineage VI. Twice a week, one of her devotees, Mugan, a landless Pannaikkar in his mid-thirties (the head of household P_{38}, son of the *varayan*, P_{37}), becomes possessed by this goddess and does "foretelling" and the exorcism of *peeys* for anyone who comes to the goddess. People do come, both from the Colony and the village, and in some cases from surrounding villages. The occasion itself, and Mugan's role while doing it, is called *kuṛi meedai* (*kuṛi* = "sign" or "omen," *meedai* = "platform" from which the foretelling is done). Mugan's *kuṛi meedai* is worth examining in some detail, as a case study in the limits of an Untouchable's ritual role towards non-Untouchables, and as a convenient entry into some indigenous notions of divinity and of divine action in Endavur.

To begin with the nature of the goddess, Periyapalaiyattar is a form of Mariyamman, the "goddess who changes," about whose character more will be said below. Mariyamman is in turn a fallen form of Parvati, wife of the high god Siva, exiled by Siva from her life with him because of an impure sexual thought on her part. Mariyamman and her alternate form Periyapalaiyattar are thus intermediate divine beings, lower than the high gods but higher than the guardian gods and the demons, closer to their human worshipers than the high gods, but also very dangerous to them because of their "anger."

The cultural relations of these goddesses to other divine beings mentioned so far can be summed up by a "genealogy" of divine control adapted from Wadley, as is done in Figure 6-1. As in the north Indian pantheon analyzed by Wadley, there are in the Endavur pantheon roughly six levels of divine beings, beings who are linked to one another across levels by a heterogeneous set of "genealogical" links. These links are stated in myths and in songs of praise to the divine beings. Thus, for example, Mariyamman is linked to Siva as "fallen wife." And Kudiraikaran is linked to the goddesses as a transgressor (the boy who told about the goddesses), and as servant and watchman.

The nature of the deities at the various levels of the Endavur pantheon also accords with what Wadley found in north India. Thus at the highest level, *KaDuval* or *Iraivan*, god is pervasive but has no nature. Since god at this level is unembodied in images or other material forms, it cannot be transacted with; it cannot be dealt with by human worshipers. At the second level, that of deities such as Siva, Parvati, and Vishnu (the last is not important in Endavur), god is embodied and is therefore worshipable. Deities at this

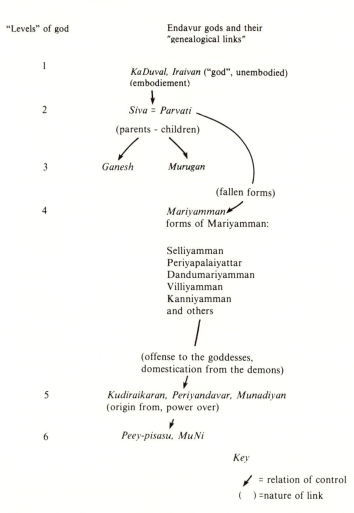

"Levels" of god | Endavur gods and their "genealogical links"

1   *KaDuval, Iraivan* ("god", unembodied) (embodiement)

2   *Siva = Parvati*

(parents - children)

3   *Ganesh*   *Murugan*

(fallen forms)

4   *Mariyamman*
forms of Mariyamman:

Selliyamman
Periyapalaiyattar
Dandumariyamman
Villiyamman
Kanniyamman
and others

(offense to the goddesses, domestication from the demons)

5   *Kudiraikaran, Periyandavar, Munadiyan*
(origin from, power over)

6   *Peey-pisasu, MuNi*

Key

= relation of control
(   ) = nature of link

FIGURE 6-1. Genealogy of Divine Control for the Deities of Endavur

Note: This figure is an adaptation of Wadley 1975: 137, 138, 145. All the divine beings shown on the figure are prominent in Endavur, and all are known to members of all castes either as personal gods, lineage gods or territorial gods.

232

level are "pure" beings with general, wide-ranging powers over the world order. They are basically beneficent in character, but will also occasionally "curse" a lower being. The regional gods Ganesh and Murugan constitute a third level in the divine hierarchy. They are mostly important as intermediaries to the higher beings, and have natures similar to those at the second level, though they are less powerful than they, and have less general powers. The fallen goddesses of the fourth level are quintessentially intermediate beings, alternately pure and impure, beneficent and maleficent, peaceful and angry (see Beck 1969a). They are sometimes only equal to, or even lower than, their human worshipers in rank, though they can also rank above them. These goddesses' powers are still more restricted and specific—over human fertility, epidemic disease in humans and cattle, rain, and against the demons of the sixth level. The role of beings at the fifth level, the guardian gods (some of whom are domesticated demons, *peey* who have been brought under the control of the goddess), has been noted for many of the lineage cults of Endavur. And the sixth level of divine beings, the evil, impure, and fundamentally low *peey-pisasus* (literally "demons/flesh-eaters") and *muNis* ("giants") are the agents against whom many of the powers of the higher gods are defined. The *peeys* are entirely maleficent beings, often the spirits of the unhappy human dead, given to unpredictable attacks on higher beings, human or divine. Occasionally, in myths, these beings become as powerful as the gods, by winning "boons" from the gods and then using these against the higher beings. Demons like this must eventually be brought once more under control by the higher gods, either by trickery or by force (cf. Wadley 1975: 127-47).

Though this divine hierarchy is an analytic construct, its structuring principles are entirely explicit in the statements of the Endavur Harijans and of other Endavur villagers about the nature of the divine. And the eventual subordination of all these specific and diverse forms of god to a supreme unifying monistic principle is as clear to the Endavur

Untouchables as it is to Brahmin theologians. A frequent and frustrating reply of Untouchable respondents to annoying questions about the specific natures of every distinct low god was: "what does it matter? They're [the various lower gods] really all the same, for god is one."

Thus, like the human hierarchy that it interpenetrates, the divine hierarchy in Endavur consists of a ranked set of interdependent beings whose states vary from pure to impure, whose natures vary from high to low, and whose powers vary from general to specific. Like the caste order, the divine order is also a hierarchy of control; lower beings are ultimately controlled by higher beings. But as in the caste order, lower beings have a kind of right to their specific powers, and they have a certain autonomy of action in the exercise of these rights.[4] As Wadley writes for the lower beings in the divine hierarchy of her north Indian village: "a deity

---

[4] This comparison of the divine hierarchy and the human hierarchy is only for illustrative purposes, and is not meant to suggest that the hierarchies are indigenously thought to be distinct and parallel. For if they were, humans would have to be considered fundamentally different from gods. The caste order, a purely human matter, could then be opposed to the divine order, a purely spiritual matter. Evidence that humans and gods are not so opposed, however, or that their opposition is a far subtler matter culturally than Western dualism suggests, is as follows. Human actors of any caste rank (as we shall see below with Mugan) can be thought to rank above certain gods, and therefore to be capable of commanding them, even when they still desire favorable action from the definitive *shakti* of the lower divine beings. Also, humans can themselves possess or acquire *shakti*, and be worshiped as gods by other humans (and possibly by other gods). Finally, humans often become gods after death (in the case of the *puuvaaDais*), and gods continually incarnate themselves as humans, both openly and covertly. All this suggests, with Wadley, that the key distinction of Indian religion is not between "human" and "supernatural," but between worshipers and worshiped (the latter having, distinctively, *shakti* or "power" relative to the former). Beings that we would define in Western terms as human and nonhuman can fall in either category in indigenous Indian terms. My thanks again to McKim Marriott for this interpretative point.

234

with only a few powers is, if ritual patterns are correct, more recognized and in some senses more powerful [in the specific domain of the deity's powers] than a higher-level intermediary with many powers" (Wadley 1975: 138). In the ritual life of Endavur, the beings with these specific and most immediately available powers are the goddesses. Which brings us back to Mugan and to the possession cult of the goddess Periyapalaiyattar.

Periyapalaiyattar is, as we have said before, Mugan's lineage deity. She is thus worshiped on a regular basis by Mugan and by all of his *pangalis* in the Endavur Colony, by all the members of Harijan Pannaikkar lineage VI. For three years, this goddess has been bestowing her "grace" (*aRul*) on Mugan; she has been "coming down" into him, and possessing him. Mugan, and all other persons given to becoming periodically possessed, are called *saamiyaaDis* ("god-dancers") or *saamiyaaLs* ("god-persons"). Possession, and the *saamiyaaDi* role, are regular features of the worship of family goddesses, lineage deities, and territorial deities in Endavur. What is unique to this possession cult (for Endavur) is that here the goddess is in essence "going public": Mugan is offering Periyapalaiyattar's power and her services to anyone who wishes to use them. Ultimately, in terms of the sociological categories of worship, Mugan is making his lineage goddess highly available as a personal deity to anyone who wishes to choose her, regardless of the chooser's lineage, caste, or village.

Mugan has only been offering Periyapalaiyattar to the public for a few years, and the reputation of her power is still unestablished; it is doubtful that many of her petitioners have as yet taken her as their chosen god. If her cult succeeds in the village, however, she will attract more regular worship from non-Pannaikkars, and since a deity's specific nature is in part the transactional result of the amount of worship she receives (the *shakti* being increased with the amount and type of devotion of the deity's worshipers, cf. Wadley 1975: 149-79), her power will therefore increase

235

and she will in turn become a more effective being. In indigenous terms, both the power of this particular form of the goddess, and the authenticity of Mugan as her *saami-yaaDi*, remain to be proven to the village at large. In religiously sceptical terms, Mugan's ability to carry off the elaborate masquerade involved in foretelling and in exorcism remains to be demonstrated.

In any case, Mugan-as-the-goddess at present attracts a small and shifting clientele on the Sunday and Tuesday afternoons when possession is induced. The goddess is brought down into Mugan in a standard way. First, Mugan and an old male *pangali* relative of his purify her small temple, and "wash" and "dress" the small image to her in the inner shrine of the temple. Mugan then presents himself to the inner image of the goddess in a pure state, bathed, cleanly dressed, and sexually abstinent and vegetarian for the past few days. Assisted by a *bambai* drummer from the Harijan Vannan caste, who acts as *pucari*, Mugan "describes" the goddess by playing the *uDukkai* drum to her and singing her songs of praise. These songs tell of Periyapalaiyattar's power and describe her genealogy—her descent from Parvati, her relation as alternate form to Mariyamman, her power over men and over lower divine beings. The goddess then comes down into Mugan, rather quickly and easily compared to other less frequent possessions.[5]

When any human devotee is possessed by a god or goddess in Endavur, it is said that that person "is" the divine being for the time of the possession; the deity has incarnated itself in a human body, in order to speak directly to the worshipers. So it is with Mugan and Periyapalaiyattar: from the moment of possession, it is the goddess rather than Mugan who is present, and Mugan says (as does every other *saami-*

---

[5] An exception to Mugan's generally easy possession, noted by all who were in attendance, was when my research assistant and I attended a possession with a tape recorder, to record the songs of praise. On this occasion, it took the goddess over one-half hour of listening to her songs before she descended.

yaaDi) that he must ask onlookers after the possession what the goddess did and said, for he is, he says, totally unconscious during the period of the possession.

The particular sign for the onset of possession varies from god to god, and from *saamiyaaDi* to *saamiyaaDi*. Mugan's possession is relatively mild; his limbs go stiff, his eyes close, and his breathing becomes heavy and spasmodic. He does not really lose control in the manner of many other *saamiyaaDis*, which is just as well, since the inner shrine of Periyapalaiyattar's temple is tiny and crowded with ritual paraphernalia. The *pucari* drummer signals the possession with a rapid, heavy beat, and the onlookers shout "Govinda! Govinda!" Mugan-as-the-goddess then rushes out of the temple, his eyes now open and staring, his hair loose and long, and circumambulates the temple three times, at a run, inspecting its preparations. He carries with him some of the weapons which "are" the goddess's power or *shakti*—a whip in his right hand, and a heavy rod in his left. When the goddess is satisfied, he reenters the temple and sits in the outer shrine, in the area called *kuṛi meedai* ("foretelling platform") and faces the goddess's petitioners from behind a small stone to her low guardian god, a male being called *Munadiyan* ("he who comes before"). The goddess is now ready to hear the "problems" and "grievances" (*kastams* and *abitus*) that have been brought to her.

Most of Periyapalaiyattar's petitioners are women, and they come both from the Colony and from *uur* castes, and occasionally from outside the village. Their problems cover a wide but highly specific range: a lost valuable, a difficulty with their husbands, their own infertility or sickness, some undefined fear, or possession by a demon. In most cases, the petitioners want the goddess's advice, or her prediction for the future. In the case of demonic possession, the petitioners (or relatives who have brought in an incoherent petitioner) want the goddess to drive out the *peey*. Normally the women talk directly to the goddess and Mugan-as-the-goddess replies with allusive and general questions and comments, using

Tamil forms that are both more formal and more archaic than Mugan's ordinary speech. The colloquies between the petitioner and the goddess often have the effect of a hard-fought negotiation. In this negotiation, the petitioner evaluates the possible accuracy and usefulness of the goddess's words, and the possible effectiveness of her *shakti*. The goddess, on the other hand, evaluates the petitioner's "trust" in the goddess, and the petitioner's potential as a regular worshiper and devotee to the goddess. Eventually, a bargain is struck, a transaction is made between petitioner and goddess, and the petitioner leaves—perhaps to return, if the advice is good, perhaps not, if the advice is useless.

The following partial text gives a sense of the interaction between petitioner and Mugan-as-the-goddess. Here, the petitioner is a woman from a higher *uur* caste in Endavur, with a complex physical syndrome. She has seen the goddess recently, and now she is returning for more aid.

> GODDESS: What, how do you feel now?
>
> WOMAN: The diarrhea is better now, but the tiredness in my legs and hands still continues.
>
> GODDESS: [in a severe tone] What, mother! In a single day, your diarrhea should stop, your leg and hand pains should stop, you want all this to happen in a single day? . . . I can reduce your diseases day by day only. If you have the idea that I should cure you in a single day, it is impossible.
>
> WOMAN: I am not saying you cannot cure me.
>
> GODDESS: How do you feel now? I'm asking you that only. It is slightly better, is it not?
>
> WOMAN: Yes.

With this minimal admission of the beneficent effect of the goddess's powers on her, the woman—with the highly vocal encouragement of a man and woman accompanying her—tells the goddess that she is thinking of going to the "T. B. hospital" with her problem, but that she still wants access to the goddess's aid as well:

238

GODDESS: So you say you will go to the hospital and then
you will return to this temple—that is what you promise? I think you will first see what they do for you and
then you will decide whether or not to return here.
. . . By all means, go. Even after going there, you will
realize that your disease can be cured only by returning
to Periyapalaiyattar. So go, don't be afraid, I will save
you in the end.

WOMAN: I know you can cure me definitely of my stomach pain and diarrhea. But for the T. B. . . .

GODDESS: No, I will cure them all. But you must go away
now.

WOMAN: First give me this fruit after doing a *mantiram*
[saying powerful words] for it.

GODDESS: No, only when you return will I give you the
fruit. If I give you the fruit now, will you say you were
cured because of Periyapalaiyattar, or . . .

WOMAN: No, it is not like that, *saami*! Even in the hospital [on an earlier occasion] the diarrhea did not stop.
It only stopped because of you.

GODDESS: All right, agreed. Give me the fruit.

The argument here is over the precise range of the goddess's powers. The woman wishes to get the benefit of as
many sources of medical aid as possible, and doubts that the
goddess's powers cover the full range of her syndrome. The
goddess is concerned with building her reputation for more
general powers, and with the hospital not getting credit for
a cure that she has caused. The goddess may also be avoiding blame for the woman's possible future deterioration, by
letting her go to the hospital in the end; if she does not get
better, it can always be blamed on the hospital rather than
on the goddess. And the goddess wants the woman to make
some clearly witnessed statement of her trust in the goddess
before she aids her. This is a constant theme of these ses-
sions: the goddess's dissatisfaction to the irregular nature
of her worship, the goddess's demand for the more regular

worship that will build her powers. In her own words to the petitioners as a group: "You don't behave properly toward Periyapalaiyattar. You only come when you have a grievance [*abitu*]. You don't come at other times." Without a regular source of devotees who pay their devotions to her regularly, and who demonstrate their subordination to her by taking her *prasadam* (the leftovers of food offerings to her), Periyapalaiyattar's recognized powers outside the *kulam* that worships her regularly will remain restricted to very narrow matters. As they do at present.

In the particular case quoted here, the outcome of the negotiation between the woman and Periyapalaiyattar is a transaction. The woman gives the goddess a fruit, which the goddess gives back to the woman, having transformed it by saying the *mantiram* over it. When the woman then eats the fruit, some the goddess's *shakti* will enter her, and work against the illness in her body.[6] The transaction can be viewed in another way: the woman gives the goddess a rather narrow expression of her devotion to her (her implicit willingness to return at least one more time), and the goddess gives the woman the benefit of her *shakti*.

The goddess's power is given or demonstrated in other ways with other petitioners. Some petitioners she whips directly with margosa leaves, the "cooling" leaves of the *neem* (or *veepumaram*) tree, thought to be particularly efficacious against smallpox and other heating diseases, and particularly disliked by the *peeys*. Others she simply advises. When she does so, however, there is a set of physical contacts by which the goddess's power is transmitted from one actor to another. First Mugan-as-the-goddess meditates on a problem while

---

[6] According to Brenda Beck, in similar "foretellings" in the Coimbatore area, the goddess places three fruits before the petitioner before listening to her problem. The goddess decides in advance which one she wants the petitioner to give her. If the petitioner then hands the goddess the correct fruit, the goddess knows that her advice will be taken seriously. (Beck, private communication). We may have missed observing a similar action here.

240

connecting the *Munadiyan* stone of the goddess's divine guardian to his own forehead, with a wooden rod held in his left hand. Then, when he-and-the-goddess give the goddess's advice, Mugan places the same rod on the forehead of the petitioner. The genealogy of divine control is constantly referred to in these advisings. A woman comes to Periyapalaiyattar complaining of disturbance by a *peey*, and admitting that she has made an unfulfilled vow to go in pilgrimage to a far-off major temple to the relatively high god Murugan. Periyapalaiyattar, having heard this, refuses at first to act: "Periyapalaiyattar cannot remove this grievance; how can a younger sister remove a curse placed by an older brother?" Later Periyapalaiyattar relents somewhat, and suggests that the woman make substitute pilgrimages to all the local deities, to a Ganesh shrine and a local Murugan shrine in particular. But, the goddess warns, the woman may still have to go to the far-off site for relief.

When no higher-level gods are involved in a complaint concerning *peey*, Periyapalaiyattar deals directly with these lowermost maleficent divine agents. A person's possession by a *peey* is unexpected and involuntary, though it is often brought on by the person's proximity to the *peey*—by going out in the fields at night, by traveling through the "crossroads" particularly inhabited by these low beings. The symptoms of *peey* possession vary widely; nearly any physical or mental complaint can be attributed to *peey* possession, or to the "nearness" of a *peey*. It is the task of Periyapalaiyattar to deal with these troublesome beings: to force them to identify themselves, to strike a bargain with them, and ultimately to force them out of the persons they have "caught." In Mugan's description of exorcism (which we witnessed only at a distance) the logic of Periyapalaiyattar's exorcism is very clear:

> People who go out in the hot sun, or to strange places, can get possessed by *peey-pisasus*, especially at noon and at midnight. Then they will come to the Goddess. Just as

241

I get possessed by the Goddess, so that person has gotten possessed by the *peey*. The Goddess questions the *peey* [that is, the person possessed by the *peey*] and the *peey* must answer: "I am the spirit of so-and-so, I died in such-and-such a way [generally by accident or suicide], and I was alone and this person passed by. I liked him or her." Then the Goddess asks, "when are you going to leave, and what do you want?" The *peey* must say, "next Sunday, or next Tuesday" [the days Mugan becomes possessed]. It may also ask for arrack or toddy, or goat or chicken. If it was a student in life, it might ask for a pen or books. These things will be brought, *tiv artanai* will be done to them, and they will be presented to the afflicted person.

Then [on the day when the spirit has agreed to leave] the Goddess uses her whip on the afflicted person. The *peey* is afraid of the goddess, and leaves. The *peey* declares, "I am going to such and such a tree." The Goddess [Mugan] plucks some hair from the person's head, and nails it to the tree. Then the afflicted person becomes unconscious, and two or three pots of water are poured over him. Finally, a small fire is made beside the tree, and everyone jumps over the fire. They are then safe. The *peey* is on the other side, and the fire is a boundary.[7]

A low divine being who possesses people without their control—a *peey*—is thus dealt with by a higher divine being whose *saamiyaaDi* can control his possession by this being—the goddess. In order to exorcize the *peey*, the goddess forces the *peey* to identify itself so that its exact and often low desires (meat and liquor) can be known. The *peey* is driven out in part by a transaction, by a gift of those things that it desires, but it is also forced out by its fear of the goddess. And the actions of its removal from the afflicted person are very clear in Mugan's account: its physical beating with the goddess's whip, its removal in the form of substance from the

---

[7] See Harper 1957 and Dumont 1957a: 407 for comparable descriptions of south Indian village exorcisms.

body of the afflicted (the hair), and its placement on the other side of a barrier protected by powerful things, by water and by fire.

In these specific interactions between humans and divine beings in the Endavur Periyapalaiyattar cult, Mugan's identity as an Untouchable Harijan is mostly irrelevant. The only connection between his Untouchability in an unpossessed state and his role as *saamiyaaDi* to the goddess Periyapalaiyattar is a loose one of initial identity. That is, deities tend to "like" and to possess those with a nature similar to their own. Periyapalaiyattar is relatively low in the divine hierarchy of Endavur, a potentially ferocious being whose identity is partly defined by her love for meat offerings. It is thus appropriate that she possess a meat eater. Since meat eating (not to be confused with beefeating) is found in most village castes of middle to lower rank in Endavur (and in most of Tamilnadu), it is then appropriate that a goddess of this nature possess anyone of middle to low-caste rank in the village. It is thus fitting that she possess Mugan, but it is not necessary that she only possess a member of an Untouchable caste. In Endavur, the similarly low goddess Selliyamman possesses a Kavundar, and in surrounding villages, *kuṛi meedai* is performed by non-Untouchable Villis and Idaiyars.

Periyapalaiyattar, a relatively low divine being, thus possesses Mugan, a relatively low human, but not a human who *must* be Untouchable by caste identity. And once her selection of a *saamiyaaDi* has been made, that *saamiyaaDi*'s caste identity is irrelevant to the interactions of human petitioners with the goddess. For when Mugan is possessed, he "is" the goddess, and Periyapalaiyattar's petitioners deal with a being with her attributes, not with his. Hence the willingness of *uur* women to accept from the Mugan-as-the-goddess things such as uncooked fruits, acceptances that they could never make from Mugan in an unpossessed state. The location of Periyapalaiyattar's temple facilitates access to her by those of higher castes. Though the old *kula devam*

243

stone to Periyapalaiyattar was located in the Pannaikkar section of the old Colony, after Mugan started doing *kuṟi
meedai*, he relocated the goddess in a new mud-and-thatch
temple outside the Colony living site itself, in the empty
space between the Colony and the *uur*, just to the Colony
side of the *uur*/Colony boundary stone. Though *uur* caste
petitioners have to pass this boundary stone to visit Periyapalaiyattar, they do not have to make a more polluting
entrance into the Colony living space itself when they petition the goddess. When a *peey* is exorcized by Periyapalaiyattar, by the way, it is often placed in a palmyra palm on
the other side of this boundary stone, outside the social
space of the Colony. That it is now technically in the social
space of the *uur* does not bother anyone, for it has not actually been placed inside the residential boundaries of the
uur. The placement of the *peey* on the other side of the Colony boundary, however, accords with the Harijans' view of
the Colony in other contexts as a central living space, an *uur*
like other *uurs*. Evil things like *peey* must be removed not
only from the persons they afflict; they must also be removed
from the social space of the Harijans (see Map 6-1).

Mugan himself makes an uncertain living as Periyapalaiyattar's *saamiyaaDi*, taking small cash contributions in return for the goddess's services. If he is no worse off economically than when he worked as a day laborer, neither is
he any better off. Mugan's wife complains of his neglect of
her and of their children since he has become Periyapalaiyattar's "god dancer." "Now he only has time for *shakti*,"
she says, alluding to his sexual chastity before each biweek-
ly possession by the goddess. His chastity and his meatless
diet, says Mugan, are necessary to build up sufficient *shakti*
for dealing with the goddess. He further maintains that he
is, in fact, purer in his life style than is the goddess, and that
he thus has "command" over her. In his behavior and his
personal style, Mugan has some characteristics of a *sannyasin* "renouncer." He is sexually abstinent, he is half withdrawn from his family duties, and he is mostly withdrawn

244

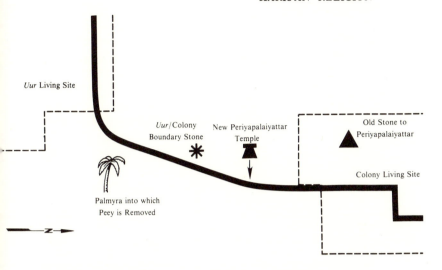

MAP 6-1. The Goddess Periyapalaiyattar and the Use of Social Space

from the caste-defined work nexus of the village. Though he is still clearly identified as Harijan when unpossessed, he is profoundly uninterested in such social facts. Of the Harijans of the Colony, he was perhaps the dullest and most uninformative about the details of daily social life. His passionate interests are reserved for the goddess alone.

The goddess Periyapalaiyattar remains a *kula devam* for Mugan and for his *pangalis* in the Endavur Colony. That she does not yet have a steady following of non-Harijan devotees is not a result of her relative lowness as a divine being, nor is it a result of the lowness of Mugan. It is the result of her history, or her lack of it: she has not yet demonstrated her power in the village and the region by a string of well-known successes, by a series of spectacular or effective cures. She may never, and this form of the goddess and her public cult may fade away in Endavur.[8] But if Periyapalai-

[8] See Berreman 1972a: 378-395 for a good description of the rise and fall of a similar Untouchable "shaman" in a north Indian village.

245

yattar should succeed in Endavur, there is nothing in the cultural logic of the situation to prevent non-Untouchables from taking this goddess as their personal divinities, as their *ista devams*. Here, too, as with the gods of person, of family, and of other lineages, the caste of individual religious actors does not limit their access to forms of divine power. Just as Harijans can among themselves "worship up" to personal gods of the highest natures, so too higher-caste villagers in Endavur can "worship down" to deities otherwise associated with Untouchables.

The Hamlet God: The Exclusive Goddess Mariyamman

In their identical worship to the gods of family and lineage, all the villagers of Endavur are turned equally inward. In caste terms, persons of different castes are equally cut off from one another at these levels of worship, for the relevant kin gods are worshiped in common only by small segments of a single caste. Nor are specialists from other castes generally brought in to help in the worship of these deities. Here everyone code-switches into "age" to find priesthood: it is generally the oldest male of the relevant group who officiates in family and lineage worship.

We enter another domain with the territorial deities Mariyamman and Selliyamman. These goddesses are worshiped in common by all those who share a territory—hamlet or village—and they are thus the only deities in Endavur whose cult includes by definition persons from a range of castes, high to low in varying degrees. Persons of these castes do not commonly worship the same territorial goddesses out of choice, as members of two different castes might worship a common "chosen deity"; they worship them out of necessity, by definition, as long as they share a common territory. In their relations of worship to these goddesses, all worshipers are the one hand equal: they all express their equal subordination to the goddess by accepting her *prasadam*,

246

and they all receive the goddess's equal protection over the territory they inhabit. Some worshipers are, on the other hand, more equal than others. In ritual practices to these territorial beings, members of the higher castes take precedence over members of the lower castes, and higher-caste persons play specialized ritual roles of a higher nature than do lower-caste persons. Inequality thus once more intrudes into the worship of these apparently equalizing beings. The inequality of the Untouchable castes of the village has two different expressions, according to the territorial goddess in question. In the cult of the inclusive village goddess Selliyamman, the Untouchables are the last among equals. In the cult of the exclusive *uur* goddess Mariyamman, the Untouchables are entirely excluded from worship and from the goddess's protection. Their response is, as we have indicated above, to replicate among themselves the same cult to the same goddess.

The goddess of the Endavur Colony is the same as the goddess of the *uur*, Mariyamman. Her freshly painted, cast concrete temple, in the center of the old Colony, differs from the *uur* Mariyamman temple only in being in better repair than the higher-caste temple. Some Harijans simply say the Colony Mariyamman "is" the same being as the *uur* Mariyamman; others say she is the "younger sister" of the *uur* goddess. The Colony Mariyamman has the same powers as the *uur* Mariyamman: to guard the boundaries of her territory, to protect all those inside these boundaries against disease in humans and cattle, particularly epidemic disease, and to bring rain for those who worship her. The Colony Mariyamman has the same myth of origin as the *uur* Mariyamman, the same dangerously ambivalent nature, and, so far as we could determine, the same set of ritual acts performed on her behalf.[9] And for these acts, a set of higher

---

[9] We were not able to conduct firsthand observation of the *uur* Mariyamman festival in Endavur, due to limited time and due to our desire to maintain primary ethnographic identification with the local Untouchables. This comparative generalization is based on in-

and lower-caste ritual specialists is mobilized, replicating
structures of human interaction in the higher castes' cult to
the *uur* goddess Mariyamman and in the village castes' cult
to the *kiraama* goddess Selliyamman. Let us consider in more
detail these facets of the goddess Mariyamman as she is
worshiped by the Endavur Untouchables: her origin, her
character, her cult, and the social structure of her worship
in the Colony.

The goddess of Mariyamman is, as we have indicated
above, a fallen form of Parvati, cursed by Siva to become a
lower being due to an impure sexual thought on her part.
Her myth of origin in the Endavur states her ambiguous
nature in a stunningly explicit image: she is part-Brahmin
and part-Untouchable in her bodily form. The myth, which
applies to the *uur* Mariyamman and the Colony Mariyamman alike (and to the other goddesses as well, since they
are all in turn forms of Mariyamman) is as follows:

M₈ *The Origin of Mariyamman*

Once Siva took the form of the great [Brahmin] *rishi* Nilakandar, and Parvati took the form of his wife Renukai.
They had four sons. Every morning Renukai would go to
a pond, swirl her fingers in the water, and a mud pot full
of water and flowers would emerge from the pond. This
she would carry to Nilikandar for his morning puja. One
morning, however, as she was leaning over the pond, she
saw the reflection of a divine messenger of the gods pass-
ing overhead [a Gandarva], and admired his figure. Because of this mere thought, she lost her chastity [*karpu*],
and she was unable to make the pot and the flowers
emerge from the pond. When she returned home to Nilakandar and told him what had happened, Nilakandar
cursed her and sent her away from his house.

formant work with *uur* persons in Endavur, on observation of *uur*
Mariyamman festivals elsewhere in Tamilnadu, and on written sources
(Thurston 1909, Whitehead 1921, Harper 1959, 1964, and Beck
1969a).

Nilakandar then called his four sons to him and asked, "which one of you will behead your mother?" Three refused, but the fourth, Parasaraman, agreed to do so, saying "you are my father, and there is nothing above a father's word." Parasaraman then chased his mother with a long knife [a *vaaLaayadam*] until he caught up with her at an [Untouchable] Chakkiliyan house. Out of fear, Renukai embraced the Chakkiliyan woman, and at that moment Parasaraman swung his knife and beheaded both women.

Parasaraman carried his mother's severed head back to his father, and told his father, "now that I have fulfilled your desire, I request a boon [*varam*] from you." Nilakandar agreed, and Parasaraman said he wanted his mother brought back to life. Nilakandar gave him a magic stick, told him to return the head to the body and to touch the stick to it, and his mother would be returned to life. Parasaraman went to do so, but in his confusion he put his mother's head on the Chakkiliyan woman's body, and the Chakkiliyan woman's head on his mother's body, and restored them both to life. When he returned with the former being, Nilakandar saw what had happened, and told Renukai/Parvati, "your body has changed, and you are no longer welcome here. Go out as a changed body [*uDal maari*]. Sprinkle and remove pearls [*mutal*; the reference is to smallpox, whose pustules are compared to pearls]. Earn your food from puja offerings. Since you have the head of a Brahmin and the stomach of a Chakkiliyan, you may receive both vegetarian and meat offerings." So Renukai went about changing forms as Mutalamman, Mariyamman, Periyapalaiyattar, Sengeniyamman, Kaliyamman, Selliyamman, Dandumariyamman.[10]

[10] This myth and the myth of Selliyamman below have been slightly condensed and slightly simplified. For the original versions, see Moffat 1975: 297-329, 339-40. The motif of the transposed head is very common in Indian folklore. For its application to similar goddesses in south India, see Whitehead 1921: 116-17 and Dumont 1957a: 385.

One message of this somewhat macabre myth of domestic morality is the intertranslatability of the human and the divine hierarchies in south Indian collective representations. Two high divine beings take the form of humans. One of them is then lowered first by a bad thought, and then by the most extreme human intermixture—that of a Brahmin and a Chakkiliyan. The lower being incorporated in this mixture of unequal human substance is finally worshiped by humans as an ambivalent divine being. She is clearly *Maariyamman*, the "goddess who changes" in Endavur folk etymologies. Her name, whose actual Sanskritic root lexeme is *maari*, "death," as also locally glossed as *MaReyamman*, the goddess of rain (*maRe* = "rain").

But though this goddess is part-Untouchable in her bodily form, she is in no way differentially worshiped by the lowest castes of Endavur. She is the goddess of everyone, in two different images, in the *uur* and in the Colony. In her worship in the Colony as in the *uur*, she is alternately present in her low form and in her high form, as a dangerous, impure, and bloodthirsty being, and as a benign, pure, and tranquil being. As in her origin myth, so too in her yearly festivals she changes her nature by context, and the appropriate rank of the ritual specialists who deal with her similarly changes by context. Mariyamman has the same bivalent character for the Harijans as she does for the higher castes, and for them as for the higher castes the lower half of this character is powerfully represented by her Untouchable body. Let us consider the ritual sequence of Mariyamman's worship in the Colony, to see how the various aspects of her character emerge through time, and how the Untouchables mediate this changing character.

The festival (*tiruviRaa*) for the Colony Mariyamman is held yearly, on a date determined by the Harijan headmen in consultation with the temple trustee and with all the male heads of household in the Harijan caste; it is doubtful that the Harijan Vannans or the Chakkiliyans have a role in this decision. In some neighboring villages, the Colony festival date is a determinate number of days (often eight) after the *uur* festival, but in Endavur this is not the case; it is merely at the same general time of year as the other goddess festivals, between April and July. During this period, agricultural work is at a minimum, temperatures are the hottest, and rainfall is the scantiest. Time is thus available for ritual activities, and the appropriate outcome of these festivals—a propitiation and "cooling" of Mariyamman and later of Selliyamman, both associated with the bringing of rain—is thus generally followed over the course of several months with the onset of occasional late summer showers, and later with the heavier rains of the period from September to December. We shall see what happens when these rains do not come.

After setting a date for the festival, which is announced through the Colony by the *varayan*, the Harijan headmen collect a house-tax within the Colony, one and a half rupees per household, toward the festival expenses. This tax they collect from all households of the Harijan caste, the Harijan Vannan caste, and the Chakkiliyan caste. Neither the Valluvar Pandarams nor the Kurivikarans, the two Untouchable castes who live outside the Colony boundaries, by preference and by exclusion respectively, benefits from the power of this goddess, and neither contributes to her festival. A second fund-raising activity is a dance called "Gangaiyamman masquerade" (Ganaiyamman *vesham*), in which a group of Harijan men and boys dress as women and go through Endavur and neighboring villages with the *parai* band, doing dances and singing songs of praise for Gangaiyamman, the form Mariyamman takes when she stays in a well ("the Ganges") in the fields. The donations that the Harijans receive for these dances go toward the Colony Mariyamman festival. This same group does a second set of dances "for fun" at the same time, and they are allowed to keep the contributions from these dances for themselves. In

251

the second set of dances, they mock the Kurivikarans, stereo-typing them as vulgar, loudmouthed, lazy, and sexually lax. For example:

> HARIJAN DANCER REPRESENTING KURIVI HUSBAND: "I'm leaving this house now, to go loaf around."
> KURIVI WIFE: "If you want to go, go. Some other man will come to me."
> HUSBAND: "Listen to what this woman dares to say!"

These stereotypes of the Kurivikarans coincide with *uur* stereotypes of Harijan character, and the chance to act out the same stereotypes on a lower group may account for much of the pleasure that the Harijans take in these dances.

The main day of the festival is a lengthy and apparently complex one, but it in fact consists of three principle move-ments. First, the goddess is incarnated as a fierce being near a well in the fields, and is at the same time installed as a higher being in her immovable image in the temple at the center of the old Colony. Second, she is processed through the Colony in her fierce form, in a decorated pot called a *karagam*, to which bloody sacrifices are made. Third, toward evening, she moves through the Colony in her higher form, as a movable image in her temple car, to which vegetarian offerings and cooked meat offerings are made. Each of these movements is punctuated by a ritual action (an *abiiSegam* or a puja) conducted by the Valluvar *purohit* at the temple. When the goddess is present in her lower form, she is dealt with by her Harijan devotees and by *pucaris* from the Hari-jan caste. When she is present in her higher form, the Vallu-var *purohit* mediates all interactions between worshipers and goddess.

There were omissions and condensations in the Colony festival in the year we observed it, though the ideal form is well known and the Harijans are embarrassed by the degree to which they deviate from it. The main day, for example, should be the "eighth day" (an even week by Western count-ing) after the goddess has been "tied" in place with sacred

252

threads (*kapus*) and offered daily puja by the Valluvar *purohit*. On the year of observation, she was only tied on the main day of the festival, which might have been due to antagonisms between the Harijans and the Valluvar *purohit*—to the Harijans' unwillingness to pay the *purohit*'s fees for eight days. Also, the goddess should receive a third procession through the Colony on the morning of the "ninth day" (the day after the main day), when her car and her movable image receive the cooling "festival of turmeric water." This third procession was omitted on the year of observation, due to an argument within the Harijan caste over the festival finances. Bearing these conflict-motivated omissions in mind, let us consider the three main movements of the Colony Mariyamman festival, as we observed them in June 1972.

The first movement of the Colony Mariyamman festival has three parts: installation of the goddess's high form in the temple, possession by the goddess's low form near a well outside the Colony, and procession of the goddess's possessed low form to her benign high form. The goddess's installation in the temple is accomplished by the Valluvar *purohit*, who comes at dawn and "wakes" the goddess, dresses her, bathes her with a "cooling" set of offerings (*abiiSegam*), and ties her and her *shakti* in place for the day with sacred black threads called *kapus*. All these actions the Valluvar performs on the immovable image of the goddess (the *muulaStaanam*) in the inner room of the temple (see Map 6-2), which is a figure of the goddess's head only. For, following the origin myth, "the Chakkiliyans have her body." The immovable image of the goddess is thus quite literally only her pure, high, Brahmanic part. The goddess's *shakti* includes the *bambai* and *uDukkai* drums used to evoke her. These, and the various images to the goddess used during this day, "are" the goddess's power and her being. They are not mere symbols or representations of her, standing for her in some abstract sense. Rather, during the events of this central day of the festival, the goddess is thought to be liter-

253

Well, "the Ganges"

Mariyamman-as-
Gangaiyamman

(Location of Possesion)

Sacred Pots
(Karagams)

UDukkai and
Bambai Drums

X (Location of *Parai* Band)

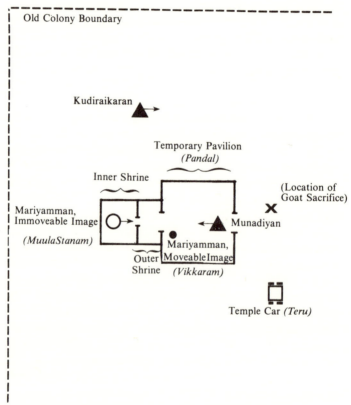

Old Colony Boundary

Kudiraikaran

Temporary Pavilion
(Pandal)

Inner Shrine

(Location of
Goat Sacrifice)

Mariyamman,
Immoveable Image

(MuulaStanam)

Munadiyan

Outer
Shrine

Mariyamman,
Moveable Image

(Vikkaram)

Temple Car *(Teru)*

Map 6-2. Locations and Forms of the Goddess, Colony Mariyamman Temple

254

ally present in the Colony, a being who can both bless and endanger the Colony, and a being with whom asymmetric exchanges can be made.

At the same time that the Valluvar *purohit* "ties" the goddess and her *shakti* in place, he also ties threads on the right wrists of five young Harijan devotees, called "thread-persons" or *kapukarans*. These men act as ritual assistants throughout the festival, and come repeatedly in contact with the goddess, especially with her lower form. If the thread-persons are not sexually pure (*suttam*, without *tittu*), the goddess will be greatly offended by their contact with her; for this reason, the Harijans say that it is best to choose unmarried young men as thread-persons, for the self-control of married men before the festival cannot be relied upon. With the tying of the threads, the high form of the goddess Mariyamman is present in her main temple, which has been purified and cooled by the actions of the *purohit*. This form of the goddess is now ready for the events of the day.

The second part of the first movement of the festival consists of the invocation of the lower aspect of the goddess, at the Gangaiyamman stone near a well just outside the northern boundary of the old Colony. The goddess is said to be in "the Ganges" (the well) when she is not embodied in humans or in other images, and her lower form is at this time drawn out of the well and into two embodiments: into decorated *karagam* pots and into a human *saamiyaaDi*. Consistent with the lowness of this occasion, the Valluvar *purohit* does not attend. The main officiants here are *pucaris* from the low-ranking Harijan Vannan caste, assisted by the Harijan thread-persons and by Harijan Vettiyans playing their *parai* drums.

The *pucaris* prepare the *karagam* pots and the Gangaiyamman stone much as the Valluvar has prepared the main temple to Mariyamman. The *karagam* pots are new mud pots that the *pucaris* fill with water from the well and with other pure and cooling liquids (including milk and lime juice), and decorate with a conical cap of margosa leaves and flowers (identified by one Harijan informant with the *gopuram* towers of temple gateways).[11] The *pucaris* wash and decorate the Gangaiyamman stone (and two ancillary stones of attending male deities whose identities are unclear to the Harijans), light an auspicious lamp (a *paDi velakku*), and tie together with a long white thread the well, the Gangaiyamman stone, the *shakti* of the goddess (here, not only the *bambai* and *uDukkai* drums, but a *VaaLaayadam* knife like the one with which Parasaraman beheaded his mother in the myth), and the *karagam* pots, of which there are three. Along this thread, they say, "power (*shakti*) comes to the goddess, life (*uyir*) comes to the goddess." The *pucaris* finally sprinkle well water over all the ritual paraphernalia and all the assembled devotees and declare: "this has become a pure (*sutamanaa*) place." Mariyamman's temple in the fields is now a suitable place for the incarnated presence of the goddess, and her invocation begins.

On the year of our observation, Mariyamman's possession proceeded much as did Periyapalaiyattar's possession of her devotee Mugan. The three *pucaris* who were present (all of them were Harijan Vannans by caste, some from outside the Endavur Colony) played the *bambai* and *uDukkai* drums of the goddess, shook silver *silambu* rattles (ankle bracelets that are also part of Mariyamman's *shakti*), and sang songs of praise to Mariyamman. These songs stressed the goddess's power and her divine genealogy, and emphasized the inferiority and unworthiness of her worshipers. After some time, the Harijan Talaiyari Gengan (T_3) went stiff and fell to the ground, limbs twitching, seemingly entirely out of control. Everyone announced the Goddess's presence: the devotees shouted "Govinda! Govinda!" the *pucari* drums beat a loud steady beat, and the *parai* band, standing outside the "pure" area of the temple, beat an even louder drum roll. The thread-persons rushed around Gengan and restrained his spasmotic motions, which threatened to loosen entirely his

[11] See Whitehead 1921: 38 for an illustration of these pots, whose use is widespread in south Indian village ritual.

only garment, a waist-cloth. Eventually Gengan came under control, pulled himself from the ground, and moved around with a stiff-legged walk, eyes almost closed, inspecting the ritual preparations. Though he made a rhythmic whimpering noise, he said nothing, and the *pucaris* finally poured water on him to bring him out of his possession, declaring: "The goddess came, but she didn't give permission [for the festival to proceed]."

Goddess possession is always a difficult matter, for the goddess in this form is a "fierce figure" (*agora ruuBam*) whose human worshipers can never fully satisfy her. She always finds some fault with the preparations, and no matter how carefully the worshipers have prepared for her, they must negotiate with the goddess at this time to get her "permission." In this case, the *pucaris* sought the aid of Periyapalaiyattar and Mugan. They began again their songs of praise, Gengan became repossessed, Mugan became quickly and easily possessed by his more controlled goddess Periyapalaiyattar, and Periyapalaiyattar served as an intermediary between the worshipers and Mariyamman. At first the two goddesses simply agreed on the unworthiness of their worshipers:

Pucari TO MUGAN-AS-PERIYAPALAIYATTAR: "Is everything all right? We may have done tens of millions of wrongs (*pavums*)."

PERIYAPALAIYATTAR: "Ask my younger sister."

GENGAN-AS-MARIYAMMAN: "They haven't given what I asked."

PERIYAPALAIYATTAR: "Yes!"

MARIYAMMAN: "I am a god, you are a god, Maduraiviran is a god. They [the devotees] are children. They have called me and they have not given what I asked."

HARIJAN DEVOTEES: "What is wrong? Where have we failed?"

PERIYAPALAIYATTAR: "You people cannot satisfy me."

MARIYAMMAN: "It is impossible for you to satisfy me!"

257

Mugan-as-Periyapalaiyattar then whipped Gengan-as-Mari-yamman, saying that "whipping is food for Marriyamman," that it would help to satisfy her appetite. Finally the two goddesses told the worshipers that the *karagam* pots needed minor changes, and that the goddess required a second bloody sacrifice in addition to the chicken sacrifice already planned—that of a goat. These demands the worshipers agreed to, and the goddess finally gave her "permission."

With the goddess's permission, the third part of the first movement of the festival commences: the procession of the lower form of Mariyamman into the Colony, to her temple. On the year in which we observed, Gengan grew calmer after the goddess's permission, though he remained possessed. He put one *karagam* pot on his head, reeling under its weight as though it were tremendously heavy, and started walking toward the temple. The other two pots, variously said to represent other forms of the goddess, or male guardian gods, were picked up by Mugan (still possessed by Periyapalaiyattar) and Sami, the Vettiyan headman (V_{31}), who had become possessed by the goddess *DanDumaari*, who was not identified in any other context, but might have been Sami's *ista devam*. Earlier, during Mariyamman's initial invocation, a young Pannaikkar boy had become possessed by his *kula devam*, a goddess. The *pucaris* had carefully ascertained the identity of this goddess, and had politely asked her to leave, saying that she was not wanted at this time—which she did. That all these goddesses come at the same time is evidence of their fundamental oneness; they are simultaneously the same being, and slightly different forms of the same being, with slightly different attributes and personalities. Their multiplicity gives the worshipers a number of different channels to the same fundamental sort of power.

The three *karagam* pots, carried by the three possessed men, were then lead in procession to the Mariyamman temple at the center of the Colony. In the procession, the *parai* band came first, followed by two thread-persons carrying a firestick and a trident (another weapon of Mariyamman's), followed by the *pucaris* still singing their songs of praise to the goddess, followed by the three *karagam* carriers. This order is identical to that of goddess processions in other festivals: the inauspicious *parai* band leads the way, to mediate downward against demons attracted by bloody offerings to the goddess, and the auspicious band follows, closer to the ritual focus. Here the *pucaris* replicate (and conflate) the role of the *uur pucaris* and the roles of the *uur* barber band in goddess festivals among the higher castes. When the procession crossed the boundary of the old Colony, the *pucaris* sacrificed a lime, said to represent "a life," quartered it and threw it to the four directions, probably as a propitiation of the *peeys*. The procession then circumambulated the stone to the Vettiyans' lineage god Kudiraikaran, and finally arrived at the main Mariyamman temple, which it circumambulated three times (all these circumambulations were in the auspicious direction, clockwise) preparatory to the entrance of the goddess into the temple.

At this point in the festival, the two forms of the goddess had come together. The low, angry form that Gengan incarnated entered the temple to inspect the ritual preparations made for the higher image of the goddess, vegetarian offerings called *paDiyaaL*, prepared under the supervision of the Valluvar *purohit*. Gengan emerged after some commotion, shouting angrily that the *paDiyaaL* was not correct, and the Harijan onlookers abused the Valluvar freely: "the Valluvar has no sense; he is a son of a dog." In other contexts on this day, abusive language was not tolerated, particularly in children: "how dare you use language like that on this day?!" But here, as usual, the Valluvar *purohit* received no visible respect from the Harijans. Gengan-as-Mariyamman was in this case again pacified by the *pucaris*, a minor adjustment was made of the vegetarian offerings, and the goddess gave her final verbal "permission" for the festival to proceed.

Finally, the goat sacrifice promised to the goddess at the wellside was made to her, in front of the temple. For this

259

event, the two aspects of the goddess had to be clearly bifurcated; a white cloth was held up between the sacrificial
spot and the inner image of the goddess, shielding both the
higher form of the goddess and the Valluvar *purohit* from
the sight of the blood. On the other side of the cloth, the
lower *pucaris* officiated while the possessed forms of the
goddess looked on. A Harijan Vannan *pucari*, assisted by
thread-persons, sawed rather slowly at the neck of a live
goat with a dull *vaaLaayaDam* knife, drawing the angry
comment from Sami-as-Dandumaari: "Do it correctly!"
When the goat was killed, its body was dragged off for a later
offering, the head of the goat was left in front of the temple,
and the white cloth was dropped, for the blood had soaked
into the ground, and it was no longer visible to the goddess.
The meat from the goat sacrifice was not offered in puja to
the goddess until evening; at this time, it was said, she received the "life" (*uyir*) of the animal.

The second and third movements of the main day of the
goddess festival are far less complex than these initial invo-
cations and permissions. The later movements consist of two
processions of the goddess through the territory that she protects, the Colony (the goddess should in fact have made
three such movements, for only odd numbers are auspicious in
ritual contexts). The bifurcation of Mariyamman's character
is maintained in these processions. First, immediately after
the goat sacrifice in front of the temple, the goddess moves
through the Colony in her low, possessable form. With the
pucaris in attendance, the *karagam* carriers go from household to household, and the goddess receives puja from each
family. At this time, she receives both vegetarian offerings
and bloody sacrifice; in the latter, as at the temple, she takes
the "life" of the animal, while the family keeps the body as
"leftovers" to be offered again later. These bloody sacrifices
are in repayment of vows (*piratanais*) made by family members during the past year. A person might promise the goddess a "life" at her next festival if she spares a life in the
family, usually that of a child or a cow. Now is the time to

repay this life, on the basis of strict reciprocity ("a life [*uyir*] for a life"), or risk the goddess's wrath. Three such family sacrifices were made during the festival we observed: one more goat, and two chickens. During this procession, the men carrying the *karagam* pots were mostly unpossessed, but if any woman in the Colony was now "caught" by *peey* and "danced before the pots," Mugan would again be possessed by Mariyamman, and the goddess would drive out the demons, in the manner of Periyapalaiyattar's exorcism in Mugan's *kuṛi meedai* cult. The procession of the *karagam* pots does not mark grade precedence within the Colony (the Talaiyaris are not visited ahead of the Pannaikkars and the Vettiyans) but it does mark caste precedence; it begins with the Harijan families, moves on to the two Harijan Vannan families, and ends with the three Chakkiliyan families at the far side of the new Colony.

After the *karagam* procession has visited all the households of the Colony, the devotees return to the main temple, where the Valluvar *purohit* performs "noon puja" to the goddess. He formally offers to the goddess the vegetarian *paDiyaaL* as food. The goddess is believed to partake of this food, and what remains of it is then eaten by the goddess's worshipers as *prasadam*. By this act, the Harijans and the others demonstrate unambiguously their inferiority to the goddess, for eating any being's leftover food is an extremely lowering act in south Indian culture. Among humans, it is done only by Untouchables, who will take food leftovers from the households of the higher non-Untouchable castes (cf. Wadley 1975: 152-53; Babb 1975: 53-57). A key ingredient of the *paDiyaaL* offered to Mariyamman is *ragi* (finger millet), thought to be particularly cooling and thus efficacious against smallpox, which the goddess brings and takes away. In eating *ragi*, the goddess and the worshipers are thus both cooled and calmed, an appropriate transition to the next movement of the festival. At this time, extra *ragi* is also prepared and distributed "to the poor." This distribution replicates offerings at the village level, when servants and Untouchables are fed at the end of high-caste life-cycle rituals, kin-god rituals, and territorial-god rituals, to earn merit for the givers of the food. In the Colony, there are only the Untouchable devotees to be fed, though if the Kurivikarans are in the Colony on this particular day, they will happily play this lowering role and take cooked food from the devotees to the Colony Mariyamman.

The third and final movement of the main day of the Colony Mariyamman festival is the goddess's procession through the Colony in her high form, embodied in her movable image (*vikkaram*) carried in a temple car. Consistent with the higher nature of this form of the goddess, she is now accompanied by the Valluvar *purohit* who, as he did at the temple, mediates between the worshipers and this form of the goddess. The Harijan Vannan *pucaris* do not deal with this form of the goddess directly, though they do continue to play their replicatory role of "auspicious band," beating their *bambai* and *uDukkai* drums and singing their songs of praise near the goddess during her procession.

The car procession (*teru tiruviRaa*) begins in the late afternoon, after everyone has rested for three or four hours following "noon puja." The Valluvar *purohit* initiates the procession, returning to the main temple and, after a second ceremonial bathing (*abiiSegam*) of the immovable image, supervising the preparation of the movable image. This form of the goddess, a papier-mâché figure of her body and head together, is assembled under the ceremonial pavilion in front of the temple, dressed, and honored by being "shown the light" (*tiv artanai*). The goddess is now in this image, which is placed by the thread-persons in a small temple car (*teru*) that belongs to the Harijans of the Endavur Colony. That they should possess such a resource as a temple car is an index of the relative prosperity of the Endavur Harijans, though in the year we were in Endavur, the car had been the subject of conflict. For the village Acaris had been paid one hundred rupees to renovate it, and there was grumbling among the Harijans about the crudeness of their work, and about the honesty of the temple trustee Cinnapayyan's accounts on this matter.

An *uur* Acari came into the Colony at this point in the festival, to supervise the pulling of the car, for which he was given a new waist-cloth in payment. A member of the *uur* Pandaram caste also came at this time, decorated the car with flowers for a fee of five rupees, and left before the beginning of the procession. As noted above, the Acaris and the Pandarams are two *uur* castes who do not deny their ritual services to the Untouchables, and whose services thus need not be replicated among the Untouchables. One reason that these higher castes do not refuse their services to the Harijans is that they are not by these services implicated in particularly lowering transactions. To give flowers and carpentry in exchange for money and new clothes is not to be lowered much by the acceptance of impure substances from the Untouchables. Another reason that the Acaris and the Pandarams can enter an Untouchable festival at this point is that they are here serving the goddess more than the devotees, and the goddess is now present in a relatively high and pure form.

After the goddess's installation in her car and the decoration of the car, the Acari sacrifices the "life" of a white gourd (a *pushanikaay*, said to represent an elephant) to the car and the procession begins. The Valluvar *purohit* takes up a position on the car, just below the goddess to her right. His position exactly replicates that of Brahmin priests in the processions of divine beings among the higher castes, as does his general intermediacy between worshipers and "god" in its higher forms. In our year, antagonisms between the Harijans and the Valluvar *purohit* once more entered the picture at this point. The *purohit* claimed he was being underpaid, and said he would not ride in the car unless he was given two new waist-clothes, which he claimed were his "right" for this particular service. The Harijans pleaded that they had already spent too much money on the car, but they had to give in in order to obtain this essential service, and the *purohit* took up his correct position.

The car was then dragged through the Colony (first toward the *uur* side of the old Colony, then back into the new Colony), and as in the *karagam* procession, puja was offered to the goddess in the car, household by household. Here the offerings differed in an interesting way, however. While in the *karagam* procession, the lower form of the goddess was offered bloody sacrifice and "lives," now she was offered the cooked meat from the earlier sacrifices—cooked together with vegetarian *paDiyaaL* in a mixture called *kumbam*. This *kumbam* was shown to her on a banana leaf, and taken back by the family to be consumed as *prasadam*. A second set of purely vegetarian offerings was then made to this higher form of the goddess, and these the Valluvar *purohit* took on behalf of the goddess. He removed one or two betel nuts from each of these offerings, and returned the rest to the family, as more *prasadam*. At the end of the procession, the car was dragged back to the temple, where one last puja ("evening puja") was performed for the goddess in her immovable image. Here, meat *kumbam* from the goat killed after the goddess's "permission" earlier in the day was placed before the temple, and then taken one last time as inferiorizing *prasadam* by all the devotees who were present.

There was some disagreement about who was getting what here. The Harijans stated that this last meat offering was "for Mariyamman," as were the meat offerings to the temple car. The Valluvar *purohit* violently disagreed, saying that these offerings were "wages" (*kuli*) for the lower guardian god Munadiyan. He was thus implicitly stating that the high form of the goddess incarnated as a head alone, inside the temple, could not appropriately receive low offerings such as meat. A possible resolution to this dispute is to say that the *purohit* might have been correct for the temple image, while the Harijans were correct for the movable image in the car. For that second image, which consisted of both the head and the body of the goddess, might have represented the only being sufficiently intermediate in character to receive both vegetarian and meat offerings.

After the completion of evening puja, the *kapu* threads that had restrained the *shakti* of the goddess since the early morning were untied from the goddess, from her drums, and from the wrists of the thread-persons. Adumbrating this end of ritual restraint, the generally serious mood of the devotees during the day had been changing in the last stages of the car procession; many of the Harijans had begun drinking country liquor and their fear of the goddess's power seemed less salient than it did earlier, when she was present in her fiercer form. The *kuttu* drama now began, and continued all night in a field to the east of the old Colony. These dramas have a religious theme, but they are in no necessary way tied to the goddess festival that they follow. In this year, the drama was entitled "The fight of Siva and Kali, or Vinayagar's marriage." The parts were acted by Endavur Harijans, under the direction of an old Harijan who had had no particular role in the earlier festival. The spectators, of whom there were several hundred, were both Harijans and *uur* people, from Endavur and from nearby villages.

The period of the goddess's physical, incarnated presence in the Colony, and of her Untouchable devotees' transactions with her, was now almost over. On the morning of the day after this main festival day, the so-called "ninth day," the Harijans were supposed to conduct a third procession of the goddess through the Colony, the second car procession, called the "festival of turmeric water" (*mangaL niraaTTu viRaa*). This was to be a joyous occasion, when the Harijans further "cooled" the goddess by splashing her with turmeric water, and "playfully" splashed each other with the same. The Harijans did rather offhandedly so spray the car, which had been left beside the temple, and they then disassembled the movable image and stored it away in the temple rafters with no particular ceremony. There was no procession, however. Instead, most of the morning was spent in an unresolved dispute over the temple finances. A Vettiyan faction accused the Talaiyaris and the Pannaikkars of the Colony of insufficient interest in the Colony goddess, and of inadequate contributions to the festival; the Talaiyaris and the Pannaikkars replied that the Vettiyans and the temple trustee Cinnapayyan, in particular, had cheated on the accounts and kept some of the money for themselves.

Later in this day, Cinnapayyan and a few of his relatives conducted the final ritual act of the Colony Mariyamman festival, called "drowning the *karagam* pots." They took the three pots to a well outside the village (not to the same one where Mariyamman had been evoked), honored them one last time by "showing the light," and dove into the water with them. Here, they removed the *karagam* decorations under water; if these were left lying around in the fields, someone might unknowingly "do some impurity" to them and bring down the goddess's anger. With this final act, the goddess Mariyamman was entirely gone from the Colony, and definitively cooled. Though her high form would be evoked in the main temple from time to time during the next year, her total being would not return to the territory until her next annual festival.

To summarize the cultural logic of the Colony festival, the character of the goddess Mariyamman has followed a basically rising curve through the ritual sequence. Though she is present in the Colony in both forms from the time of her "permission," she is dealt with first in her low, fierce, impure form, mediated by the *pucaris*, and then later in her higher forms, mediated by the higher-ranking Valluvar *purohit*. In all these interactions, worshipers continually cool her and feed her—first impure foods appropriate to her lower form (blood and lives), later purer foods appropriate to her higher form (*paDiyaaL*). They also give her their devotion, demonstrating their inferiority to her by taking the "leftovers" both of her low and her high foods as *prasadam*. She is slowly transformed by these actions from a predominantly low, angry, and "hot" being into a higher, beneficent, and "cool"

266

being.[12] The purpose of her worship is to turn away the anger of the goddess's low form, and to attract the beneficence of her high form: to prevent her from bringing diseases and other "curses," to encourage her to give rain and her general "protection" to the Colony and to its inhabitants. Power and purity are constant themes in this ritual, and here the Harijans are as careful of their personal purity as is any higher-caste actor in a ritual context. For to be in a state of impurity when this goddess's *shakti* is present in the Colony is to risk bringing down her wrath on the Colony.[13]

The forms of social-structural replication in the Untouchables' worship to the exclusive territorial goddess Mariyamman have been amply noted above. The key replicatory structure among the Untouchables is found in the relation of the Valluvar *purohit*, the devotees, and the Harijan Vannan *pucaris*, which is isomorphic with the relation between the Brahmin priest, the devotees, and the *pucari* and barber castes in the higher-caste cult to the *uur* Mariyamman. The Harijan Vannans not only mediate downward with the lower form of the goddess, as do the *uur pucaris*; they also replicate the role of the auspicious barber band in the *uur* festival, though they cannot play the music of the barber band. This, then, is a second replicatory response to the barber band's

[12] See Beck 1969b for a systematic analysis of the pervasive categories "hot" and "cold" in south Indian village ritual.

[13] These data are too thin on the *uur* castes of Endavur to prove that the conceptual structure found in Harijan worship is identical to that found in higher-caste worship in Endavur. One reason for indulging in this much description here is to allow others with some knowledge of south Indian village representations to form their own opinion on possible identities, and to facilitate future comparative work on the issue. Near identity seems likely here, however. For these representations are remarkably similar to those found among higher castes in other parts of Tamilnadu (see especially Dumont 1957a, Beck 1968, and Beck 1969a). Furthermore, the Harijan data from Endavur are also remarkably amenable to an analysis worked out by Susan Wadley among high castes in north India, suggesting that what the Harijans are in consensus with here is not simply a Tamil pattern, but a deep, all-India pattern.

nonperformance for the Harijans, in addition to the code-switching by the *parai* band discussed above. Other lowering functions in the Colony Mariyamman festival are performed mostly by the lowest grade within the Harijan caste, by the Harijan Vettiyans—once again a replicatory response to exclusion in which the code of rank is switched from "caste" to "grade." The entire set of replicatory roles between the *uur* Mariyamman cult and the Colony Mariyamman cult is summarized in Table 6-1.

The result of the Untouchables' exclusion from the higher-caste cult to the goddess Mariyamman is thus, once again, structural replication and probable cultural identity. "Religion" is often seen anthropologically as the core of a people's cultural consciousness, and those who wish to demonstrate that the consciouness of south Indian Untouchables differs from that of the higher castes often point to the absence among Untouchables of some putatively fundamental "religious" concept such as *karma* (e.g., Gough 1960: 54). The Untouchables of Endavur do not in fact place much stock in *karma*, but neither is *karma* a particularly central religious concept among most higher castes in Tamilnadu. What *is* religiously central for members of all castes in Endavur is "god" and its appropriate worship. These matters of divine beings are central even for those Untouchables who are most critical of the system. Witness the Talaiyari schoolteacher Ram, who would like to renounce caste and to embrace Buddhism, but cannot because "we must have a god" and only the Hindu gods are available (cf. p. 168 above). Therefore Ram, like all other Untouchables in the Endavur Colony, worships orthodox Hindu gods in an orthodox way.

We have demonstrated this religious orthodoxy with respect to the most critical type of worship in a social-structural sense, that of a deity whose cult excludes the Untouchables by definition, the hamlet territorial goddess Mariyamman. Let us now move to the last level of worship and to the last divine being to be treated here, to the village goddess

TABLE 6-1. Comparative Ritual Roles, *Uur* and Colony Mariyamman
Festivals Compared

Role	Social identity of performer, uur	Social identity of performer, Colony
Purohit	Brahmin (also called *gurukkal*)	Valluvar Pandaram
Command of the festival, dominance	Reddiyar zamindars	Harijan headmen
Devotees (*bhaktas*)	All *uur* castes, down to Villis	Harijans, Harijan Vannans, Chakkiliyans
God-dancers (*saamiyaaDis*)	Any devotee "liked" by the goddess, here a Chettiyar	Any devotee "liked" by the goddess, here the Harijan Talaiyari Gengen
Temple trustee	A Chettiyar acts as festival "contractor"	Any trustworthy devotee, here the Harijan Vettiyan Cinnapayyan
(Artisan, command of the temple car)	(*Uur* Acari)	(*Uur* Acari)
(Florist, decoration of the goddess)	(*Uur* Pandaram)	(*Uur* Pandaram)
Pucari	Vettaikaran (in other *uur*s: Pandaram, Occan, Tambiran)	Harijan Vannan
Auspicious band	Ambattan	Harijan Vannan
"Announcer"	Harijan	Harijan, Pannaikkar grade
Parai band	Harijan	Harijan, Vettiyan grade
Nondevotees, fed as "the poor"	Harijans and other Untouchables	Kurivikarans

269

Selliyamman, whose cult includes in a common body of worshipers members of all the castes of Endavur, Untouchables and non-Untouchables alike.

THE VILLAGE GOD: THE INCLUSIVE GODDESS SELLIYAMMAN

The goddess of the village or *kiraamam*, Selliyamman, is worshiped in a yearly festival conducted by members of all the residential castes of Endavur, Brahmin through Chakkiliyan. It is not known if the Kurivikarans are permitted to worship Selliyamman, but it is doubtful that they are: their claim to "territory" in Endavur is intermittent at best. The festival to Selliyamman must be conducted jointly; if the Untouchables and the higher castes cannot agree on its timing and its finances, it cannot be held. The Untouchables and the Harijans in particular have two general roles in the worship of Selliyamman. First, they are her coequal worshipers, and the necessity for them in her worship is acted out in an explicit ritual of integration that comes before the processions of the goddess: Colony and *uur* play the roles of the groom's family and the bride's family, respectively, in a marriage of the goddess to a form of Siva. But the Harijans are also the last among Selliyamman's coequal worshipers, inferiorized to the higher castes in the ritual by a series of separations in space and time. The Harijans must stand further from the goddess's main temple than *uur* caste persons in the marriage of the goddess. They are treated as inferior beings by members of the higher castes during worship (addressed with nonhonorific verb forms, for example). In her car processions, the goddess Selliyamman comes last to the Colony, after moving through all the streets of the *uur*, and she does not actually enter the Colony; she stays just outside its boundary stone, and the Harijans come out to her for their household puja.

The second role of the Harijans in the worship of Selliyamman is consistent with their last-among-equals position as her worshipers: they are intermediaries downward in the worship of Selliyamman, intermediaries on behalf of other, higher humans and on behalf of the goddess herself. As ever, they mediate with the lowermost *peey*, the bloodthirsty maleficent beings who live (in this ritual context) mostly outside the village boundaries and who are attracted to the bloody sacrifices made to Selliyamman. Here, the Harijans' relation to this goddess becomes complex and polyvocal. The Harijans are simultaneously watchmen for the goddess, standing precisely in the position of the low male guardian gods Munadiyan and Kudiraikaran, between her and the lowermost demons; and they are "like" the goddess, performing for the village the same function that she provides for the village: guarding its boundaries at night. The Harijans and the goddess Selliyamman are linked together by a complex set of metaphors of protection, summed up in the term *tai* or "mother." The Harijans are the goddess's "mother's house" (*tai viiDu*) in her marriage, and they once protected her "like a mother." Both the goddess and the Harijans guard the village, as a mother guards her children; they are both therefore *tai* to the *uur*. And the goddess has in the past guarded the Harijans like a mother; she has been *tai* to them.

The result of these metaphors is a special closeness between the goddess Selliyamman and the Harijans, one not detectable in the case of the comparably low goddess Mariyamman. The importance of one of her functions in the village, guardianship, represents the importance of one of the Harijans' *toRils*, village watchmanship. The Harijans thus take a kind of pride in the festival to Selliyamman that the *uur* castes do not. Which is not to say that the Harijans have differential access to this goddess's power, or that the worship of Selliyamman constitutes a holi-like ritual of inversion in which the Harijans become for a day superior to the higher castes (cf. Marriott 1966). For the *uur* castes of Endavur have the same access to the powers of the goddess Selliyamman as do the Untouchables, and the higher castes keep the Untouchables very much in place during her worship. The point is only one of emotional emphasis or ethos: one has the

271

HARIJAN RELIGION

impression that the Harijans go through the worship of Selliyamman enthusiastically and proudly, while the higher castes
worship this goddess more as a matter of necessary routine.
Selliyamman is said to be one of the many forms of Mariyamman, the "goddess who changes." She thus has the same
general powers and the same general character as Mariyamman, but the emphases of her power and nature are different.
Both goddesses control rain, disease, and fertility for the
beings within the territories they protect, and both protect
the boundaries of these territories against evil things such as
peeys. Mariyamman, however, is in Endavur more specifically associated with the control of disease, while Selliyamman
is the being immediately responsible for rain, for the fertility
of the fields, and for boundary guardianship.[14] Selliyamman
also has a lower nature and a lower rank relative to her
worshipers than does Mariyamman. She is thought to be an
angrier being than Mariyamman, one whose power grows at
night, one who *must* stay in her temple in the fields most of
the time, for the sounds of domestic activity "enrage her."
Most respondents in Endavur said that Selliyamman had
no separate origin story, that she was simply a form of Mariyamman.[15] The Harijan Pannaikkar elder Velagiri did, however, eventually tell a little-known story of Selliyamman's
origin, one that hints at her low character and at her special
ties to the Harijans:

M₉ *The Story of Selliyamman*

Once Siva became angry with Parvati for some reason, and
cursed her and sent her away. She came to earth in three

[14] This duality corresponds rather exactly to one summed up in a
different, female-male pair in a village in Madurai—there a duality
between the goddess Mariyamman and the god Aiyanar. See Dumont
1959.

[15] A suggestion of mine that this goddess might be the result of
the unused bodily parts in Mariyamman's origin myth—the Chakkiliyan head on the Brahmin body—was roundly denied by all.
"That's *not* the story," I was told. Such is the story, however, in parts
of Andhra. See Whitehead 1921: 116.

272

forms—Selliyamman, Pungoliyamman, and Villiyamman. Selliyamman founded a kingdom and began to rule over it. One day a demon came and performed a thousand human sacrifices to Selliyamman, and asked her for three boons. Selliyamman said she would grant them, with a condition. The demon asked for everlasting life, for a body that could not be consumed by fire, and for property that could not be diminished. He also asked for Selliyamman's weapons, her whip, her *bambai* drum, her flag, and her trident. The goddess said she would give the demon all these things if he would first sacrifice to her a woman pregnant with her first child, thinking that no woman would agree to such a thing.

After searching everywhere for such a woman, the demon convinced his own wife, pregnant with her first child, to be so sacrificed. Selliyamman then had to give the demon his boons, and had to give him her weapons. She was now without power, without her *shakti*. The demon took over Selliyamman's kingdom, and out of vengence for the loss of his wife, he made Selliyamman his slave (*adimai*), forcing her to do low domestic tasks and field labor. Selliyamman called on her son Virabatra, her brother Vishnu, and her husband Siva to defeat the demon, but none of them could. Finally the trickster Narada came, studied the situation, and said that only Lakshmi could do anything about it. So Vishnu took the form of Lakshmi, and the demon was attracted to her. Lakshmi asked him for the weapons he had gotten from Selliyamman, and he gave them to her. Lakshmi was then able to kill the demon, and to return Selliyamman to her kingdom.

During the time of her slavery to the demon, Selliyamman had done all the unpleasant tasks in the village, so the villagers were grateful to her and worshiped her thereafter.

The story of Selliyamman is mostly divine genealogy, relating her both to the higher gods and the lower demons. Note the nonsymbolic quality of the story; her weapons do not simply stand for her power or *shakti*, they are her *shakti*. To lose them is to lose power, to regain them is to regain power.

As far as the Harijans go, the story states an identity between Selliyamman and themselves. For in the time of her subjugation to the demon, she acted toward the demon as Untouchables now act toward higher castes—as a "slave" or *adimai* who did all the low things of the village. Implicitly, then, by worshiping the goddess for these services, the villagers must therefore also be honoring the Harijans. Higher-caste persons in Endavur do not actually state the meaning of Selliyamman's worship in these terms, but they are aware of a special relationship between the goddess and the Harijans. "Once," they will say, "she lived in the Colony," or "she was born in the Colony, though she herself was not a Harijan." The Harijans, however, are much more explicit about their protection of the goddess, of their mother-like *tai* relationship with her. The Harijan Veligiri, when asked to explain the Harijans' role of "mother's house" (*tai viiDu*) in the marriage of the goddess, added an appendix to the story of Mariyamman: "When the demon had his power, he turned the elephants, horses, camels, and the army of Selliyamman to stone. But he didn't think about the poor Colony people, who took Selliyamman in, fed her, and cared for her. Only because of their care did she stay alive. Therefore they are 'mother's house' to her."

And, according to the Harijans, the goddess Selliyamman has reciprocated by protecting them, as is indicated in the following story:

M₁₀ *Selliyamman and the Stolen Cow*

Once a Harijan stole a cow, killed it in front of Selliyamman's temple, cut off its head, and began to eat its flesh. Then the cow's owners came in search of the animal, and the Harijan was frightened; his wrong (*tapu*) would become known. So he took the cow's head into the temple, covered it with a basket, and prayed to the goddess, "if you are a real goddess, if you have *shakti*, change this into the head of a deer." When the cow's owners entered the temple and lifted the basket, all they saw was a deer's head, and the Harijan was saved.

The "wrong" in this story is not beefeating, according to Harijan interpretations, nor apparently is Selliyamman offended by the killing of a cow before her temple. The wrong is the theft of the cow, and Selliyamman here demonstrates her power and her special protection of the Harijan by destroying the evidence of his wrong.

The goddess Selliyamman and the Harijans have thus mutually protected one another as *tai*. And both finally protect the village like a mother, as was explained by a high caste Chettiyar in interpreting the meaning of the term "mother's house": "Why are the Harijans *tai viiDu*? Selliyamman looks after the village like a mother. The Harijan Vettiyan also looks after the village. Therefore, the Vettiyans are doing Selliyamman's part for the village. Selliyamman is mother of the Vettiyans."

The relative lowness of the goddess Selliyamman compared to Mariyamman may be linked to her partial identification with the Harijans: a divine being who is in any way like a Harijan cannot be very high. Her ferocity and her lowness are suggested by stories M_9 and M_{10}, by the human and cow sacrifices to her that she mythically permits (she does not receive beef sacrifice at present, however). She has other half-forgotten stories of ferocity. In one, she is said to have killed a woman bangle-seller. In another, she dances with a garland of human intestines wrapped around her neck. Her lowness is also reflected in her devotees' treatment of her: the devotion they pay to her is not as regular or reliable as that which they pay to Mariyamman, and they interact with her possessed form much less respectfully than they do with Mariyamman's possessed form.

The ritual sequence to the goddess Selliyamman is basically identical to that to Mariyamman. In her yearly festival, she is evoked in the fields and in her temple in the village, she gives her "permission," and she is processed three times through the territory that she protects. Like Mariyamman, she has a dual character, and this character is similarly mediated by a dual set of specialists: a Brahmin *purohit* mediating with the high form, an *uur pucari* mediating with the lower form. There are two important differences in her worship, however. Her transformation from a low being to a high being during worship is accomplished by her marriage, at which time she literally becomes "Parvati." Yet consistent with her generally lower nature and with the fact that her power "grows at night," most of the key events in her worship—her possession, her marriage, and her first procession through the village—are conducted after nightfall. Due to the basic similarities between the Selliyamman festival and the Mariyamman festival, we will not describe Selliyamman's ritual sequence in the same detail as we did for the Colony Mariyamman, but will rather focus on the two events in which her character and the Harijans' relations to her become clear: on her possession in the fields, and on her "marriage."

In Endavur, the Selliyamman festival (*tiruviRaa*) is supposed to be held annually, during the same generally hot, rainless, workless period in which the Mariyamman festivals are conducted. On the year we were in Endavur, however, for reasons that were never entirely clear, the *uur* people and the Untouchables did not bother to hold the festival during this period, perhaps out of pure lethargy, perhaps because the rains had been reliable for the past four or five years and the villagers did not feel it was necessary to worship the divine being who most specifically controlled rain. By September of the same year, however, they decided they had made a mistake, for the localized thundershowers typical of late summer in Tamilnadu had brought rain to most of the villages around Endavur, but Endavur itself had remained almost entirely dry. So the villagers agreed to hold a reduced festival for Selliyamman, one with a *karagam* pot but no car processions, one that would cost about one-third as much as the goddess's full ritual. The goddess was not pleased with the lateness or the cheapness of her ritual, as became clear during her possession in the fields.

The possession of Selliyamman followed the same format as that of Mariyamman. A group of devotees (here after dark) went to the goddess's stone in the fields near the village boundary, purified the stone and cooled it, drew *shakti* out of a well into the *karagam* pots, and began singing the songs of praise that bring the goddess down on a devotee. The devotees numbered from fifty to a hundred persons, depending on the time—men and boys only, *uur* people and Harijans (mostly Vettiyans by grade). The higher castes and the Untouchables stayed strictly separate—the higher castes in a line to the right of the proceedings, the Harijans in a line to the left. The *pucaris* here were of the low *uur* caste that does *pucari toRil* for all but Untouchables, the Vettaikarans. The *saamiyaaDi* to Selliyamman was a Kavundar. The possession of Selliyamman differed from that of the dozen or so other goddess possessions we witnessed in two ways consonant with this goddess's lowness and with her particular grievances on this year: her devotees were unusually disrespectful of her, and she herself was unusually difficult with them. The following partial text gives a sense of the difficult negotiations with Selliyamman on this year.

After an especially long "description" of the goddess by the *pucaris*, Selliyamman finally "came down" on her *saamiyaaDi*, and caused him to writhe incoherently on the ground for a considerable time. Eventually he came under a kind of control, and an *uur* person addressed the goddess nonhonorifically:

Uur MAN₁: "Who are you?" ["you" = *nii*, used for intimates, children, and inferiors].

KAVUNDAR-AS-THE-GODDESS: "The village goddess, sir, Selliyamman" ["sir" = *appa*, here a term of respect].

Uur MAN₁: "What, will you only come after taking blood

277

from some body? ! " [the reference is apparently to what the goddess is doing to the body of the man she is possessing].

The goddess did not reply further to this verbal harassing, and there was an acrimonious discussion among the devotees, with *uur* people taking the lead, as to whether the *pucari* should continue singing and playing his *uDukkai* drum. The Vettaikaran *pucari* did continue, and he tried addressing the goddess more respectfully:

> *Pucari*: "Mother, please do not delay us anymore. Give us your testimony. What are you going to tell us? ["you" = *ningal*, the second-person honorific]. Will the cattle prosper? Will the good rain come? Please tell us whether these things will happen. Even if they will not happen, please tell us."

The *pucari*'s conciliatory approach failed, and another *uur* man cut in with a different interpretation of the goddess's obligations to her devotees:

> *Uur* MAN₂: "What is this about whether it will rain or not? We have come here in order that it rain, not to ask you whether or not it will rain."

The *uur* Vettiyan then spoke up, the only Harijan to speak at this possession. He told the goddess in a respectful tone that all the people of the village were present (a considerable exaggeration), and he pleaded with her to help him in his work as regulator of the water in the irrigation tank, by bringing rain. This also brought no response, and other persons continued alternately to plead with and to abuse the goddess. They questioned her on what "faults" there were in the ritual preparations, with no reply. Finally the goddess did say something through her *saamiyaaDi*, alluding to the obvious "fault" of the lateness and the irregularity of her worship:

> KAVUNDAR-AS-THE-GODDESS: "Why have you come only now?" [that is, four months late].

Uur MAN₂: "Because there was no rain. . . . Because we are hungry. What else can we do?"

GODDESS: "You only worship me when you need me. You do not come when you should."

Pucari: "That is not so great a fault. Are you worried about your car festival [being omitted this year]? We will do that properly for you next year. Since you have come here now, give us your word."

This line produced no reply from the goddess. The villagers then attempted to bargain with her, pointing out that she was as dependent on them as they were on her:

Uur MAN₂: "If all of us die . . . if all of us are well off, only then can you be well off [that is, from offerings]."

Pucari: "If there is no rain . . . if there is nothing in this village, then nobody will light even a quarter-anna light for you. If not even drinking water exists, who will bother to spend a quarter-anna?"

Uur MAN: "Come on! Speak quickly!"

Finally, the goddess shouted: "Listen!" That was all she said. The devotees decided that she was telling them to switch media, to get her "permission" not from the lips of the *saamiyaaDi* but from the auspicious cry of a lizard. If the cry came from the north, it would be a good sign and would amount to permission for the festival to proceed; if it came from the south, it would be a bad sign. Immediately, a man standing on the bank of the irrigation tank, fifty feet away, called out: "somewhere there, [the lizard] gave permission." An *uur* man objected that the cry had to be heard by all, and the devotees returned to their abuse of the goddess, calling her at one time "widow," an exceedingly abusive epithet. After some time, the Kavundar-as-the-goddess said what proved to be his last words as the goddess: "Let two weeks pass." The devotees chose to let this mean "let two weeks pass and it will rain," rather than "let two weeks pass before starting the festival." But they had still received no "per-

279

mission." After perhaps another half hour of singing and arguing (the whole event, which generally takes a half hour, here took about an hour and a half), someone else gave the cry "Govinda!"—usually the mark of the goddess's possession, here an indication that the auspicious cry of the lizard had again been heard. This time, with everyone's tempers running out, there was no objection that the cry had not been heard by all. By consensus of the devotees, the goddess's "permission" had been given, and the procession of the possessed form of the goddess to her temple in the village (just inside the *uur* boundaries, in the northwest corner) commenced.

In this initial interaction with the goddess, the Harijans were present as essential devotees, but they gave precedence to people of the *uur* in dealing with the goddess. Though the one Harijan who did speak up was respectful of the goddess, most of the Harijans shared the basic attitude of the villagers toward Selliyamman—that they were here dealing with a particularly low divine being. As they said after the possession, it was entirely appropriate to bully such a being if she was proving difficult. Nor was it a good idea to show fear of this goddess, for it was her nature to take advantage of fear. "We had to show her," said one Harijan, "that we are men, not bullocks." In this ritual context, the Harijans thus share with the higher castes a denigratory attitude toward a being who is in many ways identified with themselves. Her lowness is as manifest to them as it is to the higher castes, and hence by implication, so is their own lowness.

There is a problem of cultural logic in the worship of a divine being as low as Selliyamman, however. Most humans, regardless of their own caste standing, are unwilling to demonstrate their inferiority to such a being by taking the leftovers of her food offerings as *prasadam*. Yet Selliyamman does protect the village, and she must be brought into it as an honored deity if her protection is to extend to the territory and to its inhabitants for another year. The villagers of Endavur, and of surrounding villages, respond to this implicit problem in a neat way. Before they move the goddess through the village, they transform the low being Selliyamman back into the high being Parvati, by remarrying her to the god Siva. She is then for the period of her presence in the village a high and beneficent being, one to whom it is appropriate to demonstrate subordination, one whom it is safe to have as a presence in the village living areas.[16] In terms of the divine hierarchy of Endavur, the villagers are here using a higher divine being as an intermediary to a lower divine being, working through Parvati so as to influence Selliyamman. Selliyamman-as-Parvati still partakes of some of Selliyamman's identity, however, and after her processions, she returns to her temple in the fields, and to her "angry" unmarried state for another year (cf. Beck 1969a and Babb 1975: 222-25).

In the marriage of the goddess Selliyamman, the Harijans or "the Colony" play the role of the groom's family, bringing to the marriage "donations" (*varasai*) appropriate to this role: a sari, a comb, a mirror, flower garlands, fruits and sweets, and most important, a marriage necklace or *tali*, the distinctive feature of south Indian marriage. The Harijan *uur* Vettiyan and his wife are leading actors in this marriage of the goddess. The higher castes or "the *uur*" play the complementary role of bride's family in the marriage. The Harijans' position in the marriage is referred to as *tai viiDu*, "mother's house," and the *uur*'s is called *maamiyaar viiDu*, "mother's brother's wife's house" or "female *mamaan*'s house." These

[16] It is possible that Mariyamman was similarly married just before her procession in the Colony and in the *uur*, and that we missed the action. One hint of this is that the Harijan Vannans in the Colony are said to be *tai viiDu* or "mother's house" to the Colony Mariyamman. In the Selliyamman festival, this term marks the Harijans' role as groom's family in the marriage of the goddess. If a similar marriage does occur in the Colony Mariyamman festival, by the way, we have another relation of replication in which appropriate relative rank by caste is maintained: Harijan Vannans are to Harijans (in the Colony Mariyamman festival) as Harijans are to *uur* castes (in the village Selliyamman festival).

terms are obscure in strict genealogical terms, and it is not known if they apply to the same sides in human marriages in Endavur. Their only exegesis in Endavur is that noted above: from the metaphors of "motherlike" protection between Harijans comes the Harijans' role as "mother's house." There is no doubt about which side is which, however, for the "donations" that the Harijans bring to the marriage are those that the man's side brings to a marriage among humans —gifts for the bride.

Nor is there any doubt about who is marrying whom in this marriage. It is very important to be precise here, since marriage is perhaps the key symbolic marker of human integration and of divine integration in south Indian culture. Contrary to certain appearances, the Colony is not marrying the *uur*, nor is the *uur* Vettiyan marrying the goddess. Rather, the goddess is being remarried to the high god Siva, to transform her back into the high being Parvati. The marriage is in fact a double one: at the same time that the goddess is remarried to Parvati, the Harijan *uur* Vettiyan is remarried to his own wife. Let us examine this intriguing act, and the Harijans' role in it, in more detail.

We observed the marriage of Selliyamman not during her late and diminished festival in Endavur, but during her festival in the neighboring village of Morsapakkam, where the goddess was given a full-scale ritual at the correct time for her, here in late June. In Morsapakkam, *kapu* threads were tied on the goddess's temple image, on her "weapons," and on her thread-persons (*kapukarans*) eight days before the main day of the festival. She thus received the full period of worship, which the Harijans of Endavur had neglected to offer to the Colony Mariyamman. The thread-persons in the Morspakkam Selliyamman festival were all Harijans, and the most important among them was the *uur* Vettiyan. He had been "tied" for the same eight-day period as the goddess, and he had remained for this time in a chaste state, sequestered from his own wife in a small hut in front of Selliyamman's temple.

On the eighth night after the goddess's "tying" in her village temple, her fierce form was evoked at her temple in the fields by a range of her male devotees and by the *uur pucari* (here of the low but non-Untouchable Tambiran caste), and brought in procession to the main temple, where the *saamiyaaDi* gave the goddess's second "permission" for the festival to proceed. The procession then went off toward the *uur* boundary, where it met a separate procession of Harijan women, coming out of the Colony. There were seven of these women, all "chaste" married women, led by the wife of the *uur* Vettiyan, and they carried the Harijans' *varasai* donation for the goddess's wedding. These two processions combined and headed back for the Selliyamman temple, led by the Harijan *parai* band, followed by the auspicious band of the *uur* barber caste (which had joined the former procession after it had left the fields), followed by the *uur pucari*, followed by the seven Harijan women, followed by the rest of the devotees. They were met shortly by the five Harijan thread-persons, including the *uur* Vettiyan, who had just returned from a particularly dangerous task of mediation downward. For the thread-persons had gone (at night) to the four boundary-stones of the village and thrown bloody sacrifices across them to the *peeys* and *bhuts* who lived outside, to appease these beings and to prevent them from crossing the boundaries into the village. This sacrifice was said to have once consisted of a goat who was killed and quartered, but it was now replaced by a white pumpkin similarly quartered and mixed with blood-soaked rice. The thread-persons were called "sacrifice-doers" (*bolikarans*) at this point in the ritual, and they took up a position at the head of the procession. The sacrifice-doers now led the procession toward the temple, making wild, aggressive cries that represented their ferocity and their power against the demons. Country fireworks and the beat of the *parai* band completed the cacophonous effect, an effect intended to scare away the *peeys* and shield the goddess and her worshippers from sounds more inauspicious than the *parai* drums.

When this procession arrived at Selliyamman's main temple in the village, the devotees segregated themselves by caste category: *uur* persons formed two lines under the temporary ceremonial pavilion (*pandal*) attached to the temple, and the Harijan devotees stood at a greater distance, outside the pavilion, facing the central shrine (see Map 6-3). A Brahmin (Ayyar) *purohit* stood inside the inner shrine of the temple, to perform the marriage of the goddess. The *pucari* of the *uur* Tambiran caste ranged between the Brahmin and the devotees. In a line in front of the Harijan devotees, but still outside the pavilion, stood the seven Harijan women with their *varasai* donations. The *uur* Vettiyan took up a position next to his wife, who was the principle *varasai* carrier (it was she who carried the goddess's marriage *tali*), and the two marriages were quickly accomplished.

First, the goddess Selliyamman was married to the god Siva, accomplishing her temporary transformation into the higher goddess Parvati. The *pucari* made one last ritual reference to Selliyamman's basically low character, by sacrificing two white pumpkins (representing "lives") to the goddess and to her temple-car. The Harijan sacrifice-doers gave their wild cries during these sacrifices. Then the *pucari* took the goddess's marriage *tali* from the Harijan *uur* Vettiyan's wife and handed it to the Brahmin *purohit* inside the temple, who tied it around the goddess's neck while the auspicious band and the *parai* band both played from their respective positions inside and outside the pavilion. The goddess was now married; she was "Parvati," the bridegroom Siva being represented by an inconspicuous brass pot to the goddess's right. The second marriage was then accomplished by the *pucari*, who garlanded the Vettiyan's wife, tied a *kapu* thread on her right wrist, and handed the Vettiyan a second, crude marriage *tali*. While the goddess's *tali* had been a proper one with a metal ornament (kept by the Harijans between festivals, and reused every year), this one was a cord stained with turmeric powder, with a piece of turmeric root as an ornament. The Vettiyan tied this second *tali* around his wife's

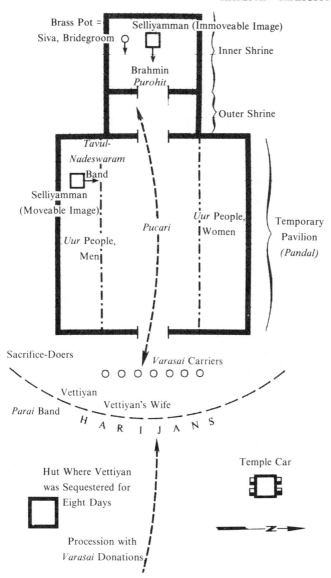

MAP 6-3. Selliyamman Temple at Morsapakkam during the Marriage of the Goddess

neck while the sacrifice-doers howled and the *parai* drum played (with no accompaniment from the auspicious band, however), and the Vettiyan's period of sexual abstinence and of nonmarriage was over; he was remarried to his own wife. Finally, the *pucari* took the sari, three bananas, and one mango from the remainder of the Harijans' *varasai* donations, and passed them to the goddess by way of the Brahmin *purohit*. The two marriages were now over, and the first procession of the goddess through the streets of the village (which lasted most of the night) began.

The marriages of the goddess and of the Vettiyan were quite clearly distinct and separate ritual actions, though they somehow depended on one another. The *pucari* differentiated the two in his actions toward them: toward the goddess and the Brahmin *purohit* he was deferential and respectful, while toward the Harijans he was abrupt and commanding. In one case, he was clearly working up, in the other, he was working down. The two marriages were also differentiated by distinct *talis* and by distinct forms of music. In each case, the goddess received more honor than the Vettiyan and his wife; the ornamental *tali* versus the crude *tali*, the auspicious band versus the inauspicious band. What are we to make of these two marriages, and what is the meaning of their nearly simultaneous occurrence?

The villagers of Endavur and of Morsapakkam, Harijan and non-Harijan alike, had little to say about the "meaning" of the marriages, other than that the goddess became Parvati by them, that they were somehow linked with the Harijans' position as *tai viiDu*, and that the Vettiyan was emphatically *not* marrying the goddess in them. It does not seem rash to give them the following interpretation, however. As watchman for the village, the Harijan *uur* Vettiyan is both "like" and "is" part of the goddess Selliyamman's power, which guards the village against demons and which grows at night. When the goddess is present in her temple in her unmarried form (during the eight preliminary days after the *kapu* threads have been tied), the Vettiyan must therefore be in a similar state: unmarried, chaste, devoted only to the goddess, serving her as do the low male gods Munadiyan and Kudirai-karan (the position of his hut outside the goddess's temple is very much like the position of these divine beings, the watch-man's position). The Vettiyans' role as sacrifice-doer against the *peey* demonstrates the fact that he is identified with that aspect of the goddess's power which mediates downward against the demons. According to this logic of partial identi-fication between goddess and Vettiyan, when the goddess changes her nature by her marriage, so too must the Vettiyan. When she becomes remarried to Siva, so too must he to his own wife. The two marriages do not bring these two figures together into a closer identification, however; rather, they separate them for a time. For after the marriages, the goddess is honored by the villagers not as a Vettiyan-like being, but as a higher, more generally protective being. Accordingly, in the subsequent car processions, the Vettiyan and the rest of the Harijans have no special relation to the goddess Selli-yamman. They are now only her devotees, worshiping her last in accordance with their low position among the total set of devotees (see Table 6-2 for a summary of high- and low-caste ritual roles in the Selliyamman festival).

If the two marriages do not integrate the Vettiyan and the goddess, however, they do integrate the Colony and the *uur*, the two parts of the village that are most clearly separate in other ritual contexts. For the Harijans are here essential actors in an essential act of marriage for the goddess. If the Harijans did not join with the *uur* castes to form the two "houses" necessary for Selliyamman's marriage, her *shakti* could not be carried through the village, and her protection would not extend to the territory for the next year.

Thus in their ritual relation to the inclusive territorial goddess Selliyamman, the Harijans are complementary rather than replicatory. As intermediaries downward and as "mother's house" in the marriage of the goddess, the Harijans complete a bipartite whole, one which is equally necessary for all in the village, one which is fundamentally incomplete

287

TABLE 6-2. High- and Low-Caste Ritual Roles in the Selliyamman Festival

Role	Role description	Social identity of performer
Purohit	Intermediary between devotees and high form of the goddess; performs goddess's marriage	Brahmin
Command of the festival	Common agreement of all *uur* castes and all Untouchable castes	All adult male devotees in the village
Devotees (*bhaktis*)	Worship of the goddess through offerings of food and devotion; recipients of the goddess's protection	Members of all residential castes of the village
God-dancer (*saamiyaaDi*)	Bodily incarnation of the goddess	Any devotee whom the goddess "likes"; in Endavur, a Kavundar
Pucari	Intermediary between the devotees and the goddess in her low, possessed form; intermediary between the Brahmin *purohit* and the Harijans	A member of a low *uur* caste; in Endavur, a Vettaikkar; in Morsapakkam, a Tambiran
Auspicious band	Playing of auspicious music near the goddess	*Uur* barber (Ambattan)
"Mother's brother's wife's house"	Bride's side in the marriage of the goddess	The *uur*
"Mother's house"	Groom's side in the marriage of the goddess	The Colony
Uur Vettiyan	"Like" the goddess in his protection of the village; "tied" to the goddess during her eight days	Harijan, Vettiyan grade
Varasai donation carriers	Representatives of Colony's role as "mother's house"	Harijan, "chaste" married women, including *uur* Vettiyan's wife
Parai band, sacrifice-doers	Guarding the ritual against lower *peey* and other inauspicious beings; intermediaries downward	Harijan, Vettiyan grade, including *uur* Vettiyan

without the Harijans. In their replicatory worship of the exclusive goddess Mariyamman, the Harijans did not have to take an inferior position to any human coworshipers who ranked above them, for there were none in that context of exclusion. In their worship of Selliyamman, on the other hand, the Harijans concede to act as lower beings whose actions will benefit both higher beings (the goddess and higher-caste devotees) and themselves. This concession has a factor of force behind it, for if the Harijans attempted to abandon their low roles in the worship of Selliyamman, the higher castes would react coercively. But, as with other issues of lowness, consensus, and coercion treated above, the Harijans would not be abandoning these roles because of disagreement with the cultural or conceptual system that defines them as low; they would be abandoning them because they themselves did not wish to act as low beings.

That the Harijans do agree with the postulates of the religious system, that they do consider the goddess Selliyamman as low a divine being as do the higher castes, is revealed by their actions during the possession of the goddess. For during the possession, the Harijans join with the higher castes in a bullying and abusive treatment of the goddess in her unmarried form. Yet at the same time, the Harijans take pride in their ties of "protection" with the goddess Selliyamman, for they share with her the function of village guardianship. When this goddess's function is honored by all the castes of the village as essential to the village's well-being, so too is theirs. And by playing their low complementary roles toward Selliyamman, the Harijans assure themselves of the protection of this goddess's *shakti*. Here again, as at the other social levels of worship, the Harijans are not cut off, due to their Untouchability, from a specific divine being or from a specific type of divine power. Here again, every fundamental entity, relationship, and action found in the religious system of the higher castes is also found in the religious system of the Untouchable Harijans.

CHAPTER VII

Conclusion: Consensus and Its Implications

THE present structural argument for pervasive cultural consensus among Indian Untouchables was set up, some chapters ago, in theoretical opposition to a set of "disjunctive
models" of Untouchables and caste. One set of these disjunctive models analyzed Untouchables as those at some distance from a single dominant high-caste culture (the outcaste image); another set saw them as possessors of alternate
cultural and social systems, whose characteristics were somehow controlled by the Untouchables' position at the bottom
of the Indian social order (the models of diversity). Both
sets tended to note and analyze only cultural differences between the high and low in caste, and to ignore (as self-evident, as unimportant, or as nonexistent) possibly concomi-
tant cultural continuities. These disjunctive approaches also
tended to see caste atomistically, as a set of self-contained,
bounded social units; and they tended to treat "culture"
either as an epiphenomenon of behavior, or as the most ac-
cessible features of informants' conscious statements about
caste and about their positions in caste.

The model being argued here takes a different theoretical
view of caste and culture. It views caste, following Dumont,
as a structure of meaningfully as well as functionally interdependent elements, as a structure to which disjunctive Untouchables would be a distinct embarrassment if they were indeed fundamentally disjunctive. And it views culture as a
complex, layered system of definitions, meanings, values, and
attitudes, some conscious and some tacit, some articulated
and some implicit in other articulated statements and in behavior. We are arguing, in common with Dumont and with
the ethnosociologists, that at the deeper levels of Indian vil-

290

lage culture so conceptualized, Untouchables and higher-caste actors hold virtually identical cultural constructs, that they are in nearly total conceptual and evaluative consensus with one another.

The structural paradigm employed here has revealed a few genuine disjunctions between the higher castes and the Untouchables of Endavur. Culturally and relationally, the five Untouchable castes of Endavur are excluded from four things: the Sanskritic ritualism of the Brahmin *purohit*, the auspicious music of the Ambattan barber band, and the services of lower-ranking barbers and midwives. The Untouchables are truly cut off from the first two, and they apparently do not have the resources to replicate among themselves the second two. For reason of these deletions, then, the Untouchable subsystem is slightly less complex than the higher caste system from which the Untouchables have been excluded. But while the Untouchable subsystem is slightly simplified around these relations, it is at the same time made more complex around the replicatory relation "Harijan to the Harijans." A single set of roles played in the *uur* by actors with a single salient identity, Harijan, is in the Colony played by a multiplicity of actors: by the Harijan Pannaikkar *varayan* announcer, by the Harijan Vettiyan,[1] and by the Chakkiliyans and the Kurivikarans. When these replicatory complexities are balanced against the deletionary simplifications, it is impossible to say that the Untouchable subsystem of ranked relations is specifiably more simple than the higher-caste system.

Nor do the deletions in themselves represent any real change in consciousness among the Untouchables of Endavur. The Harijans substitute for the first two as best they

---

[1] It is true that the Pannaikkar *varayan* and the Vettiyan also play their distinctive roles toward the *uur* castes, but the distinction between these two actors is not relevant relationally in the *uur*. From the point of view of the *uur*, a Harijan is a Harijan. The grade differences, and the division of the role "Harijan to the Harijans," become salient only within the Harijan caste.

can, with the Tamil ritualism of the Valluvar *purohit* on the one hand, and with the *pucari* band and the code-switching *parai* band on the other. The second two deletions the Harijans can do nothing about, except by developing the material resources to induce a few persons of a separate caste to begin serving them.

What of the other disjunctions predicted by the outcaste models and the models of diversity reviewed in Chapter I? Most of them are either entirely absent among the Endavur Untouchables, or must be reinterpreted with reference to cultural consensus as delineated above. Two of the deletions just mentioned amount to the sort of blocked communications that Cohn predicted systematically between non-Untouchables and Untouchables—the Brahmins' Sanskrit and the barbers' auspicious music. But each of these traits is blocked for very particular reasons: each is a uniquely complex skill whose esoteric knowledge *can* be protected. These specific blocks do not leave the Endavur Untouchables as the carriers of a distinctive little tradition, however, one that is more "Dravidian" and less "Aryan" than is found among the higher castes, for these Harijans share everything else with the higher castes, in a social and cultural system in which such possible historical disjunctions have long since become blended into a single conceptual whole.

The Harijans of Endavur are not, following Gough's and Berreman's outcaste images, in a state of cultural or psychological removal from the cognitive orientations of the higher castes. They not only share these orientations, but they appear to believe in them as strongly and unquestioningly as do those higher in the system. They may be cynical, but the focus of their cynicism is personal rather than social. Thus the Harijans delight in stories of how the Reddiyars actually manipulated their way to dominance in Endavur, and in stories of the Reddiyars' occasional political pratfalls. But they never question the right of certain actors to play such roles in the system. Likewise, the Harijans may be sceptical about the Valluvar *purohit* who serves them, but they are sceptical in terms of entirely orthodox ideas of proper religious action, and their skepticism does not challenge their need for ritual actors such as the Valluvar *purohit*.

The Harijans of Endavur may be materialistic, as suggested by Mencher. For they desire material prosperity and they see that others have achieved status in caste as a result of material gains. But this amounts only to an accurate perception of the workings of the system, and it is a perception also found at higher levels of the system. For throughout its range, high and low, between castes and within castes, the hierarchical system of Endavur does permit slow and micropolitically enacted tradeoffs between material gains and social rank. The system also sets limits on such tradeoffs, however. It requires that certain people be available to play certain distinct lowering roles, making Untouchables particularly unlikely to cross the dividing line between Untouchability and touchability. And it continually reproduces economic dominance in such a way that material success among the very low is strictly limited.

There may be in some of the theoretical statements of the Harijans Ram, Adimelem, and Velam the seeds of the sort of ideological revision that Berreman and Miller would have us anticipate among Untouchables. But these ideas are at present thin and inconsistent in the minds of those who articulate them, and they in no way control the behavior of these three men, for all are entirely orthodox socially and religiously.

A few of Gough's social distinctions appear to fit the Endavur data. Thus lineality and territorial organization are more developed among the high castes than among the Untouchables, and it is only among the higher castes that "double negative" property of marriage alliance (see p. 176) is overridden. Yet there is evidence that this particular disjunction does not appear distinctively at the dividing line between the Untouchables and the touchable castes in Endavur. Likewise, a close reading of Gough indicates that most of the non-Brahmin castes in her village approximate far more

293

CONCLUSION

closely the kinship patterns said to be found most "purely" among the Untouchables than they do the opposed patterns of the Brahmins (Gough 1956: 826-27).[2] This fact suggests that the diversity in Gough's data is found more clearly at the very top of the system, between the Brahmins (and, where they are a different caste, the dominant caste) and everyone else, and not near the bottom of the system, between the main village castes and the Untouchables. The reasons for this possible diversity at the top are not the subject here, though they are probably linked to the involuted ritual role of the Brahmins, to their ethnic distinctiveness, and to the political needs of village dominance. The same supposition might be directed at religious diversity, however. Thus belief in transmigration and *karma* doctrine, for example, may mark the Brahmins and their political allies off from everyone else, rather than uniquely marking all the main villages castes off from the disbelieving Untouchables.

As for other social disjunctions, the Untouchables of Endavur are not discernibly more egalitarian than the higher castes, a difference that Gough claims to find among the Pallans of Tanjore. To put the issue of rank among the Endavur Untouchables quantitatively, there exists in the Untouchable subset of the village a population of 109 households. This subset is divided vertically into five castes, consisting of 5, 98, 2, 3, and 1 households, respectively (the Valluvar Pandarams, the Harijans, the Harijan Vannans, the Chakkiliyans, and the Kurivikarans). The largest of these castes is in turn divided into three ranked strata of 11, 48, and 39 households (the Talaiyari, Pannaikkar, and Vet-

[2] Some excellent recent quantitative work by George H. Conklin suggests a uniformity of kinship beliefs and practices in a south Indian region more pervasive than that sketched by Gough. Working with a sample of 766 rural families and 382 urban families in northern Karnataka, Conklin finds that "caste" does not predict any statistically significant variations in the actual incidence of joint families, in "traditional" family practices (certain kin avoidances), or in stated preferences for the joint family, for a full range of castes including Brahmins and Untouchables (Conklin 1976).

294

tiyan grades), and the largest of the strata is internally divided in half by a ranked distinction (between "clean" and "dirty" Pannaikkars). There is no way that internal ranked differentiation of this degree can be said to reflect egalitarian values.[3]

Nor is there among the Endavur Harijans any of the political solidarity that Gough suggests is determined among Untouchables by low rank and material impoverishment. The Harijan headmen of Endavur do not have the tight authority over their caste's behavior that Gough found for Pallan headmen in Tanjore, and the five headmen rarely met as a united council. In poorer Colonies in the Endavur area, however, more authoritarian Harijan headmen were discovered. These leaders were rarely perceived by their own people as agents defending the interests of the Harijans as a whole; they were more often seen as agents of the higher castes, coopted by them to keep the Harijan caste in check.

Finally, Harijan religion in Endavur shows few of the disjunctions that Gough and others attribute to the changing functions of religion among the very low. Gough's Weberian "this-worldly/other-worldly" distinction has no indigenous significance in Endavur, but if for the purposes of argument we label the goddesses "this-worldly" (due to their specific powers) and the higher gods "other-worldly," it is still not possible to say, with Gough, that the Harijans are dif-

---

[3] Gough's own data contains hints of similar unanalyzed internal stratification patterns among the Untouchable Pallans of Tanjore. Her map of the Untouchable *ceeri*, for example, shows three Pallan "streets," internal divisions each with its own headman. The map also shows separate cremation grounds for each of the streets (Gough 1960: 19). Differential purity in life persists in death in Tamil culture; the three separate cremation grounds thus suggest ranked relations between Pallans of separate streets, relations analogous to those found between Harijan grades in the Endavur Colony. In the same vein, Gough does not comment on the relations between the main subcaste of Pallans in her village, the Devandra Pallans and a separate Pallan subcaste, the Tekkatti Pallans, who inhabit a separate smaller *ceeri* outside the main caste *uur*.

ferentially "this-worldly" in their religious orientation. For the Harijans have as much access to the other-worldly, higher gods as do the higher castes, and persons of all castes (with the possible exception of the Brahmins) seek benefit of the specific and pragmatic powers of the goddesses when necessary.

Nor is it the case among the Endavur Untouchables that "ascetic control of sexuality for its own sake does not increase a man's spiritual strength" (Gough 1956: 847). The *saamyaaDi* Mugan most regularly, the young Harijan thread-persons, and virtually all Harijans during the annual Colony goddess festival—all these persons increase their personal purity and their *shakti* prior to interacting with the goddess. Possession states are not peculiar to the Untouchables of Endavur, nor are they confined to the lower ranges of the caste hierarchy, for even Brahmins can become possessed (see Jha 1969). And if lower-caste persons sometimes become more violently possessed than higher-caste persons, this is not because there is a different notion of divinity among the low; it is because, as everyone agrees, lower and more violent divine beings are more likely to possess lower human beings.

Finally, it is true that, following Kolenda, *karma* doctrine is weak or absent among the Untouchables of Endavur, but there is no convincing evidence in holistic cultural descriptions of higher south Indian castes (Dubois 1959 [1815], Dumont 1957a, Barnett 1970, Beck 1972) that *karma* plays an ideologically central role at higher levels of the system in the south. *Karma* seems to be articulated more pervasively at the village level in north India than in south India; for a detailed example of a fully *karmaic* north Indian Untouchable, see Berreman's description of an Untouchable blacksmith who attributes his present low rank to bad actions in a past life (actions undertaken, as in the Paraiyan origin myth, with the best intentions) (Berreman 1972a: 222-23). In the south as in the north, however, the central religious fact is not *karma* but "god" and its appropriate worship.

Here the Endavur Harijans are at one with everyone else, as they are on the central social facts of caste, on rank and its legitimacy.

Kolenda, Gough, and the other disjunctive analysts of Untouchables are, of course, each analyzing a different Untouchable caste in a different part of India. Yet the ultimate determinants of "difference" in their analyses are so general (exclusion, psychology, material and political asymmetry) that the analyses should apply with equal force to Endavur. What then of the typicality of Endavur, and what of the generality of the structural analysis employed here? In a strict sense, the present analysis applies only to a single set of low castes in a single large multicaste village in the northern Tamil lowlands. But the broad outlines of the replicatory structures analyzed in Endavur were verified in villages up to twenty-five miles from Endavur, and the ethnographic literature contains many hints of similar replicatory unfoldings all over south India. In Parangudi, in the Pudukottai area, the same relations existed between Valluvar Pandaram, Harijan and Harijan Vannan, though there was not to my knowledge a set of grade distinctions within the much smaller local populations of the Harijan caste itself. Unfoldings as elaborate as the one found in Endavur undoubtedly require a certain critical mass of Untouchables of a single caste, a mass that in turn sets the preconditions for dominance within the Untouchable subset. If grade was not an important ranking principle among Untouchables in the Parangudi area, however, subcaste (relatively unimportant in Endavur) was more significant, for there were in close proximity to Parangudi a diverse set of separate Harijan (or Paraiyan) and Pallan subcastes. The details of intersubcaste ranking among these units were not determined in Parangudi, but it was clear that they represented further segmentations among the very low, that there were few signs of solidarity or equality of any sort between these units.

In general, the structural paradigm used here could be applied to rural Untouchable groups all over south India. The

297

replicatory structures within different Untouchable subsets in other parts of the south might have quite different contents (for instance, with different numbers of Untouchable castes and grades, and with different allocations of rank-enhancing and rank-lowering *toRils* between these castes and grades), but I suspect that in most areas the analysis would contribute to the same interpretation suggested here, to a "proof" of pervasive cultural consensus among the very low in caste. Equally importantly, this analytic strategy also contains "disproof." If, for example, we found a situation where the Untouchable population was sufficient for replication, and none occurred, or if the internal relations in this Untouchable population were either inversions of relations found higher in the system, or were quite new relations, then we would have strong structural evidence for cultural disjunction at the bottom of the system. No such case is known to this ethnographer, though in some purely theoretical social thinking, Adi-Dravida radicals have begun to revise, often by inverting, the meaning of such key symbols of Untouchability as beefeating (see Barnett and Barnett 1973).

The present analysis of cultural consensus among the very low castes of Endavur is compatible with Dumont's assumption of ideological homogeneity throughout the caste order, and incompatible with Berreman's view of individual castes as bounded social and cultural units, each with a unique inner conceptual system, each necessarily bonded together only by power. Marriott and Inden put the actual relation between caste stratification and cultural diversity very exactly: "Caste units differ from social classes in being necessarily defined by rather than incidentally distinguished by occupation, descent and marriage. *Castes have no other necessary cultural markings*" (Marriott and Inden 1972, emphasis added). That is, in a given local caste hierarchy, caste units are marked off from one another by a small number of distinctive features, such as *toRil* in Endavur. But these few cultural differences should not be taken as evidence for more total cultural diversity. The cultural situation is, in fact, just the opposite; the few distinctive features are necessary to mark functionally distinct social units in a context otherwise characterized by pervasive cultural homogeneity. A caste system *can* incorporate more cultural distinctiveness than this. Thus a new, ethnically distinct, tribal unit can be incorporated into an older caste order without immediately surrendering its inner distinctiveness. But cultural distinctiveness is not an essential feature of caste; caste does not exist in order to hold down those in cultural dissension with the dominant social order. For more often than not, the lowest in caste carry its ideology as thoroughly as anyone above them.

What then is the more general comparative significance of the present analysis? The first is negative: simple comparisons of caste with other forms of structured social inequality, especially those found in modern, complex pluralistic societies (racism or class and ethnic stratification) are exceedingly perilous. They are especially perilous when a certain essence, "birth ascription" in particular, is drawn out of all of them, and other particularities are ignored as secondary. Consider once again, for example, Berreman on caste and race. Race *is* caste, Berreman asserts, for both are founded on postulates of cultural and behavioral ascription, and both deny individual mobility between their respective strata. Formal ideology is secondary in both, Berreman continues, for white southerners are unblushingly racist (the formal egalitarianism of American ideology is irrelevant to them), and low-caste Indians are no more in consensus with the caste system than are low-race blacks. In both systems, then, the higher stratum espouses inequality and enforces it by naked power, while the lower stratum somehow denies inequality but is forced into it by power (Berreman 1960).

We have considered data on south Indian Untouchables at some length here, and it supports very little of Berreman's typification of caste. Let us look for a moment at the other half of his comparison, at racial stratification in the American south before World War II. The prewar field studies of

299

CONCLUSION

John Dollard and Davis et al. suggest a relation between culture and racial stratification that is somewhat more complex
than that outlined by Berreman. The Southern situation is,
however, amenable to the structural framework developed
for the Endavur Untouchables. The southern colorbar is
analogous to the dividing line in Endavur between the non-
Untouchables and the Untouchable castes (this analogy is
also drawn by Berreman, it should be noted); it defines a
set of relations from which Southern blacks are excluded
for reasons of their inborn racial features. Southern blacks
are, however, no more in dissension with the dominant class
ideology and the dominant racial ideology than are Indian
Untouchables with the hierarchical postulates of caste. For
they replicate among themselves, to the best of their materially limited abilities, the class-based stratification system
found among the Southern whites who have excluded them.
In "Southerntown," Dollard finds a strong distinction between lower and middle classes among the blacks (the upper
class is missing due to economic limitations); in "Old City,"
Allison et al. find all three major white classes (upper,
middle, and lower) replicated among the blacks. And the
distinctive features of class ideology are basically the same
among the blacks as among the whites: formal egalitarianism
modified by the work ethic, and differential rank explained
by differential achievements and attributes such as "lineage,"
education, occupation, community involvement, church
membership, and "respectibility."

There is one additional distinctive feature of class among
the blacks, however, one not found among the whites. For
among themselves, in a manner analogous to the Harijans of
Endavur with "beef" and "Paraiyan *toRil*," the blacks of
Southerntown and Old City have segmented the characteristics by which they are inferiorized racially to all white persons, and applied them ideologically to their class system.
Thus middle and upper-class blacks consider lower-class
blacks to have darker skins, woolier hair, and a worse smell
than themselves. In fact, virtually every criterion by which

300

the blacks as a whole are stereotypically opposed to the whites (laziness, dependency, stupidity, and so on) is among the blacks used to distinguish the lower class from the higher two classes, and some are also apparently used to set up distinctions between the upper and middle classes (see Dollard 1937, chapter 5; and Davis, Gardner, and Gardner 1941, chapters 3 and 10).

The blacks in these two Southern studies thus replicate among themselves the cultural features of both class stratification and of racial stratification. They are in themselves no more demonstrably egalitarian compared to the dominant white group than are Indian Untouchables compared to the dominant castes. There are important differences between Endavur and the American South, however, even at this abstract level. One is in the logical status of the ideology being replicated. For the break between touchables and Untouchables in India is only one expression of a consistent set of ranking principles in Indian society, while the racial bar in the American South is in apparent contradiction to the American value system being replicated elsewhere between blacks and whites (egalitarianism and class). Or perhaps more subtly, following Dumont, racial ideology is the exception that proves the rule in egalitarian ideologies. If there are inequalities between individuals that cannot be imputed to the social domain, to differences in achievement and hard work, they are relegated to a natural domain, to differences in inborn ability and in innate humanness. The inequality of Southern blacks does not in itself contradict the natural equality of all men, if the proviso is added that Southern blacks are not fully men.[4] A difference remains between In-

---

[4] Dollard indicates that, contrary to Berreman, there is considerable tension between formal egalitarianism and racism in southern white ideology, and that a common solution to this tension is exactly what Dumont predicts. That is, by maintaining in a number of ways that blacks are racially inferior, that they are not quite men, Southern whites can consistently "rationalize" the fact that they are racists toward Negroes, and ideologically egalitarian toward other whites (see Dollard 1937: 364-90).

dian Untouchables and American blacks, however, one that may relate to the relative stability of the two systems. For if all men are born unequal, and have ranked relations to one another based on relative purity and impurity, then Untouchables are merely the lowest and the most impure of men so defined. If all men are born equal, on the other hand, Southern blacks are the specific exception that defines what is meant by "men"—*white* men. Untouchables are the logic of caste writ large; blacks are much more contingently related to the logic of American egalitarianism.

There are many other differences between "caste" and "race," differences in the scale and type of society in which they are embedded, differences in the economic matrix, differences in the historicity of each as ideology. The point of this brief initial comparison is to suggest that the two phenomenon *can* be compared, but that such a comparison requires a structural perspective in which difference as well as analogy is retained, in which the specificity of each pole of the comparison is maintained, and in which culture and ideology are not necessarily taken as secondary to abstracted social structure. The point of this comparison is, following Dumont, to draw out features both of caste and of race that we might not otherwise see without dialectically opposing the two. Thus it is possible that the specific structural understanding of caste developed here can provide insights into race as ideology and as structured social inequality. Such an augmented understanding of race might then "feed back" to our structural understanding of caste. The opposite comparative strategy, following Berreman, tends to be misleading concerning both of race and of caste. It is also amenable to the logical criticism that Oliver Cox directed somewhat polemically at the older "caste school of race":

> [these analogies between caste and race operate as if the analyst said:] "This animal before us is not a horse, but *for our purpose* it is convenient to call it a horse. If you examine it closely, you will discover it is a water buffalo.

That does not matter, however, for we are not going to use it in a water-buffalo sense. Obviously, you cannot say the animal is not a horse; it is, in so far as it has four legs; and four legs are generally understood to be the essence of all horses and water buffalos" (Cox 1948: 493).

To close by referring back to India, it is worth making a few final disclaimers as clearly as possible. First, this argument concerning south Indian Untouchables and cultural consensus is not meant to deny the existence of elaborate and enriching forms of diversity in India. It is meant to suggest that this diversity can be properly understood, especially for cross-cultural purposes, only when it is evaluated with reference to possibly cooccurring unity and consensus in Indian culture and society. Second, the present analysis is not meant to rule out the existence of conflict, or the operation of power, in south Indian village hierarchies. It is instead intended to delineate the agreed-upon cultural framework within which such conflict occurs and power operates. Third, this approach to Indian Untouchables is not meant to suggest that nothing ever changes in India, for Untouchables in the cities are in different social environments from those of Untouchables in the villages, and are often the carriers of new and clearly disjunctive ideologies.

Finally, and most importantly, the present analysis is not meant to contribute to a defense of the traditional Indian social order that operates by "blaming the victim." The fact that south Indian rural Untouchables replicate a system that makes them fundamentally inferior, that they participate willingly in what might be called their own oppression, does not mean that they therefore "deserve" their position. For this replication, this ideological and social conformity, is the result of social forces beyond the control of south Indian Untouchables, and beyond their comprehension in their present state of consciousness. The nature and understanding of these forces would make a separate book and a separate frame of analysis. The present effort is intended only to demonstrate the outcome in one south Indian village of these forces, an outcome that must be taken seriously by all those who seek to transform India. This outcome can be simply stated: those persons who are, in egalitarian terms, among the most oppressed members of Indian society are also among the truest believers in the system that so oppresses them.

Bibliography

Aiyappan, A.
   1937   *Social and Physical Anthropology of the Nayadis of Malabar.* Madras: Government Press.
Babb, Lawrence A.
   1975   *The Divine Hierarchy: Popular Hinduism in Central India.* New York: Columbia University Press.
Barbosa, Duarte
   1866   *A Description of the Coasts of East Africa and Mala-*
   [1516]   *bar in the Beginning of the Sixteenth Century.* Translated from an Early Spanish Manuscript in the Barcelona Library. London, Hakluyt Society, Vol. 35.
Barnett, M. and Steve Barnett
   1973   *Contemporary Peasant and Post-Peasant Alternatives in South India: The Ideas of a Militant Untouchable.* Transactions of the American Philosophical Society 63.
Barnett, Steven A.
   1970   "The Structural Position of a South Indian Caste: *KonDaikkaaTTi VeeLaaLar*-s in Tamilnadu," Ph.D. dissertation, University of Chicago.
   1973   "Identity Choice and Caste Ideology in Contemporary South India." Preliminary draft of paper presented to the Ninth International Congress of Anthropological and Ethnological Sciences (ICAES) Meetings, Chicago.
   1976   "Coconuts and Gold: Relational Identity in a South Indian Caste," *Contributions to Indian Sociology* NS 10 (1): 133-156.
Barnett, Steven A., Lina Fruzzetti, and Akos Ostor
   1976   "Hierarchy Purified: Notes on Dumont and His Critics," *Journal of Asian Studies* 35 (4): 627-646.
Beck, Brenda E. F.
   1968   "Social and Conceptual Order in Kongu: A Region of South India." D.Phil. dissertation, Oxford University.
   1969a   "The Vacillating Goddess: Sexual Control and Social

Rank in the Indian Pantheon," paper presented at the ASA Meetings, Boston.

1969b "Colour and Heat in South Indian Ritual," Man, NS 4 (4): 553-572.

1972a *Peasant Society in Konku: A Study of Right and Left Subcastes in South India.* Vancouver: University of British Columbia Press.

1972b "Subcaste Boundaries: Empirical Observation and Our Theoretical Models," paper presented to the American Anthropological Association, Toronto.

Berreman, Gerald

1960 "Caste in India and the United States," *American Journal of Sociology* 66: 120-127.

1965 *Behind Many Masks: Ethnography and Impression Management in a Himalayan Village.* Ithaca: The Society for Applied Anthropology.

1967 "Stratification, Pluralism and Interaction: A Comparative Analysis of Caste," in *Caste and Race: Comparative Approaches*, A. de Reuck and J. Knight, eds. London: Churchille.

1971 "The Brahmanical View of Caste," *Contributions to Indian Sociology* NS 5: 16-23.

1972a *Hindus of the Himalayas: Ethnography and Change.* Berkeley and Los Angeles: University of California Press.

1972b "Race, Caste and Other Individious Distinctions in Social Stratification," *Race* 13 (4): 385-414.

Buchanan, F.

1807 "Buchanan's Journey through Mysore, Canara, and Malabar," in *Voyages and Travels to All Parts of the World*, F. Pinkerton, ed., vol. 8. London.

Census of India

1961 *Scheduled Castes and Tribes (Report and Tables).* Vol. IX, *Madras*, Part V-A (i). New Delhi.

Cohn, Bernard

1954 "The Camars of Senapur: A Study of the Changing Status of a Depressed Caste." Ph.D. dissertation, Cornell University.

1955 "The Changing Status of a Depressed Caste," in *Vil-*

lage India, McKim Marriott, ed. Chicago: The University of Chicago Press.

Conklin, George H.
1976 "Family Structure, Caste and Economic Development: An Urban-Rural Comparison from Dharwar," in *Family and Social Change in Modern India,* Giri Raj Gupta, ed. Durham, N.C.: Carolina Academic Press.

Cox, Oliver C.
1948 *Caste, Class and Race: a Study in Social Dynamics.* Reprinted, Modern Reader Paperback Edition, 1970. New York: Monthly Review Press.

Crole, Charles
1879 *The Chingleput, Late Madras, District. A Manual.* Madras: Government Press.

David, Kenneth
1972 "Hierarchy and Equivalence in Jaffna, North Ceylon: Normative Modes as Mediator," preliminary draft, paper presented to the ninth ICAES meetings, Chicago.

Davis, Allison, John Davis, and W. Lloyd Warner
1941 *Deep South.* Chicago: University of Chicago Press

Djurfeldt, Goran and Staffan Lindberg
1975 *Behind Poverty: The Social Formation in a Tamil Village.* Scandinavian Institute of Asian Studies Monograph Series. London: Curzon.

Dollard, John
1937 *Caste and Class in a Southern Town.* New York: Doubleday.

Dubois, Abbe J. A.
1959 *Hindu Manners, Customs and Ceremonies.* Oxford:
[1815] Clarendon.

Dumont, Louis
1957a *Une Sous-caste de l'Inde du sud.* Paris: Mouton.
1957b "For a Sociology of India," *Contributions to Indian Sociology* 1: 1-22.
1957c *Hierarchy and Marriage Alliance in South Indian Kinship.* Occasional Paper No. 12. London: Royal Anthropological Institute.
1959 "Structural Definition of a Folk Deity," *Contributions to Indian Sociology* 3: 75-87.

307

1960   "Caste, Racism and 'Stratification': Reflections of a Social Anthropologist," reprinted in Dumont 1970, appendix.

1966   "Marriage in India, the Present State of the Question." *Contributions to Indian Sociology* 9: 90-114.

1970   *Homo Hierarchicus.* Chicago: University of Chicago Press.

1971   "On Putative Hierarchy and Some Allergies to It," *Contributions to Indian Sociology* NS 5: 58-81.

1977   *From Mandeville to Marx.* Chicago, University of Chicago Press.

Fuchs, Stephen

1950   *The Children of Hari: A Study of the Nimar Balahis in the Central Provinces of India.* Vienna: Verlag Herold.

Gough, Kathleen

1956   "Brahmin Kinship in a Tamil Village," *American Anthropologist* 58: 826-853.

1960a   "Caste in a Tanjore Village," in *Aspects of Caste in Southern India, Ceylon, and Northwestern Pakistan,* E. R. Leach, ed. New York: Cambridge University Press.

1960b   "The Hindu Jajmani System," *Economic Development and Social Change* 9: 83-91.

1973   "Harijans in Thanjavur," in *Imperialism and Revolution in South Asia,* K. Gough and H. P. Sharma, eds. New York: Monthly Review Press.

Hardgrave, Robert L., Jr.

1969   *The Nadars of Tamilnadu: the Political Culture of a Community in Change.* Berkeley and Los Angeles: University of California Press.

Harper, E. B.

1957   "Shamanism in South India," *Southwest Journal of Anthropology* 13: 267-287.

1959   "A Hindu Village Pantheon," *Southwest Journal of Anthropology* 15: 227-234.

1964   "Ritual Pollution as an Integrator of Caste and Religion," in *Religion in South Asia,* E. B. Harper, ed. Berkeley and Los Angeles: University of California Press.

Hart, George L. III
1975 "Ancient Tamil Literature: Its Scholarly Past and Future," in *Essays on South India*, Burton Stein, ed. Hawaii: The University Press of Hawaii.

Hocart, A. M.
1950 *Caste, a Comparative Study*. London: Methuen.

Hutton, J. H.
1963 *Caste in India: Its Nature, Function and Origins*. Fourth edition. Oxford, Oxford University Press.

Inden, Ronald B.
1975 *Marriage and Rank in Bengali Culture: a History of Caste and Clan in Middle Period Bengal*. Berkeley and Los Angeles: University of California Press.

Inden, Ronald B. and Ralph Nicholas
1972 "A Cultural Analysis of Bengali Kinship," in *Prelude to Crisis: Bengal and Bengal Studies in 1970*, Peter J. Bertocci, ed. Michigan State University Studies Series. East Lansing.

Isaacs, Harold
1965 *India's Ex-Untouchables*. New York: John Jay.

Jha, Makhan
1969 "Spirit Possession among the Maithil Brahmins," *Eastern Anthropologist* 22 (3): 361-368.

Karve, I.
1961 *Hindu Society: An Interpretation*. Poona: Deccan College Postgraduate and Research Institute.

Kolenda, Pauline
1964 "Religious Anxiety and Hindu Fate," in *Religion in South Asia*, E. B. Harper, ed. Berkeley and Los Angeles: University of California Press.

Kumar, Dharma
1965 *Land and Caste in South India*. Cambridge: Cambridge University Press.

Lewis, Oscar
1970 "The Culture of Poverty," in *Anthropological Essays*, Oscar Lewis, ed. New York: Random House.

Lynch, Owen
1969 *The Politics of Untouchability*. New York: Columbia University Press.

BIBLIOGRAPHY

Mahar, J. Michael
1972 *The Untouchables in Contemporary India.* Tucson: University of Arizona Press.
Manu
1969 *The Laws of Manu.* Georg Buhler trans. Sacred Books
[1886] of the East 25. New York: Dover Books.
Maranda, Pierre
1972 "Structuralism in Cultural Anthropology," *Annual Review of Anthropology* 2: 329-348.
Marriott, McKim
1968 "Caste Ranking and Food Transactions," in *Structure and Change in Indian Society*, Milton Singer and Bernard Cohn, eds. Chicago: Aldine.
1969 "Review" of Louis Dumont, *Homo Hierarchicus: Essay sur le système des castes, American Anthropologist* 71.
1974 "Hindu Transactions: Diversity without Dualism." Association of Social Anthropologists, Symposium on Transactional Analysis, Oxford.
Marriott, McKim and Ronald Inden
1973 "Towards an Ethnosociology of Hindu Caste Systems," Ninth ICAES Conference, No. 2206.
1974 "Caste Systems," *Encyclopedia Britannica*, 15th edition. Chicago.
Mencher, Joan
n. d. "Group and Self-Identifications: The View from the Bottom," unpublished paper.
1972 "Continuity and Change in an Ex-Untouchable Community of South India," in *The Untouchables in Contemporary India*, J. Michael Mahar, ed. Tucson: University of Arizona Press.
1974 "The Caste System Upside Down, or the Not-So-Mysterious East," *Current Anthropology* 15: 469-493.
Miller, Robert
1966 "Button, Button . . . Great Tradition, Little Tradition, Whose Tradition?" *Anthropological Quarterly* 39: 26-42.
Moffatt, Michael
1968 "The Funeral Ritual in South India," B.Litt. thesis, Oxford University.
1975 "Cultural Continuity and Structural Replication in a South Indian Untouchable Community," Ph.D. dissertation, University of Chicago.

310

Montgomery, Edward
1977 "Human Ecology and the Population Concept: Yelnadu Reddi Population in India," *American Ethnologist* 4 (1): 179-189.

Reddy, N. S.
1952 "Transition in Caste Structure in Andra Desh with Particular Reference to Depressed Castes," Ph.D. dissertation, University of Lucknow.

Sastri, K. A.
1955 *The Colas*. Madras: University of Madras Press.
1963 *Development of Religion in South India*. Bombay: Orient Longmans.

Singer, Milton
1958 "Traditional India: Structure and Change," *Journal of American Folklore* 71: 191-205.

Srinivas, M. N.
1962 *Caste in India and Other Essays*. Bombay: Asia Publishing Company.

Stein, Burton
1967 "Brahmin and Peasant in Early South Indian History," *Adyar Library Bulletin*, vols. 31-32.
1968 "Social Mobility and Medieval South Indian Hindu Sects," in *Social Mobility in the Caste System in India*, James Silverberg, ed. Paris: Mouton.
1969 "Integration of the Agrarian System in South India," in *Land Control and Social Structure*, R. E. Frykenberg, ed. Madison: University of Wisconsin Press.

Subrahmanian, N. S.
1966 *Sangam Polity: The Administration and Social Life of the Sangam Tamils*. Bombay: Asia Publishing Company.

Tambiah, S. J.
1973 "From Varna to Caste through Mixed Unions," in *The Character of Kinship*, Jack Goody, ed. Cambridge: Cambridge University Press.

Thurston, Edgar
1909 *Castes and Tribes of Southern India*. 7 Vols. Madras: Government Press.

Valentine, Charles
1968 *Culture and Poverty*. Chicago: University of Chicago Press.

311

BIBLIOGRAPHY

Wadley, Susan
   1975   *Shakti: Power in the Conceptual Structure of Karimpur Religion*. The University of Chicago Studies in Anthropology. Series in Social, Cultural and Linguistic Anthropology, No. 2. Chicago: Department of Anthropology, University of Chicago.

Whitehead, Henry
   1921   *The Village Gods of South India*. London: Oxford University Press.

Yalman, Nur
   1967   *Under the Bo Tree*. Berkeley and Los Angeles: University of California Press.

Index

Acari (artisan): in Untouchable goddess festival, 263; its *toRil*, 96

acceptance: of lowermost position in caste, 141-142, 147; of caste principles, by Untouchables, 147-148. *See also* consensus

"accretion at the bottom," 41, 63

acre: adjusted, 103; standard, 68n

Adi-Dravidas, 17, 56, 112n

adimai ("slave"), 45-46

Adimelum (Endavur Harijan), xl, xli, 172, 181, 183, 185-186, 210

Aiyappan, A., 150-151

Ambattan (barber), 94, 95

Ambedkar, B. R., 32, 56, 129, 168

"anonymous people" among Harijans, 170-171, 173, 189n, 203

Arichandran (mythic slave of Untouchables), 195-196

astrology as duty of Valluvar *purohit*, 102

auspicious band: of barbers, 113, 135-136; compared to *parai* band, 199. *See also parai* drum, drumming

Babb, L. A., 220, 261, 281

Balahi caste of central India, 8

barber: lack of among Endavur Harijans, 135; presence of in some Colonies, 153n

Barbosa, D., 42, 88n

Barnett, M. and S. Barnett, 57, 298

Barnett, S., 24n, 175n, 214n, 296

baseline for change, xv, 15, 19, 20, 50, 72

Beck, B.E.F., xxvi, 137, 154n, 175n, 213, 220, 233, 240n, 248, 267n, 281, 296

beef-eating: actual, among Endavur Harijans, 193-194; and Harijan grades, 157, 165, 181-182; and Harijan lowness, 114, 122; Harijan attitudes toward, 119

Berreman, G., xxvi, 11, 12, 21-22, 245n, 292, 296, 298, 299, 301n

Beteille, A., 87

bhakti (devotionalism), 19, 38-39

Block (administrative unit), 70

boundaries: and divine beings, 116, 243-245, 247, 259, 283; of social space, *see* Colony; *uur*; village

Brahmins: as disjunctive, 294; in Endavur, 92; in Pudukottai, xxix, xxx, xxxvi, 39n; vs. Untouchables, 17-18, 27, 30n, 87

"Brahmins to the Harijans," 102, 105-106. *See also* Valluvar Pandaram

British effects on Untouchables, 44-52

Buchanan, F., 8

Buddhism, 39; neo-, 19, 56, 129, 168

Camar caste of north India, 14-15, 44, 55n

Candala (early Untouchable), 34, 196

Harijan Vannan caste, of Endavur, 131-139, 258
Harper, E. B., 220, 242n, 248
Hart, G. L., 37n
headmanship, Harijan: and goddess festival, 250; and paradox of Pannaikkars, 170-171; and Vettiyans, 191; of Harijans, 79, 110, 163-164; Periyasami in, 210
hierarchy in Dumont, 25, 27
history: of Pannaikkars, 172-173; of village of Endavur, 66-84; of Untouchability, 32-57
Hutton, J., 50, 87n, 132
hypergamy, 33
hypogamy, 33, 34

Idaiyar caste (herdsman), of Endavur, 67, 96
identity, religious, between high castes and Untouchables, 250, 268, 280, 289, 290-291. See also consensus
ideology: and caste, 25; anti-Brahmin, 107; of caste and rate, 301, 302; revision of, 20, 129, 293, 298
images: high caste, of Untouchables, 125-127; self-, of Harijans, 121-125, 129-130
impurity, see purity
inclusion of Untouchables: in religion, 222, 246-247, 270-289; in services of higher castes, 95-98; in village, 64. See also exclusion
Inden, R., 24, 30, 222n
Inden, R. and R. Nicholas, 87n, 92n, 158
individualism and race, 26
intercaste worship, 246-247, 270-289
intermediacy downwards: and

Harijans, 111, 113, 115, 150, 270-271, 283, 287; of pucaris, see pucari
intermediacy upwards: Brahmins and, 92; Valluvar Pandarams and, 104-105. See also purohit
internal organization of Untouchables, 18, 28, 57, 97-98, 100-218. See also grade
inversion, mythic, and Paraiyans, 123, 126
Isaacs, H., 57

Jainism, 41
Jha, M., 296

Kallar caste, of southern Tamil-nadu, xxvii-xxix, xxxv, 29, 50-51
Kannakka Pillai caste (accountant), of Endavur, 89n, 90n
karagam pots (ritual pots), 255-256, 258, 267
karma: and Brahmins, 294; and Harijan lowness, 122; its non-centrality, 268, 296-297; reported lack among Untouchables, 15-16
Karve, I., 19n, 41
Kavundar caste of Endavur, 89n
kinship system of Endavur Harijans, 154-218
kinship terminology, Dravidian, 145, 174-176
kiraamam, see village
Kolenda, P., 15-16, 20, 121, 123
kottu, see lineage
KTR (Endavur landlord), xxxviii, xxxix, 68n, 69-71, 80-81, 84
Kudiraikaran (god), 205-207, 229, 259, 287
kuli wage labor, 78, 143

317

Untouchables, 41, 52, 54; of Artisans, 40; of Pannaikkar grade, 204
mobility, individual: and migration, 173; between grades, 198, 215
mobility, putative upward, of Reddiyars, 67
models of diversity, *see* disjunctive theories of Untouchability
models of unity, *see* consensus
modernity, agricultural, of Reddiyars, 70, 73
Moffatt, M., 134, 249n
monism, fundamental, of Harijans, 233-234
Montgomery, E., 154n
Morsapakkam (village), 79, 282
"mother's house" in Selliyamman festival, 271-272, 274, 275, 281, 282, 287
Mugan (Endavur Harijan), 230, 235-246, 258-260
Munadiyan (god), 237, 287
Muni (Endavur Harijan), 211
munsif (village policeman), 47, 159
Murugan (Parangudi Harijan), xxvi

Nadar movement, 52-54
Nagamalai (Endavur Harijan), 172, 186
Naidu caste of Endavur, 90n
Nalasami (Endavur Harijan), 165, 227
name-giving ritual among Harijans, 105
Nandan (Untouchable *bhakti* saint), 38, 41, 225-226
Nayadi caste of Kerala, 150
Nayar caste of Kerala, 42
Nicholas, R., 24, 30

nuclear areas in south Indian history, 41, 61

"occupation" in caste, 92. *See also toRil*
Oddar caste of Tamilnadu, 67
opposition, structural, 27, 93
oppression and Untouchability, 11, 21-23, 43-44, 98, 303
Orans, M., 19n
origin myths: of Harijans, 120-128; of Valluvar Pandaram, 103
outcaste image: of Untouchables, 6, 8, 9-13; lack of evidence for, 292
outcasting among Endavur Untouchables, 108, 131, 168
outcasts, putative origins of Untouchables in, 7n, 39

Pallan caste of Tamilnadu, 17-18, 45-46, 50-51, 59
panchayats, 70, 84-85. *See also* headmanship
Pandaram caste of Endavur, 96, 263
pangali (sharer), 161, 175n, 189
pangali split: among Harijans, 211, 228; among Reddiyars, 68
Pannaikkar grade of Endavur, 169-187
paNNaiyaaL (tied labor) relation, 46, 68, 72, 79, 82, 110
parai drum, drumming, 111-112, 197-199, 256, 258, 259
Paraiyan caste of Tamilnadu, xxvi, 6, 36, 59. *See also* Harijan
Parangudi (village), xxiii, xxvi-xxxvi, 297
participant observation, *see* fieldwork
Parvati (goddess), 249, 281, 284

165, 182, 202-203 (*see also*
replication); and economic
position, *see* trade-offs; calculations of, 92, 142; concession
of, 93-95, 150, 172; of castes
of Endavur, 90; of Untouchable castes of Endavur, 59
"rationalization" of caste, 3, 4,
13
Reddiyar caste, of Endavur, 66-
71, 80, 91-92
Reddy, N. S., 148-149
reflexivity, 143, 188
relativism, 21, 31
religion: definition, 219; Harijan,
219
replication: and grades, 157, 189,
215, 216; and racial stratification, 300; and social control,
217; as proof of consensus, 5,
148, 298; definition, 5, 29;
generality of, 137n, 139n; in
myth, 202-203; in religion,
222, 267-269, 281n; in social
organization, 89, 92, 98-152,
216; limits of, 98, 138-139,
148, 151-152, 200, 297; of
dominance, 78, 110; simplicity
and complexity of, 291. *See
also* code-switching; consensus
right-hand/left-hand caste distinction, lack of in Endavur, 155n
ritual: to chosen gods, 224-226;
to household gods, 227-229;
to lineage gods 229-231; to
territorial goddesses, 250-267,
275-289
ritual services: of Harijan Vannan, 133-136; of Valluvar
Pandaram, 104-106

saamiyaaDi (god-person), 235.
See also possession
sacrifice, bloody, 136, 259-261

sacrifice-doers, Harijans as, 283,
284
Sami (Endavur Harijan), 211,
258
Sandegren, P., xxvi
Sangu Paraiyan subcaste, 131,
154, 195
sannyasin (renouncer), quasi,
223-224
Sanskritization by Untouchables:
14, 50-52, 79
Sastri, N., 38, 39
security and caste, 137
segmentation, territorial, of
Untouchables, 58
Selliyamman (goddess), 270-
289; duality of, 276, 283;
origin myth of, 272-273;
special closeness to Harijans,
271-272, 274-275, 287-288
Sengundar Mudaliyar caste, of
Endavur, 69, 71-72, 83-84, 97
shakti (power), *see* power
(*shakti*)
share (*pangu*), 43, 67, 68, 132,
162. *See also* pangali
Siva (god), 121, 125, 126, 231-
232, 248-249
Sivaraj, Mrs. (Congress politician), 79
social movements, lack of among
Untouchables, 46
solidarity, lack of among Untouchables, 57, 78, 82-83, 295
sorcery, of Untouchables, 44
Srinivas, M. N., 52, 71n
Stein, B., 38, 40, 41, 61
structuralism, 4, 5, 11, 24-30, 31,
152-153, 290-291, 302
subcaste: definition, 130n; of
particular Untouchable castes,
41, 108-109, 130-131, 143,
154-155
Subrahmanian, N. S., 36

Vettiyan grade of Endavur, 188-212

Vettiyan role, 47, 189, 191-192, 211, 283, 284

"view from the bottom," non-distinctiveness of, 3, 26, 28

village, 64-65

Wadley, S., 24, 31, 219, 220, 223, 231, 232n, 233-235, 261, 267n

washerman, Harijan, *see* Harijan Vannan caste

watchmanship: and Harijan closeness to Selliyamman, 271-272; and Harijan lowness, 116, 118. *See also* Vettiyan role

weaving, in Endavur, 71-72

Weber, M., 16

Whitehead, H., 248, 249n, 256n

Yalman, N., 175n

zamindari, xxiv, 47, 63, 66-69

Library of Congress Cataloging in Publication Data

Moffatt, Michael, 1944-
   An Untouchable community in South India, structure and
consensus.

   Bibliography: p.
   Includes index.
   1. Caste-India—South India.   2. Untouchables.
3. South India—Social conditions.   I. Title.
DS484.M64   301.44'94'09548   78-51183
ISBN 0-691-09377-6